THE PASTORAL COMPANION

A Canon Law Handbook for Catholic Ministry
by
John M. Huels, O.S.M., J.C.D.

THE FRANCISCAN HERALD PRESS
1434 West 51st Street — Chicago, Illinois 60609

Library of Congress Cataloging-in-Publication Data

Huels, John M.
   The pastoral companion.

   Includes indexes.
   1. Canon law. I. Title.
LAW   262.9'4   85-29316
ISBN 0-8199-0901-7
ISBN 0-8199-0900-9 (pbk)

ACKNOWLEDGEMENTS

Excerpts from the English translation of documents in the *Canon Law Digest* edited by T. Bouscaren and J. O'Connor (vols. 1-6, Milwaukee-New York: Bruce Publishing Co., 1934–1969; vols. 7–9, Chicago: Canon Law Digest, 1975–1983) are used with permission. Excerpts from *Documents on the Liturgy, 1963–1979: Conciliar, Papal, and Curial Texts* (Collegeville: The Liturgical Press) © 1982 by the International Committee on English in the Liturgy, Inc. are reprinted by permission of ICEL. All rights reserved. Excerpts from *Pastoral Care of the Sick: Rites of Anointing and Viaticum* © 1982 by the International Committee on English in the Liturgy, Inc., are reprinted by permission of ICEL. All rights reserved.

MADE IN THE UNITED STATES OF AMERICA

CONTENTS

iii

FOREWORD

The Pastoral Companion traces its ancestry back to the German work *Comes Pastoralis* by Fr. Louis Anler, OFM. In 1929, Fr. Honoratus Bonzelet, OFM, prepared the first of ten editions of a translation and adaptation of Anler's work entitled *The Pastoral Companion*. By the time the 9th edition appeared in 1943, Fr. Bonzelet had made so many changes in the original *Comes Pastoralis* that he no longer considered *The Pastoral Companion* a translation and adaptation, but published it under his own name and as his own work.

Father Bonzelet died in 1952 while he was engaged in preparation of the 11th edition of his work. Father Marcian Mathis, OFM, and Fr. Clement Leahy, OFM, took over the project and published the 11th edition of *The Pastoral Companion* in 1956. A 12th edition appeared in 1961, coauthored by Father Mathis and Fr. Nicholas Meyer, OFM. Finally, Fr. Mathis and Fr. Dismas Bonner, OFM, compiled editions of the work in 1967 (13th) and 1976 (14th).

Thus, for the better part of this century, through many changes of author and numerous alterations in the law, this publishing venture has provided a notable and eminently useful source of information and guidance for people engaged in the ministry of the Catholic Church. Doubtless, this new edition by Father John Huels, OSM, will continue that fine tradition. May it enjoy the success it so richly deserves.

Dismas Bonner, OFM
St. Louis, Missouri
July 31, 1985

PREFACE

The purpose of *The Pastoral Companion* is to provide ministers and students with a handy reference of Church laws and brief commentary on topics pertinent to Catholic ministry, especially parish and liturgical ministry. It is not intended to be a detailed or complete treatise of canon law, but a selection of norms and a treatment of canonical issues most useful to those preparing for or involved in the pastoral ministry.

The sources of the laws selected for this work are mainly the *Code of Canon Law*, the *praenotanda* and rubrics of the liturgical books, and other documents issued by the Apostolic See. Select norms of the National Conference of Catholic Bishops are also provided where applicable. Other sources of a non-legal nature from the Apostolic See and elsewhere, as well as the author's commentary, are included to help explain and exemplify the law's meaning. The approach is topical, not a canon-by-canon adherence to the Code, so that all the laws pertinent to a topic can be seen at a glance and the whole law can be appreciated in its proper context.

I wish to extend a word of gratitude to the Very Rev. Dismas W. Bonner, O.F.M., J.C.D., minister provincial of the Sacred Heart Province of Franciscans, and my former teacher at Catholic Theological Union, who invited me to take over the project of revising *The Pastoral Companion*, previously authored by him and Fr. Marcian J. Mathis, O.F.M., J.C.D. Some of the material in this predecessor volume was still useful, especially in the sections on general principles and marriage. I also wish to thank my colleagues at CTU, to whom this work is dedicated, especially Dean Robert J. Schreiter, C.PP.S., for creating an atmosphere that encourages faculty publication in areas of pastoral ministry.

General Principles

Part I

CHAPTER I
Governance and Dispensations

I. The Power of Governance

A. Division

1. Governance, also called "jurisdiction," in the *external forum* provides primarily and directly for the common and public good of the Church; it regulates the social action of the faithful, their relationship to the external and visible society of the Church. Therefore, it is exercised publicly and has public juridical effects.

> Enacting laws, exercising judgment in ecclesiastical courts, establishing censures, and conferring parishes are examples of the exercise of governance in the external forum. Such actions as the remission of certain censures and dispensations from vows and matrimonial impediments usually take place in the external forum, but may, in a proper case, fall within the internal forum.

Governance in the *internal forum*, the forum of conscience, provides primarily and directly for the private welfare of the faithful; it regulates their private actions and their moral relationship to God. Therefore it is exercised privately and confidentially, often in complete secrecy, and has no public juridical effects unless these are expressly granted by the law or by the action of some competent superior. (See can. 130.) Some examples of governance exercised in the internal forum include dispensations from occult impediments to marriage in accord with canon 1079, §3; secret marriages (cans. 1130-1133); the remission of reserved censures in accord with canon 1357.

> The power of governance in the internal forum is

1

sacramental when it can be exercised only in the administration of the sacrament of penance, such as the power of confessors to remit automatic censures of excommunication or interdict which have not been declared (can. 1357). Governance in the internal forum is *extra-sacramental* when it can be exercised apart from any relation to the administration of the sacrament of penance, though still in a private manner.

2. *Ordinary* power of governance is that which is connected with some office by the law itself; *delegated* power is that which is granted to a person not by means of an office. (Can. 131, §1)

> For governance to be classified as ordinary, it must be attached to an office *by the law itself*, i.e., either by the universal law or particular law, or by legal custom. For example, the power of pastors and clerical superiors to dispense from fast and abstinence is ordinary governance since it is granted by the Code, canon 1245.

> Governance which is granted to a person not by means of an office is delegated governance. For example, some dioceses delegate to parish priests and deacons the faculty to permit mixed marriages, a power which the universal law reserves to the local Ordinary. (See can. 1125.) Rules for delegation are given below.

3. Ordinary power of governance can be either *proper* or *vicarious*. (Can. 131, §2)

> Proper power is that which is exercised *in one's own name* in virtue of the office one has. For example, when the diocesan bishop exercises the power of his office, he does it in his own name. When the vicar general or episcopal vicar exercise the power of their office, they do it vicariously, that is, in the name of the bishop. Likewise, when a pastor is impeded from exercising his pastoral office and a parochial vicar (assistant pastor) exercises the power of the pastor, the parochial vicar exercises vicarious power in the name of the pastor. (See can. 541.) On the other hand, when the pastor exercises the power of his office, he does so in his own name, and thus he exercises proper power.

2

4. The power of governance is distinguished as *legislative, executive, and judicial.* (Can. 135, §1)

Legislative power cannot be validly delegated by anyone other than the pope or ecumenical council, unless the law explicitly provides otherwise. Thus, diocesan bishops, particular councils, episcopal conferences, and general chapters of religious institutes, cannot delegate their law-making powers to others. Furthermore, a lower level legislator is unable validly to enact a law contrary to the law of a superior. (See can. 135, §2.) For example, a diocesan bishop could not enact a law contrary to a canon of the Code, since the *Code of Canon Law* is papal law.

Judicial power, which judges or judicial colleges enjoy, must be exercised in the manner prescribed by law and it cannot be delegated except to carry out acts which are preparatory to a decree or sentence. (Can. 135, §3) The manner of exercising judicial power is treated in Book VII of the Code.

Executive power is enjoyed by various Church superiors and office-holders, such as diocesan bishops and their vicars, pastors, religious superiors.

B. Delegation

The following rules on delegation apply to any kind of delegation of executive power of governance. Priests and deacons in pastoral ministry will find these rules most useful in respect to delegating the faculty to assist at marriage. Although the faculty to assist at marriage is not technically considered an exercise of the power of governance, the delegation of this faculty follows the same rules as for the delegation of executive power of governance.

1. Ordinary executive power can be delegated both for a particular act or for all cases unless the law expressly provides otherwise. (Can. 137, §1)

Power delegated for a particular act is called *special delegation*; that granted for any number of cases of the same kind is called *general delegation*. For example, a pastor who is going on vacation delegates a visiting priest to perform the six marriages scheduled in the

3

parish during his absence. This is special delegation and can be used only for those six marriages. If the pastor had granted general delegation, the visiting priest could have assisted at *all* marriages in the parish, even those that had not been scheduled.

Pastors have the faculty in virtue of their office to assist at marriages within their parish of any couple, provided at least one of the parties is a Latin rite Catholic. (See can. 1109.) They can grant this faculty either by way of general or special delegation to any priest or deacon. (See can. 1111.)

Although pastors have the faculty in virtue of their office to hear confessions in their territory, they may not delegate this faculty to others. The faculty to hear confessions is granted by the local Ordinary or clerical superior in accord with canons 968-969.

Pastors and other priests with an office of pastoral care such as parochial vicars and chaplains have the faculty of confirming after baptism an initiate who is seven years of age or older as well as a baptized non-Catholic who is being received into the full communion of the Catholic Church. However, they could not delegate this to another priest; the mandate must be given by the diocesan bishop. (See can. 883, 2°.)

2. Executive power delegated by another authority having ordinary power, if it was delegated for all cases, can be subdelegated only in individual cases; but if it was delegated for a particular act or acts, it cannot be subdelegated unless by express grant of the one delegating. (Can. 137, §3)

For example, a parochial vicar or a deacon has general delegation to assist at marriages in the parish. With general delegation, he could subdelegate another priest or deacon to assist at marriages in individual cases, that is, for specified weddings. He could not grant general delegation to another priest or deacon. General delegation can only be granted by the authority having ordinary power, such as the pastor.

If a priest or deacon has only special delegation, he could not subdelegate another to assist at the marriage or marriages for which he was delegated unless

4

the one who delegated him had granted him the power to subdelegate. For example, a pastor who is going on vacation delegates a visiting priest to assist at the six scheduled marriages during his absence, but he does not mention that the visitor may subdelegate this power. In such a case, the visiting priest could not subdelegate this power to another priest or deacon even in a case of necessity; the delegation would have to come from the pastor or local Ordinary (or from a parochial vicar or deacon in the parish with general delegation, if there is one).

3. No subdelegated power can be subdelegated again unless this was expressly granted by the one delegating. (Can. 137, §4)

C. Use

One may validly exercise executive power of governance on behalf of one's subjects even though he or they may be outside the territory, unless something else is evident by the nature of the matter or by prescription of law. One may also exercise this power on behalf of travelers who are in the territory, provided it is a question of granting favors or of enforcing either universal or particular laws to which they are bound by canon 13, §2, n.2. (Can. 136)

An example of this rule for pastoral ministry is a dispensation from the law of fast and abstinence or from the Sunday or holy day obligation which the pastor can grant even for visitors in his parish, or for his parishioners even when he or they or outside the parish boundaries. (See can. 1245.)

There is an exception to this general principle regarding the faculty for assisting at marriages and the faculty for presbyters to confirm. Marriages performed outside one's territory (usually the parish) without special delegation are invalid, as are confirmations by presbyters outside their territory (unless they are baptizing someone from an Eastern rite or someone in danger of death). (See cans. 1109-1111 and 887.)

Canon 13, §2, 2° exempts travelers from all particular laws except for those laws which provide for the public order, which determine legal formalities, or which deal with immovable goods situated in that territory.

D. Cessation

1. *Ordinary power* is lost by the loss of the office to which it is connected. (Can. 143, §1)

> For example, if a pastor dies, or his term expires, or he is transferred or removed from office, or his resignation is accepted by the bishop, he loses the ordinary power of a pastor. Unless the law provides otherwise, ordinary power is suspended if one legitimately appeals or makes recourse against a privation or removal from office. (Can. 143, §2) Thus, if a diocesan bishop decrees the removal of a certain pastor and the pastor makes recourse against this decision to the Holy See, his ordinary power is not lost but he cannot exercise it until the case is resolved in his favor. (Note: The term "recourse" is to an administrative process as "appeal" is to a judicial process.)

2. *Delegated power* is lost: (a) when the mandate for which it was given is fulfilled; (b) when the time of delegation or the number of cases for which it was given has run out; (c) when the motivating cause of the delegation has ceased; (d) by revocation on the part of the delegating authority, upon direct notice thereof to the delegate; (e) by renunciation on the part of the delegate, upon direct notice to and acceptance thereof by the delegating authority. Delegated power is not lost, however, by the expiration of the authority of the one delegating, unless this is apparent from clauses appended to it. (Can. 142, §1)

E. Supplied Jurisdiction

1. *In case of inadvertence.* An act of delegated power which is exercised only in the internal forum is valid if it is done inadvertently after the grant has expired. (Can. 142, §2)

2. *In common error*, whether of fact or of law, and also *in positive and probable doubt of law or of fact*, the Church supplies executive power of governance both for the external and internal forum. This

same norm applies to the faculties for confirmation, penance, and marriage. (See can. 144.)

> For discussion of this issue in relation to the faculties for these three sacraments, see pp. 64, 124, and 224.

II. DISPENSATIONS

A. Power to Dispense

1. A dispensation, which is the relaxation of a merely ecclesiastical law in a particular case, can be granted by those who enjoy executive power within the limits of their competence, and also by those to whom the power of dispensing has been given explicitly or implicitly whether by the law itself or in virtue of legitimate delegation. (Can. 85)

> Dispensations can be granted only for *ecclesiastical laws*, not for divine laws. Thus, e.g., a dispensation from the marital impediment of prior bond is never given because the law against divorce and remarriage is considered divine law.

> Dispensations are granted only for particular cases, either for an individual or for a group. The particular case may involve many repetitions of the same circumstances for which a dispensation is given. For example, a person who for good reason must miss Sunday Mass repeatedly could be given one dispensation for as long as that reason lasts, or the Sunday obligation could be commuted to other forms of prayer or charitable deeds.

2. Laws are not subject to dispensation insofar as they define those things which are essentially constitutive of juridical institutes or acts. (Can. 86)

3. One who has the power of dispensing can exercise it on behalf of his subjects even when he is outside his territory and even when they are absent from the territory. Unless the contrary be expressly established, he also can dispense travelers who are actually in his territory, and he can dispense himself. (Can. 91)

4. *The diocesan bishop*, as often as he judges it to be for the spiritual good of the faithful, can dispense them from disciplinary laws, both from universal laws and from particular laws established by the supreme authority of the Church for his territory or for his subjects. However, he cannot dispense from procedural or penal laws nor those laws whose dispensation is specially reserved to the Apostolic See or another authority. (Can. 87, §1)

5. *Ordinaries*. If recourse to the Holy See is difficult and likewise there is danger of serious harm in delay, any Ordinary can dispense from these same laws, even if the dispensation is reserved to the Holy See, provided it is a question of a dispensation which the Holy See is accustomed to grant in these same circumstances, with due regard for canon 291. (Can. 87, §2)

> The following are considered Ordinaries in canon law besides the pope and diocesan bishops: territorial prelates, territorial abbots, apostolic vicars, apostolic prefects, apostolic administrators, diocesan administrators when the see is vacant, vicars general, episcopal vicars, and major superiors of clerical religious institutes of pontifical right and of clerical societies of apostolic life of pontifical right. (See cans. 134 and 368.)

> Canon 291 states that a dispensation from the obligation of clerical celibacy is granted by the pope alone.

> In doubt of fact, an Ordinary can dispense from the law, even from a law whose dispensation is reserved, provided the dispensation is usually granted by the authority to whom it is reserved. (See can. 14.)

6. *Local Ordinaries*, [all Ordinaries except clerical major superiors] can dispense from diocesan laws and, as often as they judge it to be for the good of the faithful, from laws established by a plenary or provincial council or by the episcopal conference. (Can. 88)

7. *The pastor and other presbyters or deacons* may not dispense from universal or particular law unless this power has been expressly granted to them. (Can. 89)

> Presbyters and deacons should consult their diocese to determine what dispensations they may give.

The law itself allows the pastor and clerical superiors to dispense in individual cases from the obligation to attend Mass on a Sunday or holy day and from fast and abstinence on a day of penance. (See commentary, p. 296.) Parochial vicars and deacons could also be delegated to give these dispensations.

The pastor and clerical superior can dispense from a private vow in accord with canon 1196. Pastors, presbyters and deacons who have delegation to assist at marriages, and confessors may dispense from certain marital impediments in danger of death and in *omnia parata* cases in accord with canons 1078–1081.

B. Just Cause for Dispensation

A dispensation from an ecclesiastical law should not be given without a just and reasonable cause, bearing in mind the circumstances of the case and the importance of the law being dispensed. Otherwise the dispensation is illicit and, unless it was given by the legislator himself or his superior, it is also invalid. In doubt whether the cause is sufficient, a dispensation is validly and licitly granted. (Can. 90)

The spiritual good of the faithful is always a legitimate cause for a dispensation.

Intrinsic reasons for granting a dispensation arise from a difficulty in observing the law (e.g., sickness with regard to fast and abstinence, bad eyesight with regard to the obligation to celebrate the Liturgy of the Hours, foul weather with regard to attendance at Sunday Mass). *Extrinsic* reasons may arise from the condition of the person who is dispensed (e.g., his special merits or great dignity, the dispensation will be especially useful to this person), from the status of the person dispensing (e.g., to manifest his kindness or liberality), or from the desire to promote the common good (e.g., avoidance of many transgressions against the law, the seeking of alms for a pious cause, increase of the common joy). (Mathis/Bonner, 12-13)

Doubt concerning the reason for a dispensation may concern the sufficiency of a reason which is known to exist, or even the very existence of a reason itself. In any case, a dispensation granted in circumstances of doubt is valid, even though it be later discovered that the reasons alleged were insufficient or completely non-existent. (Ibid., 13) The doubt, however, must be positive, i.e., there must be a reason for the doubt. If there is no reason, one is in a state of ignorance rather than doubt.

C. Use of a Dispensation

1. A dispensation which is personal can be used anywhere, e.g., an individual who is dispensed from fasting need not fast even when he is outside his own diocese.

2. A dispensation which is local is restricted to a determined place, e.g., a diocese, city, or parish. It can be used by all who are in that place, but by no one outside that place.

3. A dispensation which is mixed, i.e., both personal and local, may be used by anyone in the territory, and by the residents or subjects of the territory even when they are outside the territory.

> Dispensations given for a whole diocese or city by general indult are presumed to be local or territorial and not personal, unless the contrary is evident from the wording of the dispensation. (Mathis/Bonner, 13)

D. Cessation of Dispensation

1. A dispensation which is granted for a single act, once it has been put into effect, produces a situation where the law which was relaxed can never again be effective in the same case, e.g., a dispensation from today's fast, from the impediment of consanguinity, etc. Moreover, once such a dispensation has been granted, it does not cease, even though its motivating cause should cease during the interval between the concession and use of the dispensation. However, as long as the dispensation has not been used, it can be recalled by the legislator.

> If one is dispensed from a matrimonial impediment for the reason of legitimating a child, and the child dies before the marriage is celebrated, the dispensation is still valid.

2. A dispensation which has *recurring application*, e.g., from abstaining on Fridays or from the obligation to celebrate the Liturgy of the Hours, *expires*:

a. by revocation, provided the dispensed person is notified of this;

b. by renunciation, provided the renunciation is accepted by the dispensing superior;

c. when the period of time for which the dispensation was granted has run out, or lapse of the number of times for which the dispensation was given;

d. by the certain and complete cessation of the motive cause for the dispensation. (Cf. cans. 93, 47, 79, 80, 83.)

> A motive or motivating cause is one which is of itself sufficient to ask and grant a dispensation. It is distinguished from a subsidiary cause which adds its influence to the motivating cause, but does not of itself suffice for the dispensation. The cessation of subsidiary causes does not affect a dispensation. Moreover, for a dispensation to cease, it is required that all (not only some) of the motivating causes cease certainly (not only probably or doubtfully) and completely (not only partially). (Mathis/Bonner, 14)

3. A dispensation which has *recurring application* does *not* expire:

a. on the expiration of the authority of the person who granted the dispensation, unless he gave it *ad beneplacitum nostrum*, e.g., at my good pleasure, as long as I am bishop, etc.;

b. by the death of the person dispensed, provided the dispensation was given to the ecclesiastical office the person held, rather than to the particular individual holding that office;

c. by non-use or by contrary use, provided the dispensation is not burdensome to others (e.g., a dispensation from abstinence in no way affects others). However, should the dispensation place a burden on others (e.g., a dispensation which would involve exemption from some jurisdiction of the local Ordinary), it ceases through legitimate prescription. (Cf. cans. 93, 81, 78, 82.)

CHAPTER II
Causes which Release from Legal Obligation and Epikeia

I. Causes Which Release From Legal Obligation

Apart from dispensations, there are other causes which may release one from the obligation to fulfill a law. These may be either exempting causes or excusing causes.

A. Exempting Causes

Exempting causes are those in virtue of which one ceases to be a subject of the law. These causes may actually remove the subject from the jurisdiction of a superior.

> Thus, one who goes from a diocese where there exists an obligation to attend Mass on a certain holy day into a diocese in a foreign country where such an obligation does not bind, has placed an exempting cause by leaving the territory of the superior. (See cans. 12 and 13.) Those who profess vows in religious institutes of pontifical right place a cause which gives them greater autonomy from the jurisdiction of the local Ordinary than do those who enter institutes of diocesan right. Or, a change in legal status may amount to an exempting cause, e.g., the completion of one's fifty-ninth year exempts from the obligation imposed by the law of fasting. (Mathis/Bonner, 18–19)

B. Excusing Causes

Excusing causes are those which render the observance of the law impossible or extremely difficult. In such a situation, a person remains a subject of the law, but is not bound to observe it.

1. *Ignorance, inadvertence, and error* constitute excusing causes from the imputability of a violation of the law. Since these factors render an act involuntary, at least to some extent, they prevent a true violation of law with its consequent effects, with certain notable exceptions.

> Note that ignorance of *invalidating and incapacitating laws* does not excuse from their observance and effects, unless the law expressly declares otherwise. (See can. 15, §1.) Nor does ignorance excuse one from incurring impediments to matrimony, or irregularities and impediments to holy orders. (Mathis/Bonner, 19)

2. *Physical impossibility* exists when compliance with the law is simply beyond human capability; such impossibility certainly excuses from the observance of law, since no one can be obliged to perform what is not possible.

3. *Moral impossibility* arises when the observance of the law is rendered very difficult by reason of grave fear, serious harm, or inconvenience which may be connected with the fulfillment of the law in question. Note that the inconvenience, etc., must be *extrinsic* to the law itself; if these factors are *intrinsically* bound up with its observance, they must be regarded as foreseen by the lawgiver, and therefore borne by the subjects. However, moral impossibility sometimes excuses from ecclesiastical law, because the legislator is not presumed to impose his law on his subjects with resulting notable inconvenience. Also, the grave fear, serious harm, or inconvenience must be *accidental*, i.e., not fostered deliberately to create moral impossibility.

> Note that not even danger of death excuses in cases where violation of the law harms the common good, inflicts extreme spiritual harm on a given person, results in hatred of God or contempt of the Church. The common good is always to be preferred to the private good of an individual.

> Outside of the above cases, moral impossibility can excuse from law. In the case of ecclesiastical law, when its observance entails relatively serious fear,

14

harm, or inconvenience, it becomes by that very fact an impossible law, since human law must be observable by the application of the ordinary capacities of people. In any given case, in order to determine how much harm or inconvenience is necessary to excuse, one must look to the seriousness of the precept and the strictness with which it is enjoined. In general, negative laws oblige more strictly than affirmative ones; those which are expressions of divine natural or positive law more strictly than those which are merely ecclesiastical laws. In any event, the opinions of authors can be of great assistance in determining what constitutes an excusing cause in a given instance. Note that, in the case of invalidating or incapacitating laws, moral impossibility on the part of a private person does not excuse, since such laws are intended to safeguard the common good. However, should the moral impossibility become common, such an invalidating law would cease. Thus it is probable that diriment impediments of merely ecclesiastical law do not bind in the case of these who wish to marry when it is impossible to obtain a dispensation, e.g., because of war. (Mathis/Bonner, 19-20)

II. Epikeia

Epikeia is "a correction of law where it is defective owing to its universality." (Aristotle, *Nichomachean Ethics*, 5, 10) It is a correction made by a subject who deviates from the clear words of the law in order to uphold some other value. Because the legislator cannot foresee all the consequences of the law in every situation, individuals and groups can invoke the virtue of epikeia and not observe a law, or not observe it strictly, when its observance would conflict with some other, greater good.

According to Thomas Aquinas, a law is "an ordinance of reason, for the common good, made by the one who has care of the community, and promulgated." (*Summa Theologiae*, I-II, 90, 4) Laws are intended to be ordinances of reason; if in particular circumstances a law is not rational, if it does not promote good ends, then it ceases to be what a law is supposed to be. In such a case an individual or group can correct the law by invoking epikeia in order to uphold the true purpose of the law, namely to promote and protect values—especially for the good of the community. The principal criterion for invoking epikeia, therefore, is whether the results of not observing the law, or not observing it strictly, would be more just, charitable, and prudent than if the law had been observed with full rigor.

> Epikeia is a species of equity, which may be defined as a benign interpretation and application of the law, by which its rigor and severity are somewhat tempered by kindness and mercy because of particular circumstances. Obviously, such an attitude towards the law of the Church must be adopted in the concrete circumstances and situations of pastoral practice whenever the law is to be applied.

> Certain similarities exist between epikeia and excusing causes. However, the excusing cause implies a situation in which the observance of the law ceases altogether, whereas epikeia implies a correction of the law for the sake of some other value. (Mathis/Bonner, 21)

The following rules, developed by the author, may be helpful in determining whether epikeia may be invoked in a given case.

1. Epikeia may not be applied to precepts of the natural law and the divine positive law. Its use is limited to ecclesiastical laws.

2. Epikeia may not be applied to invalidating laws which of their very nature exclude in practice deviation from them. Epikeia is not a legal act, but a virtue that corrects a law in a particular case; it cannot make valid that which legally is invalid.

3. Epikeia ordinarily should not be applied to categories of laws from which no dispensation is possible, including procedural laws, constitutive laws, and penal laws. (See cans. 86-87.)

4. Epikeia should not be used if it results in dissension in the community. Since a chief purpose of law is to promote harmony in the community, epikeia—if it is truly to be a virtue—should not produce conflict and disagreement. Even if the majority of the group favors invoking epikeia, the view of the minority who wish to observe the law should be respected. In such a case it is best to seek a dispensation from the competent superior rather than use epikeia.

An example will help to clarify these principles. Canon 230, §3 permits deputed laypersons to administer Holy Communion "when the need of the Church requires it and ministers are lacking." It sometimes happens, e.g., at a special celebration, that more priests and deacons arrive than anticipated, and there is no real need for the service of the regularly assigned lay Eucharistic ministers. Strict adherence to the letter of the law would mean that the pastor or superior should dismiss the unnecessary lay ministers. However, the sensitive pastor who knows his people would realize the possibilities of hurt, anger against the Church, and even scandal that might arise by strict enforcement of the law. Since the prevention of such unwanted results of the law's enforcement is a greater good than the value behind the law, the pastor could invoke epikeia to enable the lay ministers to exercise their function.

CHAPTER III
Physical Persons

I. Subjects of Ecclesiastical Law

A. Subjects of the Law in General

1. Those bound to observe merely ecclesiastical law are those baptized into the Catholic Church or received into it, who enjoy a sufficient use of reason and, unless the law expressly states otherwise, have reached the age of seven. (Can. 11)

> *Divine* law binds everyone; *ecclesiastical* law binds only those specified above.

2. The canons of the *Code of Canon Law* pertain only to the Latin Church. (Can. 1)

> Although the Latin Code does not bind Catholics who belong to the Eastern ritual churches (Oriental rites), there are times when it does; e.g., when an Eastern Catholic marries a Latin Catholic, the parties are subject to the marriage laws of both rites.

3. An *adult* is a person who has completed the eighteenth year of age; a *minor* is one below this age. A minor younger than seven is called an *infant* and is considered *non sui compos* [legally incompetent]; but after the seventh birthday the use of reason is presumed. (Can. 97) Whoever habitually lacks the use of reason is considered *non sui compos* and is equated with infants. (Can. 99)

> In canon law, one completes a year of life at midnight of the day following one's birthday. Thus, e.g., one becomes an adult the day after one's eighteenth birthday; one is presumed to have the use of reason the

day after one's seventh birthday. This is the way all canonical age requirements are to be reckoned. (See can. 203.)

Adults have the full exercise of their rights. Minors remain subject to their parents or guardians in the exercise of their rights, with the exception of those areas in which minors are exempt from parental control either by divine law or by canon law. In reference to the designation of guardians and their authority, the civil law should be observed unless canon law establishes something else, or if, in certain cases and for a just reason, the diocesan bishop has decided to provide otherwise by the appointment of another guardian. (Can. 98)

B. Subjects of Universal and Particular Law

1. Everyone, for whom universal laws are made, is bound to observe them everywhere on the earth. However, when universal laws are not in force in a certain territory, all who are actually in that territory are exempt from them. (Can. 12, §§1–2)

> *Universal* laws are established for members of the Church everywhere. For example, the *Code of Canon Law* is universal law binding persons everywhere as applicable. Thus, the laws on clergy bind all clergy; the laws on religious bind all religious, etc. When there are exemptions for a particular territory, all those actually in the territory are exempt. For example, the feast of the Assumption on August 15 is a holy day of obligation in the universal Church, but not in Canada. Accordingly, all Catholics in Canada on August 15 (including non-Canadians) are not bound by the obligation to attend Mass.

2. Bound to laws established for a particular territory are those for whom they were enacted, and those who have either domicile or quasi-domicile and likewise are actually staying there, with due regard for canon 13. (Can. 12, §3)

> *Particular* laws bind only in the territory or only the persons for whom they were made. In order to be bound by the particular laws of a territory—e.g., some

diocese, province, or region—it is required that one be both *of* the territory and actually *in* the territory. In other words, the subject of particular law not only has a domicile or quasi-domicile in the territory, but is actually present in the diocese, province, or region and is not travelling elsewhere. Exceptions are given in canon 13.

3.   Particular laws are not presumed to be personal but rather territorial, unless otherwise evident. (Can. 13, §1)

> *Personal* laws bind persons wherever they go. For example, religious are bound by the constitutions of their institute wherever they go. Laws are presumed to be territorial unless it is clear that they are personal. Thus, the laws of the Code are territorial, binding Catholics everywhere. Particular laws are also presumed to be territorial, binding only those both of the territory and in the territory.

4.   Travelers are not bound by particular laws of their own territory as long as they are absent from it, unless the transgression of them would cause harm in their own territory, or unless the laws are personal. (Can. 13, §2, 1°)

> Examples of laws which cannot be violated without doing *harm to one's own territory* would be a law requiring the pastor's presence in his parish on a certain day, a law requiring his presence at the diocesan synod, or restricting his absence from the diocese. Particular laws concerning these and similar matters must be observed even when one is outside the territory. Moreover, the lawgiver may make *personal particular laws* which must be observed even when a subject is outside the territory. Thus, a diocesan bishop may make certain disciplinary rules and norms for his clergy, clearly indicating the personal character of these norms. However, this personal character must be quite evident and clear; in doubt, the presumption of territoriality takes precedence.

5.   Travelers are not bound to the laws of a territory in which they are staying except for those which pertain to public order, determine the formalities of legal acts, or pertain to immovable things located in the territory. (Can. 13, §2, 2°)

21

Laws which concern the *public order* are those which are enacted to avert harm, scandal, and other evils, to prevent crimes and disturbances, to guard and protect peace and tranquility, and to promote the public welfare. Some of them may be especially made to include outsiders. Thus, possible particular laws restricting clerics and religious in the matter of engaging in business, politics, etc. may pertain to the public order. In doubt whether a given law is one which pertains to the public order, freedom on the part of the traveler is favored. Laws which concern *legal formalities* are those which determine the acts and procedures required in the drafting of wills and contracts, the conduct of trials, etc. Laws pertaining to *immovable things* refer to buildings and property which cannot be moved.

6. Transients (*vagi*) are bound to both universal and particular laws which are in force in the place where they are staying. (Can. 13, §3)

Transients are those who have no domicile or quasi-domicile.

II. Domicile and Quasi-Domicile

A. Acquisition of Voluntary Domicile

1. Domicile is acquired by residence in the territory of some parish or at least of a diocese which is conjoined with either the intention of remaining there perpetually if nothing calls one away, or the completion of residence for five years. (Can. 102, §1)

2. Quasi-domicile is acquired by residence in the territory of some parish or at least of a diocese which is conjoined with either the intention of staying there three months if nothing calls one away, or the completion of residence for three months. (Can. 102, §2)

When domicile or quasi-domicile is acquired by actual residence for a period of five years or of three months, the time need not be absolutely continuous; moral continuity suffices. Hence, brief absences do not break the continuity of the time period.

A domicile or quasi-domicile in the territory of a

parish is called parochial; in the territory of a diocese, even if not in a parish, is called diocesan. (Can. 102, §3)

Spouses may have a common domicile or quasi-domicile; for reason of legitimate separation or for another just cause, either can have one's own domicile or quasi-domicile. (Can. 104)

A person is called a *resident* in the place where one has domicile; a *temporary resident* in the place of quasi-domicile; a *traveler* if outside one's domicile or quasi-domicile while still retaining it; a *transient* (*vagus*) if one has neither a domicile nor a quasi-domicile anywhere. (Can. 100)

B. Acquisition of Legal (Necessary) Domicile

1. Minors necessarily retain the domicile or quasi-domicile of those who have authority over them. Those who are beyond infancy [seven or older with the use of reason] are able to acquire their own quasi-domicile; and those who have been legitimately emancipated according to the norm of civil law may also acquire their own domicile. Whoever has been placed legally under the guardianship or care of another for some reason other than minority [under eighteen] has the domicile or quasi-domicile of the guardian or curator. (Can. 105)
2. Members of religious institutes and societies of apostolic life acquire domicile in the place where the house to which they belong is located; they acquire quasi-domicile in the house where they are living in accord with canon 102, §2. (Can. 103)

C. Effect of Domicile

One acquires a pastor and Ordinary through both one's domicile and quasi-domicile. The proper pastor or Ordinary of a transient is the pastor or Ordinary of the place in which the transient is actually staying. The proper pastor of those who have only a diocesan domicile or quasi-domicile is the pastor of the place in whey they are actually staying. (Can. 107)

It frequently occurs that a person has several proper Ordinaries and pastors by reason of domicile in one place and quasi-domicile in one or more other places. Which proper Ordinary or pastor is to be preferred in various cases (as for baptism or burial) is sometimes determined either by law or legal custom; in other cases one has the liberty to choose which ever proper Ordinary or pastor one prefers.

D. Loss of Domicile

Domicile and quasi-domicile are lost by departing from the place with the intention of not returning, the prescription of canon 105 remaining intact. (Can. 106)

Mere absence, even for a number of years, does not cause loss of domicile or quasi-domicile as long as the intention to return exists.

Legal (necessary) domicile of minors is not lost by departure even with the intention never to return; it is lost only when subjection to the authority of parents or guardian ceases. (Cf. can. 105.)

III. Consanguinity and Affinity

A. Consanguinity

Consanguinity is computed by lines and degrees. In the direct line there are as many degrees as there are generations, that is, as there are persons, not counting the common ancestor. In the collateral line there are as many degrees as there are persons in both lines, not counting the common ancestor. (Can. 108)

Consanguinity, or blood relationship, exists in the *direct line*, if one person is the direct ancestor of the other, e.g., grandfather, father, son, etc.; in the *collateral line*, if neither person is the direct ancestor of the other but both are descended from a common ancestor, e.g., brothers and sisters, cousins, uncles and nephews and aunts and nieces, etc.

Since carnal generation is the basis of consanguinity, the relationship arises from both legitimate and illegitimate generation.

24

A degree of relationship indicates the measure of distance of two related persons. In the direct line there are as many degrees as there are generations or persons, not counting the common ancestor. Thus, the relationship between parent and child is first degree; that between grandparent and grandchild is second degree; etc.

In the collateral line there are as many degrees as there are persons in both lines together, not counting the common ancestor. Thus, brothers and sisters are related in the second degree; uncle or aunt and nephew or niece in the third degree; first cousins in the fourth degree; great aunt or uncle and grand nephew or niece in the fifth degree; second cousins in the sixth degree, etc.

To compute the degree of relationship one must always identify the common ancestor. For example, the common ancestor of first cousins is the common grandparents. It is helpful to diagram the relationship.

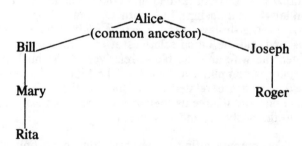

In this example, Bill and Joseph are brothers, related in the second degree, the sons of Alice. Mary is Bill's daughter and Roger is Joseph's son. Joseph is Mary's uncle (third degree) and Bill is Roger's uncle (third degree). Mary and Roger are first cousins (fourth degree), the grandchildren of Alice. Rita is Mary's daughter, Bill's granddaughter, Roger's niece. She is related by consanguinity to Joseph, her grand uncle, in the fourth degree collateral line. The rule for determining the degree is to count the number of persons taken together on both lines but without counting the common ancestor. The first line is that from Alice through

25

Rita; the other line is that from Alice through Roger. Also, descendants who are not relevant are not counted. For example, in determining that Rita is related to Joseph in the fourth degree, Joseph's descendant, Roger, is not counted—he is irrelevant to determining the relationship between Rita and Joseph.

Note: The former law had a different, more complex system for computing degrees of relationship.

B. Affinity

Affinity arises from a valid marriage, even if not consummated, and it exists between a man and the blood relations of his wife and also between a woman and the blood relations of her husband. It is computed such that those who are blood relatives of the man are related by affinity to his wife in the same line and degree as they are related by consanguinity to the man, and vice versa. (Can. 109)

Affinity arises from valid marriage, whether ratified only or both ratified and consummated. It is the "in-law" relationship, i.e., father-in-law, daughter-in-law, brother-in-law, etc. It exists only between the husband and the blood relatives of the wife and the between the wife and the blood relatives of the husband. Affinity is computed as follows: The blood relatives of the husband are related by affinity to the wife in the same line and degree as they are related by consanguinity to the husband, and vice versa.

To compute affinity, therefore, one need only determine the line and degree of consanguinity, because it is exactly the same line and degree for affinity. Thus, a man is related to his mother by consanguinity in the first degree of the direct line; his wife is related to his mother (her mother-in-law) by affinity also in the first degree of the direct line.

Some other examples; the husband's brother is related by affinity to the wife in the second degree of the collateral line; the wife's first cousin is related by affinity to the husband in the fourth degree of the collateral line.

26

IV. Membership in a Ritual Church

A. By Baptism

1. If both parents belong to the Latin Church, their child becomes a member of it by receiving baptism in it. If one of the parents does not belong to the Latin Church, they may decide by common agreement to have their child baptized in the Latin Church; but if they are unable to agree, the child should become a member of the ritual church to which the father belongs. (See can. 111, §1)

> Under the former law, the children had to be baptized in the ritual church, or rite, of the father. Under the revised legislation, parents of mixed rite may choose the ritual church of either for the baptism of their children. If they are unable to agree, the children are baptized in the ritual church of the father.

> There are six ancient liturgical rites in the Catholic Church: Latin, Byzantine, Alexandrian, Antiochene, Chaldean, and Armenian. These are not to be confused with the automonous ritual churches *sui iuris*, of which there are at least twenty: Armenian, Bulgarian, Byelorussian, Chaldean, Coptic, Ethiopian, Greek-Melkite, Hellenic Byzantine Rite, Hungarian Greek Catholic, Italo-Greek and Albanian, Krizevtsky (Yugoslavian, Croatian, Russine, Macedonian, Ukrainian), Latin, Malabar, Malankar, Maronite, Romanian, Russian, Ruthenian Byzantine-Catholic U.S.A., Slovak Greek Catholic, Syrian, Ukrainian.

> Of these, the following jurisdictions exist in North America at the present time: (1) the Ukrainian Metropolia of Philadelphia, with episcopal sees in Stamford, Connecticut; Chicago; and Parma, Ohio; (2) the Ukrainian Metropolia of Winnipeg, with episcopal sees in Toronto, Ontario; Edmonton, Alberta; Saskatoon, Saskatchewan; and New Westminster, British Columbia; (3) the Byzantine Catholic (Ruthenian) Metropolia of Pittsburgh with episcopal sees in Passaic, New Jersey; Parma, Ohio; and Van Nuys, California; (4) the Maronite Diocese of Saint Maron in Brooklyn; (5) the Maronite Diocese of Canada in Montreal; (6) the Melkite Diocese of Newton, Massachusetts; (7) the Melkite

27

Diocese of Canada in Montreal; (8) the Apostolic Exarchy for the Armenians, with the see in New York; (9) the Apostolic Exarchy for the Slovaks, with the see in Toronto; (10) the Apostolic Exarchy for the Chaldeans, with see in Detroit; (11) the Apostolic Exarchy for the Romanians, with the see in Canton, Ohio. (Pospishil/ Faris, 7-8, 14-15)

2. Anyone to be baptized who is at least fourteen may freely choose to be baptized in the Latin Church or in some other ritual church *sui iuris*. In such a case the person belongs to that church which he or she has chosen. (Can. 111, §2)

B. By Transfer

After baptism one can become a member of another ritual church if one:

a. obtains the permission of the Apostolic See;

b. is a spouse who, when getting married or during the marriage, declares that he or she is transferring to the ritual church of the other spouse; if the marriage is dissolved, however, he or she may freely return to the Latin Church;

c. is a child under fourteen of those mentioned in a or b; or, in a mixed marriage, is a child under fourteen of the Catholic party who has legitimately transferred to another ritual church; but when the children have completed their fourteenth year they may choose to return to the Latin Church. (Can. 112, §1)

Among the reasons on account of which transfer to another rite is usually granted, the return to the rite of one's ancestors is eminent. (*Cleri Sanctitati*, Canons on Rites and Persons for Eastern Churches, June 2, 1957, can. 8, §2)

The practice, however long, of receiving the sacraments according to the rite of another ritual church *sui iuris* does not bring about membership in that church. (Can. 112, §2)

C. By Reception into Full Communion

Catholics, one and all, as well as those who have been baptized in any non-Catholic church or community and now belong to the fullness of the Catholic communion, should, everywhere in the

28

world, retain their own rite, cherish it and, according to their ability, observe it, without prejudice to the right of recourse in special cases of persons, communities, or regions to the Apostolic See which, as supreme arbiter of inter-ecclesial relations, will itself or through other authorities provide for needs in an ecumenical spirit by issuing timely norms, decrees, or rescripts. (OE, 4, CLD 6:9)

Non-Catholic Christians, when they are received into full communion with the Catholic Church, must become members of the ritual church indicated by their baptism. Thus, all Protestants must become members of the Latin Church; a Greek Orthodox must become a member of the Greek Catholic Church; a Syrian Orthodox must become a member of the Syrian Catholic Church, etc. Exceptions constitute a transfer of rite, requiring the permission of the Apostolic See.

Baptism

Part II

CHAPTER I
Fundamental Norms

A. Juridical Effects of Baptism

1. By baptism one is incorporated into the Church of Christ and becomes a person in the Church with the duties and rights proper to Christians according to their condition to the extent that they are in ecclesiastical communion and are not impeded by a sanction legitimately imposed. (Can. 96; see also can. 849.)

> Those bound to observe merely ecclesiastical law are those baptized into the Catholic Church or received into it, who enjoy a sufficient use of reason and, unless the law expressly states otherwise, have reached the age of seven. (Can. 11)

2. The faithful are those who, inasmuch as they have been incorporated in Christ by baptism, are constituted the people of God. For this reason they have been made sharers in their own way in the priestly, prophetic, and kingly functions of Christ. They are called to exercise, according to their own proper condition, the mission which God has entrusted the Church to fulfill in the world. (Can. 204, §1)

B. Necessity of Baptism for Reception of Other Sacraments

No one may validly be admitted to the other sacraments without having first received baptism. (Can. 842, §1)

C. Relation to Full Initiation

The sacraments of baptism, confirmation, and Eucharist are so related to each other that all are required for full Christian initiation. (Can. 842, §2)

D. Matter and Form

For validity, baptism must be conferred with real water using the proper words. (See can. 849.) The Trinitarian form is required for the validity of baptism, and the baptism of non-Catholics is not recognized by the Church as valid unless the words include the Trinitarian form. The words for conferring baptism in the Latin Church are: I BAPTIZE YOU IN THE NAME OF THE FATHER, AND OF THE SON, AND OF THE HOLY SPIRIT. In the Eastern ritual churches, the form is: "The servant of God N. is baptized in the name of the Father, and of the Son, and of the Holy Spirit."

Distilled water or even a mixture in which water predominates would still be considered true water and does not affect the validity of the sacrament. For liceity, in ordinary circumstances, the water must be blessed according to the prescriptions of the liturgical books. (Can. 853) Baptism is conferred either by immersion or by pouring, observing the norms of the bishops' conference. (Can. 854)

The baptismal anointings are for liceity only. The anointing with the *oil of catechumens* on the breast in infant baptism may be omitted for serious reasons in the judgment of the episcopal conference. In the United States it may be omitted when the minister of baptism judges that it is pastorally necessary or desirable. (RBaptC, 51) This anointing in adult baptism is optional. (RCIA, 127) In infant baptism there is a mandatory post-baptismal anointing with chrism, but this again is for liceity only. In adult baptism confirmation replaces this post-baptismal anointing, unless confirmation is delayed for some special reason, such as to postpone it from the Easter Vigil to Pentecost. (RCIA, 224; 56)

The minister should use oil consecrated or blessed by the bishop at the Chrism Mass. For pastoral reasons, the oil of catechumens may be blessed by the priest immediately before the anointing during the catechumenate. (RCIA, 129) The oil used must be olive oil or an oil pressed from some other plant. Old oils, i.e., oils consecrated or blessed before the most recent Chrism Mass, should not be used except in necessity. The pastor should obtain the sacred oils from his own

34

bishop and carefully keep them in fitting custody. (Can. 847)

E. Capability for Baptism

Any person not yet baptized is capable of being baptized. (Can. 864)

F. Non-repeatability

The sacrament of baptism cannot be repeated because it imparts a character. (See can. 845, §1.) It may never lawfully be repeated once it has been validly celebrated, even if by Christians from whom we are separated. (IGIC, 4)

CHAPTER II
The Celebration of Baptism

I. Adult Initiation

The prescriptions of canon law on adult baptism refer to all who are no longer infants and have the use of reason. (Can. 852, §1) N.B. Children who are seven years old and older and have the use of reason are to be baptized using the RCIA.

RCIA = 7 yo.

A. The RCIA

1. The *Rite of Christian Initiation of Adults* (RCIA) consists of several rites of adult initiation: the *Rite of the Catechumenate Arranged in Stages*, the *Simple Rite for the Initiation of an Adult*, the *Short Rite for the Initiation of an Adult in Danger of Death or at the Point of Death*, and the *Rite of Initiation for Children of Catechetical Age*.

2. *An adult* who intends to receive baptism should be admitted to the catechumenate and, as far as possible, should be gradually led to sacramental initiation through the various stages. (Can. 851, 1°)

> The stages of the catechumenate are: evangelization and precatechumenate, catechumenate, period of purification and enlightenment (Lenten preparation), sacraments of initiation, and period of postbaptismal catechesis or mystagogy. (RCIA, 4-40) Ordinarily, adult baptism is conferred as part of this catechumenal process using the *Rite of the Catechumenate Arranged in Stages*. (RCIA, 68-239)

3. *In extraordinary circumstances* when a candidate has been unable to go through all the stages of initiation or when the local Ordinary, convinced that the candidate's Christian conversion is sincere

and that he or she is religiously mature, decides that the candidate may receive baptism without delay, the Ordinary, in individual cases, can allow the use of the *Simple Rite for the Initiation of an Adult*. (RCIA, 240)

> Clearly, the law considers the stages of the catechumenate to be normative, and there must be a good reason to use the abbreviated rite, e.g., disease, old age, change of domicile, or a long journey. (See RCIA, 274.) Permission to use the rite must be obtained from the local Ordinary.

4. *Rite of Initiation for Children of Catechetical Age.* This rite is intended for children, unbaptized as infants, who have reached the age of reason and are of catechetical age and who have been brought by their parents or guardians for Christian initiation or have come of their own accord with parental permission. (RCIA, 306)

B. Requirements for Adult Baptism

For an adult to be baptized, he or she must manifest the desire to receive baptism, must be sufficiently instructed in the truths of the faith and the Christian obligations, and must be tested in the Christian life during the catechumenate. The one to be baptized should also be admonished to be sorry for his or her sins. (Can. 865, §1)

C. Necessity of Full Initiation

Unless there is a serious reason, an adult who is baptized should be confirmed immediately after baptism and should participate in the Eucharistic celebration, including receiving Communion. (Can. 866)

> This prescription refers to *all* who receive adult baptism, including children seven and older who have the use of reason. This will be treated further in Part III on Confirmation under canon 883.

D. Baptism by the Bishop

The baptism of adults, at least those who are 14 or older, should be referred to the diocesan bishop so that, if he judges it expedient, he himself may administer it. (Can. 863)

II. Infant Baptism

A minor under the age of seven is an infant in canon law, as is anyone who habitually lacks the use of reason. (See cans. 97, 99.)

An infant, even in reference to baptism, includes anyone who is mentally incompetent—*non sui compos*. (Can. 852, §2) The baptism of such persons follows the *Rite of Baptism for Children*.

> Those who are insane are not to be baptized unless their condition has existed from birth, or from a time preceding their attaining the use of reason. In this case, they are to be baptized as infants. If they have lucid intervals, during which the use of reason is present, they should be baptized if they so request. Similarly, those who fall into coma or delirium should be baptized only when they are awake and manifest a desire for baptism. (V.C. 2:35)

A. Rite of Baptism for Children

The *Rite of Baptism for Children* consists of several rites of infant baptism: the *Rite of Baptism for Several Children*, the *Rite of Baptism for One Child*, the *Rite of Baptism for a Large Number of Children*, the *Rite of Baptism for Children Administered by a Catechist when no Priest or Deacon is Available*, and the *Rite of Baptism for Children in Danger of Death when no Priest or Deacon is Available*.

B. Preparation of Parents and Godparents

The parents of an infant to be baptized, as well as those who will be the godparents, should be suitably instructed about the meaning of this sacrament and about the obligations that go with it. The pastor personally or through others should ensure that the parents are duly instructed through pastoral exhortations and also by common prayer; several families may be brought together for this purpose and, where possible, each family visited. (Can. 851, 2°)

C. Duties of Parents

1. Parents are bound by obligation to see that their infants are baptized within the first weeks after birth. As soon as possible after birth, or even before it, they should see the pastor so that they may

request the sacrament for their child and receive preparation for baptism. (Can. 867, §1)

2. For an infant to be baptized licitly, it is necessary that: (1) at least one of the parents consents to it, or the person who lawfully takes their place consents; (2) there is a well founded hope that the child will be brought up in the Catholic religion. If this hope is utterly lacking, the baptism should be deferred according to the prescriptions of particular law, explaining the reason to the parents. (Can. 868, §1)

when to refuse baptism

In 1970 the Congregation for the Doctrine of the Faith established some guidelines for the case of "parents who are not Christian or who are 'irregular' Christians." By irregular Christians, the Congregation means "polygamous Christians, concubinaries, lawful spouses who have abandoned all regular practice of the faith, or who request baptism of the infant for the sole reason of social propriety." Although these guidelines do not have the same force as the canons of the Code, they may be helpful in handling a case where there is lacking a well founded hope that the child will be brought up in the Catholic religion.

a) It is important to make the parents become conscious of their responsibilities.

b) Further, it is important to pass judgment on the sufficiency of the guarantees regarding the Catholic education of the infants—guarantees given by some member of the family, or by the godfather or godmother, or by the support of the community of the faithful. (By guarantees we mean that there is founded hope of Catholic education.)

c) If the conditions are sufficient in the judgment of the pastor, the Church can proceed to the baptism because the infants are baptized in the faith of the Church.

d) If the conditions are not sufficient, one will be able to propose to the parents:
—enrollment of the infant with a view to baptism later;
—continuance of pastoral contacts with them as a way of preparing them for the rite of reception of their

child for baptism. (SCDF, reply, July 13, 1970, CLD 7:593-94)

Also useful on this issue is an instruction of the Congregation for the Doctrine of the Faith of October 20, 1980 which discusses the historical, theological, and pastoral issues at some length. In speaking of the "well founded hope," the Congregation states: "If sufficient assurances are given, for example, by the selection of godparents who will sincerely undertake the care of the child, or by the assistance of the faithful in the community, then the priest cannot refuse to celebrate the baptism without delay, exactly as he would do with regard to children of Christian families."

The instruction also clarified what it means to enroll the infant for later baptism. "Enrollment in a future catechumenate, if it should take place, should not be celebrated with any ritual set up for that purpose since it could easily be considered as the equivalent of the sacrament itself. It should also be clear that enrollment of this kind is not actual entrance into a catechumenate, nor are the children who are thus enrolled, connected with this state. At a later time they will have to be presented for a catechumenate suited to their age." (See SCDF, reply, Oct. 20, 1980, CLD 9:508-27, esp. pp. 524-25.)

D. Name of Child

The parents, godparents, and pastor are to see that the name given is not foreign to Christian sentiment. (Can. 855)

The law does not require that the child be given a saint's name, but only a name that is not offensive to Christians.

E. Abandoned Infants

Unless after a diligent investigation its baptism has been proven, an abandoned infant or a foundling should be baptized. (Can. 870)

F. Aborted Fetuses

If they are living, aborted fetuses should be baptized insofar as possible. (Can. 871)

III. Offices and Ministries

A. Ordinary Ministers

The ordinary minister of baptism is a bishop, presbyter, or deacon. (Can. 861, §1) The administration of baptism is a function especially committed to the pastor. (Can. 530, 1°)

B. Extraordinary Ministers

If the ordinary minister is absent or impeded, baptism is lawfully conferred by a catechist or another person who has been deputed for this function by the local Ordinary and, in case of necessity, by any person who has the proper intention. (Can. 861, §2. See also can. 230, §3.)

C. Godparents

1. There should be a godparent for the person to be baptized insofar as this is possible. In adult baptism the godparent assists the baptized in Christian initiation. In infant baptism the godparent, together with the parents, presents the child for baptism and helps the baptized to lead the Christian life expected by baptism and to fulfill faithfully the obligations inherent to it. (Can. 872)

2. There may be one godfather, one godmother, or one of each. (Can. 873)

3. To be accepted to undertake the duty of a godparent, it is necessary:
a) that one be designated by the person to be baptized or by the parents or the person who takes their place or, if these are lacking, by the pastor or minister; and that one have the aptitude for an intention of carrying out this duty;
b) that one be at least 16 years of age, unless the diocesan bishop shall have established another age or unless in an exceptional case it seems to the pastor or minister that there is just cause to admit a younger person;
c) that one is Catholic, confirmed, and already has received the Holy Eucharist, and likewise leads a life of faith in harmony with the undertaking of this duty;

d) that one is not under a lawfully imposed or declared canonical penalty;

e) that one is not the father or mother of the one to be baptized. (Can. 874, §1)

> *Exception for Eastern non-Catholics.* Because of the close communion . . . between the Catholic Church and the separated Eastern churches, it is permissible for a just reason to accept one of the faithful of an Eastern church as godparent along with a Catholic godparent at the baptism of a Catholic infant or adult, as long as the Catholic upbringing of the one being baptized is provided for and there is assurance that the person is fit to be a godparent. A Catholic invited to stand as a godparent at a baptism in an Eastern church is not forbidden to do so. In such cases the duty of looking out for the Christian upbringing of the baptized falls first upon the godparent belonging to the church in which the child is baptized. (ED, 48)

> *Godparent by proxy.* If the godparent cannot be present in person, he or she may appoint another person to serve as a proxy, but the appointment must be made in such a way that there is certainty as to the person who takes the responsibility as godparent. Ordinarily the appointment of the proxy should be made by the godparent in writing or before two witnesses, in order that there be certainty as to who is the responsible person. The custom of leaving the appointment of the proxy to the parent of the infant or to the baptizing priest tends to make sponsorship doubtful, and is to be reprobated. The real godparent must give a mandate directly or indirectly (through the agency of others but with his or her consent) to the proxy. In the record of baptism the names of both the godparent and the proxy should be entered. (SCSacr, instr, Nov. 25, 1925)

D. Sponsor

Any candidate seeking admission as a catechumen is accompanied by a sponsor, that is, a man or woman who has known and assisted the candidate and stands as a witness to the candidate's moral character, faith, and intention. It may happen that this sponsor is not the one who will serve as godparent for the periods of purification, enlightenment, and mystagogy; in that case, another person takes the sponsor's place in the role of godparent. (RCIA, 42)

E. Non-Catholic Witness

A baptized person belonging to a non-Catholic ecclesial community may be admitted as a witness to baptism but only along with a Catholic godparent. (Can. 874, §2)

> Eastern non-Catholics, however, may be admitted as a godparent along with a Catholic godparent as above under C.

F. Catechists

Catechists have an important office for the progress of the catechumens and for the growth of the community. As often as possible, they should have an active part in the rites. (RCIA, 48)

G. Parents

Because of the natural relationships, parents have a ministry and a responsibility in the baptism of infants more important than those of the godparents. . . . It is very important that the parents be present at the celebration in which their child is reborn in water and the Holy Spirit. (See RBaptC, 5.)

H. The People of God

It is important that catechists and other lay people should work with priests and deacons in preparing for baptism. In the actual celebration, the people of God (represented not only by the parents, godparents, and relatives, but also, as far as possible, by friends, neighbors, and some members of the local Church) should take an active part. (IGIC, 7)

IV. Time and Place of Celebration

A. Time of Baptism

1. *Day of Celebration.* Although baptism may be celebrated on any day, it is commendable to celebrate it ordinarily on Sundays or, if possible, at the Easter Vigil. (Can. 856) On Sunday, baptism may be

celebrated even during Mass, so that the entire community may be present and the relationship between baptism and Eucharist may be clearly seen; but this should not be done too often. (RBaptC, 9)

2. *Adult baptism.* For the times of the stages of the catechumenate and the celebration of the sacraments in adult initiation, see the *Rite of Christian Initiation of Adults*, 49-62.

3. *Infant baptism.* Parents are obliged to see that their infants are baptized within the first weeks after birth. As soon as possible after birth, or even before it, they should see the pastor so that they may request the sacrament for their child and receive preparation for baptism. If an infant is in danger of death, it should be baptized without delay. (Can. 867)

> As for the time of baptism, the first consideration is the welfare of the child, that it may not be deprived of the benefit of the sacrament; then the health of the mother must be considered, so that, if at all possible, she too may be present. Then, as long as they do not interfere with the greater good of the child, there are pastoral considerations such as allowing sufficient time to prepare the parents and to plan the actual celebration in order to bring out its true character effectively. (RBaptC, 8)

> For an infant to be baptized licitly, it is necessary that there be a well founded hope that the child will be brought up in the Catholic religion; if this hope is utterly lacking, the baptism should be deferred according to the prescriptions of particular law, explaining the reason to the parents. (Can. 868, §1, 2°)

4. As far as possible, all *recently born babies* should be baptized at a common celebration on the same day. Except for a good reason, baptism should not be celebrated more than once on the same day in the same church. (IGIC, 27)

5. *Children of catechetical age.* It is desirable that as far as possible the final period of preparation coincides with Lent and that the sacraments themselves are celebrated at the Easter Vigil. . . . As far as possible, the candidates should come to the sacraments of initiation when their baptized companions are receiving confirmation or Eucharist. (RCIA, 310)

B. Place of Baptism

1. Except in a case of necessity, it is not lawful to baptize anyone outside one's territory, not even one's own subjects. (Can. 862)

2. Outside a case of necessity, the proper place for baptism is a church or oratory. As a rule, the baptism of adults is held in their own parish church, and the baptism of infants takes place in the parish church of their parents, unless there is a just reason for having it elsewhere. (Can. 857)

> An example of a just reason for celebrating baptism in a church or oratory other than one's parish is the convenience of the faithful. The pastor of the one to be baptized (or of the parents) as well as the local Ordinary are competent to grant this permission. If the church where the baptism is held is a parish church, the baptism is recorded there. If not, it should be recorded in the parish of the baptized (or parents).

3. If on account of distance or other circumstances, the person to be baptized cannot without grave inconvenience go or be brought to the parish church or another church or oratory in the parish boundaries that has a baptismal font, baptism may and must be conferred in a closer church or oratory, or even in another suitable place. (Can. 859)

4. Except in a case of necessity, baptism may not be conferred in private homes, unless the local Ordinary has permitted it for a serious reason. Except in a case of necessity or for another pressing pastoral reason, baptism may not be celebrated in hospitals unless the diocesan bishop has decreed otherwise. (Can. 860)

V. Emergency Baptism

A. Baptism in a Case of Necessity

Baptism is administered according to the rite prescribed in the approved liturgical books except in the case of urgent necessity, in which case only those things must be observed that are required for the validity of the sacrament. (Can. 850)

There are two principal rites of baptism: the *Rite of Christian Initiation of Adults* and the *Rite of Baptism of Children*. The use of either of these rites has traditionally been called *solemn baptism*. In ordinary circumstances solemn baptism is required for liceity. However, in urgent necessity only the requirements for validity, namely, the use of water (blessed or unblessed) and the Trinitarian formula, are required. Nevertheless, if there is time the minister should use as much of the appropriate rite of baptism as circumstances allow, e.g., as found in the *Short Rite of Adult Initiation in Proximate Danger of Death or at the Point of Death* or the *Rite of Baptism for Children in Danger of Death when no Priest or Deacon is Available*. Some examples of urgent necessity are danger of death, religious persecution, and serious family disagreement about the baptism.

In necessity, baptism need not be celebrated in a church or oratory, and it may be celebrated in a home or hospital. The minister may confer baptism even outside his territory in such cases. Also, in necessity, any person with the proper intention may baptize.

B. Baptism in Danger of Death

1. *Adults.* An adult in danger of death can be baptized if he or she has some knowledge of the principal truths of the faith, manifests in some way the intention to receive baptism, and promises to observe the requirements of the Christian religion. (Can. 865, §2)

If possible, the minister of baptism should use the appropriate rite. Normally the priest or deacon uses the *Simple Rite for the Initiation of an Adult*. Catechists and other laypersons use the *Short Rite for the Initiation of an Adult in Danger of Death or at the Point of Death*. In case of emergency, however, a priest or a deacon may use this rite. If the sacred chrism is at hand and there is time, a priest who baptizes should confer confirmation after the baptism; in this case the postbaptismal anointing with chrism is omitted. Also whenever possible the priest or deacon, as well as a catechist or layperson having permission to distribute

47

Communion, should give the Eucharist to the person newly baptized. (RCIA, 280)

When a person is at the point of death or when time is pressing because death is imminent, the minister, omitting everything else, pours natural water (even if not blessed) on the head of the sick person, while saying the usual sacramental form. (RCIA, 281)

2. *Infants.*

a) If an infant is in danger of death, it should be baptized without delay. (Can. 867, §2) In danger of death the infant of Catholic parents, and even of non-Catholic parents, may be licitly baptized even if the parents are against it. (Can. 868, §2)

When no priest or deacon is available, anyone with the proper intention may baptize using water and the Trinitarian formula or, if it is prudently judged that there is sufficient time, the *Rite of Baptism for Children in Danger of Death when no Priest or Deacon is Available*. The priest or deacon may also use this shorter form if necessary. (RBaptC, 22) The pastor or any priest should confirm after baptism. In this case he omits the postbaptismal anointing with chrism. (See RBaptC, 22; can. 883, 3°). The Holy Eucharist may be administered to children in danger of death if they are able to distinguish the body of Christ from ordinary food and receive Communion reverently. (Can. 913, §2)

Infants may be baptized in danger of death even against the positive objections of the parents, provided one can prudently judge that the child will not live to attain the use of reason, and that the baptism can be administered in such a manner as to avoid anything like scandal or hatred of the faith. If necessary, the baptism can be conferred in such a case without the parent's knowledge of it.

b) *Supplying the ceremonies.* When solemn baptism has been omitted due to danger of death, the *Rite of Bringing a Baptized Child to the Church* should be used if the child lives. (RBaptC, 165-185) If solemn baptism was omitted for some other reason, this rite may be adapted accordingly by the minister. (RBaptC, 31, n. 3)

48

VI. Conditional Baptism

1. If there is a doubt whether someone was baptized, or whether the baptism was conferred validly, and this doubt remains after a serious investigation, then baptism should be administered conditionally.
2. Those baptized in a non-Catholic ecclesial community are not to be baptized conditionally unless there is a serious reason for doubting the validity of the baptism after examining the matter and the form of the words used in the baptism as well as the intention of the adult being baptized and of the baptizing minister. (Can. 869, §§1-2)

The practice of the Church in this matter is governed by two principles: (1) baptism is necessary for salvation; (2) it can be conferred only once. (ED, 9)

1. There can be no doubt cast upon the validity of baptism as conferred among *separated Eastern Christians*. It suffices, therefore, to establish the fact that baptism was administered. (ED, 12)

2. In respect to *other Christians*, doubt can *sometimes* arise.

a. *Concerning matter and form.* Baptism by immersion, pouring or sprinkling, together with the Trinitarian formula, is of itself valid, though consideration should be given to the danger of invalidity when the sacrament is administered by sprinkling, especially of several people at once. Hence, if rituals, liturgical books, or customs of a church or community prescribe one of these ways of baptizing, doubt can arise only if it happens that the minister does not observe the regulations of his own church or community. What is necessary and sufficient, therefore, is evidence that the minister of baptism was faithful to these norms. For this purpose, one should generally obtain a written baptismal certificate with the name of the minister. In many cases, the other community may be asked to cooperate in establishing whether or not, in general or in a particular case, a minister is to be considered as having baptized according to the approved ritual. (ED, 13, a)

b. *Concerning faith and intention.* Insufficient faith on the part of the minister never, of itself, makes baptism invalid. Sufficient intention in the baptizing minister is to be presumed, unless there is serious ground for doubting that he or she intends to do what Christians do. (ED, 13, b)

c. *Concerning the application of the matter.* When doubt arises in this area, both reverence for the sacrament and respect for the ecclesial nature of other communities demand that a serious investigation of the practice of the separated community and the circumstances of a particular baptism be made before any judgment is passed on the validity of a baptism by reason of its manner of administration. (ED, 13, c)

Indiscriminate conditional baptism of all who desire full communion with the Catholic Church cannot be approved. Conditional rebaptism is not allowed unless there is prudent doubt of the fact or invalidity of a baptism already administered. (ED, 14)

Since baptism cannot be repeated, conditional baptism or rebaptism should be done only after a thorough investigation has taken place, the results of which demonstrate that the baptism did not take place or was not conferred validly. If water and the Trinitarian formula was used, one can presume that the intention of the minister was to do what the Church does when it baptizes, unless there are contrary indications. A baptismal certificate is sufficient proof of baptism in ordinary circumstances.

The following are some non-Catholic churches which have valid baptism: all Eastern non-Catholics (Orthodox), Adventists, African Methodist Episcopal, Amish, Anglican, Assembly of God, Baptists, Evangelical United Brethren, Church of the Brethren, Church of God, Congregational Church, Disciples of Christ, Episcopalians, Evangelical Churches, Lutherans, Methodists, Liberal Catholic Church, Old Catholics, Old Roman Catholics, Church of the Nazzerine, Polish National Church, Presbyterian Church, Reformed Churches, United Church of Christ, Church of the Latter Day Saints (Mormons).

Some churches without valid baptism are: Apostolic Church, Bohemian Free Thinkers, Christian and Missionary Alliance, Christian Scientists, Church of Divine Science, Masons (no baptism at all), Peoples Church of Chicago, Quakers, Salvation Army, Pentecostal Churches, Christadelphians, Jehovah's Witnesses, and Unitarians.

In the absence of a baptismal certificate, proof of baptism can be had as described below, chapter III, section I.

3.   In cases 1 and 2 above, if doubt remains whether the baptism was conferred or whether it was valid, baptism should not be administered until after the one being baptized, if he or she is an adult, has received instruction on the doctrine of the sacrament of baptism. Also the reasons for doubting the validity of the previous baptism should be explained to the person or, in the case of infant baptism, to the parents. (Can. 869, §3)

4.   The local Ordinary shall determine, in individual cases, what rites are to be included or excluded in conditional baptism. (RCIA, appendix, n. 7; see also can. 845, §2.)   The formula for conditional baptism is: If you are not baptized, I baptize you in the name of the Father, and of the Son, and of the Holy Spirit.

CHAPTER III
Proof and Recording of Baptism

I. Proof of Baptism

To prove the conferral of baptism, if there is no conflict of interest, it suffices to have a declaration from one witness who is above suspicion or the oath of the baptized person, provided he or she received baptism as an adult. (Can. 876)

> Baptism is ordinarily proved by means of a baptismal certificate. In the absence of a baptismal certificate, it suffices to have the testimony of one reliable witness; if the person was at least seven years old and had the use of reason when baptized, the oath of the baptized person suffices. In either case, there can be no conflict of interest. For example, one could not prove one's own baptism by personal testimony when this testimony would be the sole indication of the decisive grounds for an annulment of marriage.

> The one who administers baptism should ensure that, if the godparent is not present, there be at least one witness who can prove the conferral of baptism. (Can. 875)

II. Recording of Baptism

1. The pastor of the place where baptism is celebrated must carefully and without any delay record in the baptismal register the names of the baptized, the minister of baptism, the parents, godparents and, if there were any, the witnesses, and the place and day that baptism was administered. He should also note the day and place of birth. (Can. 877, §1)

Illegitimate children. In the case of a child born of an unwed mother, the mother's name is recorded if there is public proof of her maternity or if she freely requests this in writing or before two witnesses. Likewise the name of the father is to be recorded if his paternity can be proved by some public document or he himself makes a declaration of his paternity before the pastor and two witnesses. In other cases, the name of the baptized is recorded without any mention of the name of the father or the parents. (Can. 877, §2)

Adopted children. In the case of an adopted child, the names of the adopting parents are recorded and also, at least if this is done in the civil records of the region, the names of the natural parents in accord with canon 877, §§ 1 and 2, and observing the statutes of the episcopal conference. (Can. 877, §3)

2. If baptism was administered neither by the pastor nor in his presence, the minister of baptism, whoever that may be, must notify the pastor of the parish in which baptism was administered so that it may be recorded in accord with the norm of canon 877, §1. (Can. 878)

The pastor of the territorial parish in which baptism was administered should be notified and should record the baptism. Notification must also be sent in the case of private baptism. If the person baptized was an infant (under seven years old or without the use of reason), notification should also be sent to the proper pastor of the parents or guardians.

Confirmation

Part III

CHAPTER I
General Norms

A. Juridical Consequences

1. By confirmation the baptized are joined more perfectly to the Church, are strengthened, and are more strictly obliged to be wtinesses to Christ by word and deed and to spread and defend the faith. (See can. 879.)

2. By baptism and confirmation the faithful are deputed to the apostolate. (See can. 225, §1.)

3. Those who are confirmed may licitly enter the novitiate (can. 645, §1), receive holy orders (can. 1033), or marry (can. 1065, §1), provided all other requirements of law have been met.

B. Relation to Full Initiation

The sacraments of baptism, confirmation, and Eucharist are so related to each other that all are required for full Christian initiation. (See can. 842, §2.) Confirmation is a continuation of the journey of Christian initiation. (See can. 879.) Unless a serious reason stands in the way, an adult who is baptized should be confirmed immediately after baptism and should participate in the Eucharistic celebration, including the reception of Communion. (Can. 866)

In certain cases, confirmation may be postponed until near the end of the period of postbaptismal catechesis, for example, Pentecost Sunday. (RCIA, 56) Even when children of catechetical age (seven and older) are baptized, they are to be confirmed and receive first Communion in the same celebration. (RCIA, 344) Adult catechumens and children who are baptized at an age when they are old enough for catechesis should ordinarily be admitted to confirmation and the

Eucharist at the same time as they receive baptism. If this is impossible, they should receive confirmation at another community celebration. (RConf, 11)

C. Non-repeatability

The sacrament of confirmation cannot be repeated because it imparts a character. If, after a diligent investigation, a doubt still remains whether confirmation was actually or validly conferred, it should be conferred conditionally. (See can. 845, §1.)

> N.B. Eastern non-Catholics (Orthodox) are confirmed at baptism. They may not be re-confirmed when they are received into the Catholic Church. Likewise, Eastern Catholics may not be reconfirmed. Even if the confirmation was not recorded, this does not give grounds for doubting that the sacrament was conferred. (ED, 12)

D. Matter and Form

1. The sacrament of confirmation is administered by the anointing with oil on the forehead which is done by the imposition of hands using the words prescribed in the approved liturgical books. (Can. 880, §1) The words prescribed in the Latin rite are: BE SEALED WITH THE GIFT OF THE HOLY SPIRIT.

> The laying of hands on the candidates with the prayer, *All-powerful God*, does not pertain to the valid giving of the sacrament. But it is still to be regarded as very important: it contributes to the complete perfection of the rite and to a more thorough understanding of the sacrament. (RConf, 9)

> The minister need not actually impose his hand on the head of the one being confirmed since the anointing with chrism on the forehead sufficiently expresses the laying on of hands. (See VatCom, reply, June 9, 1972, DOL 2529; CLD 7:611.)

2. The chrism used in the sacrament of confirmation must be consecrated by a bishop, even if the sacrament is administered by a presbyter. (Can. 880, §2)

The chrism is consecrated by the bishop in the Mass that is celebrated as a rule on Holy Thursday for this purpose. (RConf, 10) The chrism is required for the validity of the sacrament. The pastor should obtain the sacred oils from his own bishop and carefully keep them in fitting custody. (Can. 847, §2)

E. Capability for and Age of Confirmation

1. All and only the baptized who are not yet confirmed are capable of receiving confirmation. (Can. 889, §1)

2. The sacrament of confirmation is conferred on the faithful around the age of discretion, unless the conference of bishops has determined another age, or if there is danger of death, or if in the judgment of the minister a serious reason suggests otherwise. (Can. 891)

Confirmation in the Latin church is delayed until about the seventh year. If possible the proper sequence of Christian initiation should always be followed, with confirmation preceding first Communion. For pastoral reasons, the conference of bishops may set an age that seems more suitable. This means that the sacrament is given, after the formation proper to it, when the recipients are more mature. (See RConf, 11.) In the United States each diocesan bishop may establish the age for confirmation for his own diocese. (*BCL Newsletter* 19 (June/July, 1983) 23)

F. Preparation for Confirmation

1. To receive confirmation licitly, apart from danger of death, one must be suitably instructed, properly disposed, and be able to renew one's baptismal promises. Those who are in danger of death, or those who do not have the use of reason, are exempted from these requirements. (See can. 889, §2)

2. The faithful are obliged to receive confirmation at the proper time. Parents, pastoral ministers, and especially pastors should see to it that the faithful are properly instructed for receiving this sacrament and that they come for it at the opportune time. (Can. 890)

Uncatechized Adults. Adults who were baptized as infants, or baptized in danger of death or similar cases, and who did not receive further catechetical formation, should be confirmed according to the *Rite of Christian Initiation of Adults* (RCIA), chapter IV: "Preparing Uncatechized Adults for Confirmation and the Eucharist." Any confusion between such baptized persons and catechumens must be avoided.

Some of the rites belonging to the catechumenate, suited to the condition and spiritual needs of these adults, can be used to advantage. Among these are the presentation of the creed, the Lord's Prayer, and the Gospels. (RCIA, 302) Other liturgical rites for the catechesis of the baptized are described in a March 8, 1973 document of the SCDW. (See *Notitiae* 9 (1973) 274-78; DOL 2489.)

Sometimes the preparation of baptized adults for confirmation coincides with preparation for marriage. In such cases, if it is foreseen that the conditions for a fruitful reception of confirmation cannot be satisfied, the local Ordinary will judge whether it is better to defer confirmation until after the marriage. (RConf, 12) In analogous situations, such as when a person does not practice the faith, there is serious reason for the minister to delay confirmation.

G. Time and Place

1. The sacraments for the initiation of adults are to be celebrated at the Easter Vigil itself. (RCIA, 55) In certain cases, confirmation may be postponed until near the end of the period of postbaptismal catechesis, for example, Pentecost Sunday. (RCIA, 56)

When confirmation is celebrated apart from baptism, it can be administered on any day, but the Easter season is especially appropriate.

2. It is desirable that the sacrament of confirmation be celebrated in a church and also within Mass. However, for a just and reasonable cause it may be celebrated outside Mass and in any fitting place. (Can. 881)

CHAPTER II
Offices and Ministries

I. The Minister

The ordinary minister of confirmation is a bishop. A presbyter also validly confers this sacrament if he has this faculty by virtue of the universal law or a special concession of the competent authority. (Can. 882)

A. Presbyters with Faculty by Law

By the law itself the following have the faculty to administer confirmation:

a) within the boundaries of their jurisdiction, those who are equated in law with the diocesan bishop [territorial prelate, territorial abbot, vicar apostolic, prefect apostolic, apostolic administrator, diocesan administrator];

b) the presbyter who, by virtue of office or a mandate of the diocesan bishop, baptizes someone beyond infancy [seven or older with the use of reason], or who admits someone already baptized into full communion of the Catholic Church, but only for the person in question;

c) the pastor, or any presbyter, for someone in danger of death. (Can. 883)

> All Eastern priests can validly confer confirmation, either together with baptism or separately, on all the faithful of any rite, not excluding the Latin rite; the prescriptions of law, both common and particular, must be observed for licitness. Also priests of the Latin rite, in accord with faculties they enjoy regarding the administration of this sacrament, can validly administer it

also to the faithful of the Eastern Churches but without prejudice to rite; the prescriptions of law, whether universal or particular, must be observed as regards licitness. (OE, 14)

In reference to the faculty under b, not every presbyter may confirm at adult baptism or admission into full communion of the Church, but only one who has an office, e.g., the pastor, parochial vicar, chaplain. Presbyters without an office of pastoral care must have a special mandate from the diocesan bishop. The mandate does not have to be specifically for confirming, so long as it is a mandate for baptizing an adult or receiving a baptized person into full communion, but it must come from the diocesan bishop. (McManus, 665) The faculty of a presbyter to confirm is territorially limited, as noted below.

Also in virtue of the law, presbyters with an office of pastoral care or a mandate from the bishop who receive apostates from the faith back into the Church may confirm them using the *Rite of Receiving Baptized Christians into the Full Communion of the Catholic Church*. (RCIA, Appendix, 8) This also includes those baptized as Catholics who without fault were brought up in a non-Catholic religion or adhered to a non-Catholic religion. (VatCom, reply, Dec. 21, 1979, CLD 9: 527-28)

Note: Presbyters may not confirm in virtue of the law baptized Catholics who have not practiced the faith. Only those who left the Church, or who were brought up in or adhered to another faith, can be received back into the Church. Others must be treated as Catholics, even if they have never practiced their baptismal faith. To confirm in such cases, presbyters need the delegated faculty.

B. Presbyters with Delegated Faculty

1. The diocesan bishop should administer confirmation personally or should see that it is administered by another bishop. If need requires it, he may concede the faculty to one or more designated

presbyters who may administer the sacrament. (Can. 884, §1)

Cases of need would include the illness of the bishop, his necessary absence from the diocese for an extended period, a large number of parishes where confirmation is to be celebrated. (McManus, 637)

The presbyter who has the faculty to confirm must use it for those in whose favor the faculty was granted. (Can. 885, §2) Thus, for example, a presbyter who by law or mandate baptizes an adult (seven years old and older with the use of reason) must also confirm. (McManus, 637)

2. *Ad hoc delegation.* For a serious reason, the bishop and also the presbyter who by law or special concession of the competent authority has the faculty to confirm, may choose presbyters, in particular cases, to help with the administration of the sacrament. (See can. 884, §2.)

A serious reason for using this provision of the law is, e.g., the large number of those to be confirmed. (RConf, 8)

C. Extent of Faculty

1. A presbyter who has the faculty to administer confirmation may also licitly confer the sacrament in his designated territory on outsiders, unless their own Ordinary has forbidden it. However, he may not validly confer the sacrament outside his territory except in the case of danger of death. (Can. 887)

The faculty, whether conceded by law or delegation, is territorially limited. A presbyter cannot *validly* confirm outside his territory except: (1) in danger of death; (2) if he is confirming a member of an Eastern rite (OE, 14); or (3) if he receives a new faculty for that territory, including "*ad hoc* delegation." For example, a pastor or parochial vicar who confirms an adult after baptism can do so validly only within the boundaries of the parish, with the exceptions noted above.

2. Within the territory in which confirmation may be conferred, the ministers may also administer it in exempt places. (Can. 888)

D. Supplied Faculty

In common error, whether of fact or of law, and also in positive and probable doubt, whether of law or fact, the Church supplies executive power of governance both for the external and internal forum. This also applies to the faculty for confirmation. (See can. 144.)

It seems that supplied jurisdiction for confirmation should be interpreted in the same way as that for marriage. (See p. 224.) Therefore, the error must concern the "status" of the presbyter in question who lacked the faculty to confirm. For example, a priest is only in residence in a parish and does not celebrate baptisms, receive Christians into full communion, etc. On a given Sunday the pastor is away on an emergency call and the resident priest is notified by a parishioner that there is no one to celebrate the Sunday Eucharist at which there is going to be an adult baptism. The resident priest celebrates the Eucharist with the baptism, and confirms the initiate in accordance with the rite. The community is not at all surprised by this, because the priest is known to be in residence and regularly celebrates the Eucharist and even occasionally celebrates the sacrament of penance. Although he has no mandate to celebrate baptism or confirmation, nor any office, the Church supplies the faculty to confirm because the community errs regarding the status of the priest. The reason the Church supplies the faculty is not for the private good of this one individual being confirmed, but for the *common good* of the potentially many who could approach this priest under similar circumstances.

On the other hand, the Church does not supply the faculty to confirm when the common good is not at stake. For example, a priest who is a university professor receives a student into full communion and confirms him, and only later notifies the pastor to have it recorded. The confirmation is invalid because of the lack of a pastoral office or a mandate from the diocesan bishop. The community would not err concerning the status of this priest, nor is there a danger to the common good.

For further discussion of common error and of positive and probable doubt of law or of fact, see page 6.

II. The Sponsor

A. Desirability of Having a Sponsor

1. Insofar as possible, there should be a sponsor for the person to be confirmed. The sponsor's duty is to see that the one confirmed acts as a true witness to Christ and faithfully fulfills the duties inherent in this sacrament. (Can. 892)

2. It is desirable that one's baptismal godparent also serve as one's sponsor for confirmation. (Can. 893, §2) Nonetheless the option of choosing a special sponsor for confirmation is not excluded. (RConf, 5)

> Although the law speaks only in the singular, the possibility of having two sponsors, one male and one female, is not excluded, especially when they are the baptismal godparents. (SCSacr, reply, Nov. 13, 1984)

B. Qualifications of Sponsors

To be accepted to undertake the duty of a godparent, it is necessary:

a) that one be designated by the person to be confirmed or by the parents or the person who takes their place or, if these are lacking, by the pastor or minister; and that one have the aptitude for and intention of carrying out this duty;

b) that one be at least 16, unless the diocesan bishop shall have established another age or unless in an exceptional case it seems to the pastor or minister that there is just cause to admit a younger person;

c) that one is Catholic, confirmed, and already has received the Holy Eucharist, and likewise leads a life of faith in harmony with the undertaking of this duty;

d) that one is not under a lawfully imposed or declared canonical penalty;

e) that one is not the father or mother of the one to be baptized. (See cans. 893 and 874, §1.)

confirmed

Parents may "present" their children for confirmation, but may not be the canonical sponsor. The law favors the baptismal godparent or godparents to be the sponsor or sponsors at confirmation. If either of them are not available, or if they are no longer leading a life of faith in harmony with this duty, it would be appropriate to have the parents present the child rather than choosing a new sponsor for confirmation, although the latter is not excluded. If neither baptismal godparent is eligible or available for confirmation and if the parents present the child, there is no reason why a new sponsor would have to be named, since the confirmation sponsor, while desirable, is not obligatory.

III.   Other Roles

A.   In the Catechumenate

Adult catechumens who are to be confirmed immediately after baptism have the help of the Christian community and, in particular, the formation that is given them during the catechumenate. Catechists, sponsors, and members of the local Church participate in the catechumenate by means of catechesis and community celebrations of the rites of initiation. (See RConf, 3.)

B.   Parents

The initiation of children into the sacramental life is ordinarily the responsibility and concern of Christian parents. The role of the parents is also expressed by their active participation in the celebration of the sacraments. Even the parents themselves may present their children for confirmation. (See RConf, 3; 5.)

> N.B. Parents may not be sponsors at confirmation. The parent or parents may present the child to the minister for the anointing during the celebration in place of the sponsor, but they may not be recorded as the official sponsor. See commentary above under II, B.

CHAPTER III
Proof and Recording

I. Proof of Confirmation

To prove conferral of confirmation, if there is no conflict of interest, it suffices to have a declaration of one witness who is above suspicion or the oath of the confirmed person, provided he or she was confirmed in adulthood [seven or older with the use of reason]. (See cans. 876; 894.)

See the commentary in Part II on baptism, p. 53.

II. Recording of Confirmation

1. The names of the confirmed, the minister, the parents and sponsors, and the place and date of confirmation should be recorded in the confirmation book of the diocesan curia or, where it is prescribed by the bishops' conference or the diocesan bishop, in a book in the parish archives. The pastor must notify the pastor of the place of baptism that confirmation was conferred so that he might record it in the baptismal register in accord with the norm of can. 535, §2. (Can. 895)
2. If the pastor of the place was not present, the minister either personally or through another should notify him as soon as possible of the conferral of confirmation. (Can. 896)

CHAPTER IV
Receiving a Baptized Christian into Full Communion

I. Eastern Christians

In the case of Eastern Christians who enter into the fullness of Catholic communion, nothing more than a simple profession of Catholic faith is required, even if they are permitted, upon recourse to the Apostolic See, to transfer to the Latin rite. (RCIA, Appendix, 2)

> The profession of faith consists of the recitation of the Nicene Creed followed by a brief statement by the one being received and the words of reception by the celebrant in accord with nn. 15-16 of the *Rite of Receiving Baptized Christians into the Full Communion of the Catholic Church*, which is an appendix to the *Rite of Christian Initiation of Adults*.

II. Other Baptized Christians

1. Those baptized in a separated ecclesial community are received into full communion by the *Rite of Receiving Baptized Christians into the Full Communion of the Catholic Church*.

2. The rite should be seen as a celebration of the Church, with its climax in Eucharistic communion. For this reason the rite of reception is generally celebrated within Mass. (RCIA, Appendix, 3)

3. Any confusion between catechumens and candidates for reception into communion should be absolutely avoided. (Ibid., 5)

Candidates for reception into full communion are already baptized Christians, and should not be treated like catechumens. If their catechetical preparation is to incorporate certain formational aspects of the RCIA, it must be clear to all that those being received into full communion have a separate status, e.g., by being instructed separate from the catechumens. Their separate status must also be clearly recognized in the celebration of the rite of confirmation, e.g., by confirming them during a separate ceremony or at the same ceremony after all the catechumens have been baptized and confirmed.

4. It is the office of the bishop to receive baptized Christians into full communion. But the priest to whom he entrusts the celebration of the rite has the faculty of confirming the candidate during the rite of admission, unless the latter has already been validly confirmed. (Ibid., 8)

See the commentary above, p. 61.

5. At the reception, candidates should be accompanied if possible by a sponsor, that is, the person who has had the chief part in bringing them into full communion or in preparing them. Two sponsors may be permitted for each candidate. (Ibid., 10)

6. The names of those received into full communion should be recorded in a special book, with the date and place of baptism also noted. (Ibid., 13)

The Rite itself, both the *praenotanda* and the rubrics, should be consulted for additional norms.

The Eucharist

Part IV

Introduction

1. *The Code of Canon Law* divides its presentation of Eucharistic discipline into three chapters: the Eucharistic Celebration, the Reservation and Veneration of the Eucharist, and Mass Offerings. The present work adapts this structure by adding an initial chapter on the Liturgy of the Word, and reorganizing some of the material in the other chapters, especially chapter II, the Liturgy of the Eucharist, which is divided into five sections: Ministries; Participation in the Eucharist; Different Forms of Celebration; Rites and Ceremonies; and Frequency, Time and Place of Celebration. Also, the discipline on the administration of Communion outside Mass is given in the third chapter under Eucharistic reservation rather than in the chapter on the Liturgy of the Eucharist.

Chapters II-IV contain a nearly complete presentation of the canons on the Eucharist from the Code. Select norms from liturgical books are also included, but detailed, rubrical norms are avoided in accord with the original and longstanding policy of *The Pastoral Companion*. Chapter I includes select norms from the Code, the *General Instruction of the Roman Missal*, and the *Lectionary for Mass*.

2. *Principal Sources of Eucharistic Discipline*
a) *Code of Canon Law*, canons 897-958.
b) *General Instruction of the Roman Missal* (GIRM).
c) *Rite of Holy Communion and Worship of the Eucharist Outside Mass* (HCW).
d) *Lectionary for Mass* (LFM).
e) *General Norms for the Liturgical Year and Calendar.*
f) *Directory for Masses with Children* (DMC).

CHAPTER I
The Liturgy of the Word

I. Roles and Ministries

A. The Assembly

The intimate connection between the Liturgy of the Word and the liturgy of the Eucharist in the celebration of Mass should lead the faithful to be present in the celebration from the beginning and to participate attentively. As far as possible they should be prepared for listening, especially by acquiring beforehand a more profound knowledge of sacred scripture. Moreover, the connection between liturgies of word and Eucharist should arouse in them the desire to attain a liturgical understanding of the texts which are read and the will to respond in song. (LFM, 48; see also 44–48; GIRM, 62.)

B. The Presider

1. If he celebrates with a congregation, the priest should first consider the spiritual good of the faithful and avoid imposing his own personal preferences. In particular, he should not omit the readings assigned for each day in the weekday lectionary too frequently or without sufficient reason, since the Church desires that a richer portion of God's word be provided for the people. (GIRM, 316; LFM, 83)
2. The presider also exercises his proper function and the ministry of the word of God when he preaches the homily. (LFM, 41; see also nn. 78, 38-43; GIRM, 313.)

C. The Deacon

In the Liturgy of the Word at Mass the deacon proclaims the

Gospel, sometimes gives the homily when opportune, and leads the general intercessions. (LFM, 50; see also GIRM, 127-32; 34; 61.)

D. The Reader

1. The liturgical assembly needs readers, even if they are not instituted for this function. Therefore, one should see to it that there are some qualified laypersons who have been prepared to fulfill this ministry. When there is more than one reader and more than one reading, it is desirable to distribute the readings among them. (LFM, 52; see also LFM, 51-55; GIRM, 34; 66.)

> Lay men, who are of the age and possess the qualities required by the episcopal conference, are able to take on the permanent ministry of lector in accord with the prescribed liturgical rites. However, the conferral of this ministry does not grant the right to receive support or remuneration from the Church. Laypersons are able to fulfill the function of reader during the liturgy by means of a temporary deputation. Likewise, all the laity are able to function as commentators, cantors, and other ministries according to the norm of law. (See can. 230, §§1-2.)

2. The reader has his own proper function in the Eucharistic celebration and should exercise this even though ministers of a higher rank may be present. (GIRM, 66)

E. The Cantor or Psalmist

To fulfill the task of the psalmist, or cantor, it is expedient to have in each ecclesial community laypersons who are talented in the art of singing and have a facility for speaking and pronouncing words correctly. (LFM, 56; see also n. 53; GIRM, 36, 37, 47, 64, 67.)

F. The Choir and Musicians

The *schola cantorum* or choir exercises its own liturgical function within the assembly. Its task is to ensure that the parts proper to it, in keeping with the different types of chants, are carried out becomingly and to encourage active participation of the people in the singing. What is said about the choir applies in a similar way to other musicians, especially the organist. (GIRM, 63)

G. The Commentator

Also the commentator exercises a true liturgical ministry, presenting from a suitable place opportune explanations and comments which are clear, brief, accurately prepared, ordinarily written, and approved beforehand by the celebrant. (LFM, 57; see also GIRM, 68.)

II. Preaching the Word of God

A. Faculty for Preaching

Without prejudice to can. 765, presbyters and deacons enjoy the faculty of preaching everywhere, with at least the presumed consent of the rector of the church, unless this same faculty has been restricted or taken away by the competent Ordinary, or unless express permission is required by particular law. (Can. 764)

> Can. 765 states that permission of the competent superior, in accord with the Constitutions, is necessary to preach to religious in their churches or oratories.
>
> Presbyters and deacons, in virtue of their ordination, have the faculty to preach everywhere. No other permission is needed unless one or more of the exceptions mentioned in can. 764 is applicable. The faculty applies to all forms of preaching, not only the homily at Mass.
>
> Bishops have a right to preach everywhere, including the churches and oratories of religious institutes of pontifical right, unless the bishop of the place has expressly denied it in particular cases. (Can. 763; see also cans. 762, 768-772.)

B. The Homily

1. Among the forms of preaching the homily is preeminent because it is a part of the liturgy itself, and it is reserved to the priest or deacon. In it the mysteries of the faith and the norms of Christian life should be expounded from the sacred text in the course of the liturgical year.

2. There must be a homily in all Sunday and holy day Masses which are celebrated with a gathering of people. It may not be omitted except for a serious reason.

3. It is highly desirable, if there is a sufficient gathering of people, that there also be a homily on weekdays, especially during Advent and Lent or on some feast or occasion of grief.

4. The pastor or rector of the church is to see that these norms are zealously observed. (Can. 767)

C. Lay Preaching

1. Laypersons may be admitted to preach in a church or oratory if in certain circumstances necessity requires it or in particular cases it is useful. The norms of the episcopal conference are to be observed and also can. 767, §1. (Can. 766)

2. *Mass with children in which only a few adults participate.* With the consent of the pastor or rector of the church, one of the adults may speak to the children after the gospel, especially if the priest finds it difficult to adapt himself to the mentality of children. (DMC, 24)

> Qualified laypersons may preach in churches or oratories, but they may not give the homily which is a liturgical function reserved to a priest or deacon. They are not thereby excluded from "preaching" at Mass, in distinction to giving the homily. They may give a reflection on the word or a sermon in addition to the homily of the priest or deacon. Or they may preach in place of the homily when the celebrant or another priest or deacon is morally or physically impeded. (See Coriden, 553.) This can only be done in accord with the prescriptions established by the episcopal conference as, e.g., in Germany. (See SCC, letter, Nov. 20, 1973, CLD 8:941; DOL 2953.) The universal law also gives competence to the diocesan bishop to establish regulations governing preaching. (Can. 772, §1) For a good discussion of the legal issues involved in lay preaching, see J. Provost, "Lay Preaching in a Time of Transition," in *Preaching and the Non-Ordained*, ed. N. Foley (Collegeville: Liturgical Press, 1983) 134-53.

78

CHAPTER II
The Liturgy of the Eucharist

I. Participation in the Eucharist

A. The Assembly

The faithful should hold the holy Eucharist in highest honor. They should take part actively in the celebration of the most august sacrifice, receive the sacrament very devoutly and frequently, and worship it with highest adoration. (See can. 898.) They should become one body, whether by hearing the word of God, joining in prayers and song, and above all by offering the sacrifice together and sharing together in the Lord's table. (GIRM, 62)

> In the celebration of the Eucharist, deacons and laypersons are not allowed to say prayers, especially the Eucharistic Prayer, or perform actions which are proper to the celebrating priest. (Can. 907) The laity in their own way have their own part to play in the Church's sanctifying function by their active participation in the liturgy, especially the Eucharist. (Can. 835, §4)

B. Right to the Eucharist

Anyone baptized, who is not prohibited by law, may and must be admitted to Holy Communion. (Can. 912)

> The baptized have a right to the sacraments which they are capable of receiving according to the law. Besides requirements of age and use of reason, the law requires the recipient of the Eucharist to be in the state of grace and not have any penalty of excommunication

or interdict. The restrictions on the reception of the Eucharist by non-Catholics are discussed below in the section on ecumenism.

C. Prohibition of Eucharist to Manifest Sinners

Those who have been excommunicated or interdicted after an imposed or declared sentence as well as others who obstinately persevere in manifest, grave sin are not to be admitted to Holy Communion. (Can. 915)

> A manifest sin is one which is publicly known. Obstinate perseverance in such a state of sinfulness is indicated when a person persists in the sinful state and does not heed the teachings of the Church or the warnings of Church authorities. Those who have been publicly excommunicated or interdicted are obviously prohibited from receiving the Eucharist and other sacraments. (Cans. 1331, §1, 2°; 1332)

> It is difficult to determine other examples of manifest, serious sin. For example, the sin of public concubinage arising from divorce and remarriage may not always be a sin in the internal forum. The divorced and remarried person may have repented of past sinfulness, but may be unable to break off the second irregular union due to obligations to the second spouse and the children of the second marriage. Any prudent doubt about either the gravity or the public nature of the sin should be resolved in favor of the person who wishes to receive Communion.

D. State of Grace

One who is conscious of serious sin should not celebrate Mass or receive the body of the Lord without previous sacramental confession unless there is a grave reason and there is no opportunity to confess. In this case the person is bound to make an act of perfect contrition which includes the intention of confessing as soon as possible. (Can. 916)

> One who is *conscious* of serious sin is one who is *certain* of it. If a priest is in serious sin, he may not celebrate the Eucharist without first going to confession

unless there is a grave reason and there is no opportunity to confess. An example of a grave reason is when the priest cannot omit Mass (even daily Mass) without grave infamy or scandal arising, or when he must celebrate a Mass for the faithful. Likewise, the necessity to communicate must be grave, e.g., to avoid infamy or grave scandal which can arise if one does not go to Communion at a wedding Mass, a family celebration, etc. (Mathis/Bonner, 69, 87)

The *lack of opportunity* to confess may arise from various sources: e.g., there is no confessor at hand and one cannot get to a confessor without grave inconvenience (which is prudently judged from the distance to go, the time one has, one's age and physical condition, etc.;) or, e.g., because of extraordinary shame one cannot confess before a certain priest; or, e.g., one cannot go to a confessor who is present without danger of infamy, as when going to confession immediately before Mass is, according to the circumstances, an admission to others that one has committed a mortal sin. (See Genicot, II, n. 191.)

E. Children and Mentally Handicapped

1. In order that the Holy Eucharist may be administered to children, it is required that they have sufficient knowledge and careful preparation so that they can understand the mystery of Christ according to their capacity and receive the body of the Lord with faith and devotion. However, the Holy Eucharist can be given to children in danger of death if they can distinguish the body of Christ from ordinary food and receive Communion reverently. (Can. 913)

2. Parents, primarily, and those who take the place of parents, as well as the pastor have the duty to see that children with the use of reason are suitably prepared for and are refreshed by this divine food as soon as possible, having first made sacramental confession. The pastor also is to be vigilant lest children come to the holy banquet who do not have the use of reason or whom he judges are not sufficiently disposed. (Can. 914)

The law presumes that a child reaches the use of reason at age seven. Hence, children should be prepared for first Communion at this age so that they may receive the sacrament "as soon as possible." Canon 914 implies that there also should be some preparation for the sacrament of penance before first Communion so that those children who need or desire the sacrament can make use of it, since, as canon 916 requires, all those who are conscious of serious sin must go to confession before receiving Communion (unless there is a serious reason and there is no opportunity to confess, in which case an act of perfect contrition suffices). If a child does not wish to approach the sacrament of penance before first Communion and the pastor is nevertheless able to judge that the child is sufficiently disposed, the pastor should not deny the Eucharist to the child since the child has a right to the sacrament in virtue of canon 213.

Children who are in danger of death may receive Viaticum even if they lack the knowledge and preparation needed for first Communion. All that is required is that they be able to differentiate the body of Christ from ordinary food and be able to receive Communion reverently. When Viaticum is given during Mass, as is optimal, the sacred character of the liturgical action and the reverent participation of family and friends enables the child to make this distinction more easily, at least on a symbolic and intuitive level if not on the cognitive level. In other words, the child may not be able to conceptualize and articulate the difference between the body of Christ and ordinary food in abstraction of the Eucharistic action, but may well intuitively appreciate this difference during the celebration itself.

As for the reception of Communion by those with a developmental disability such as mental retardation or other mental handicaps, the universal law makes no specific provision. However, some episcopal conferences and many dioceses have policies and programs for the preparation of such persons for the reception of the sacraments, including the Eucharist. Where such local policies are lacking, it falls to the pastor and parents (or guardians) to see that mentally handicapped persons are prepared for the Eucharist according to their capacity and that they receive it when the pastor judges them to be sufficiently disposed. (See can. 777, 4°.)

F. Eucharistic Fast

1. Before receiving Holy Communion one should abstain for at least one hour from all food and drink except water and medicine. (Can. 919, §1)

> Medicine is whatever is taken to cure, ease, or prevent illness, whether prescribed by a physician or commonly recognized as a medicine. It is not necessary to avoid a medicine which contains alcohol, as long as it is truly and properly called a medicine. Other foods and beverages, although they could be said to have a medicinal effect, cannot be taken unless the communicant is elderly or sick. (Mathis/Bonner, 90)

2. Those who are advanced in age or suffer from some illness, as well as those who care for them, may receive the Holy Eucharist even if they have taken something during the preceding hour. (Can. 919, §3)

> The sick, elderly, and those who care for them are not bound to any Eucharistic fast. The typical situation addressed by this norm is Communion given outside Mass in a home or institution. Clearly, a person who is too sick or too old to go to church does not have to fast. However, even the sick or elderly who are able to attend Mass need not fast if their condition requires some nourishment. *Those who care for the sick and elderly* include not only their attendants who provide physical care but also family and friends who happen to be there insofar as they are providing emotional and spiritual care.

3. A priest who celebrates the Holy Eucharist twice or three times on the same day may take something before the second or third celebration, even if the interval of one hour has not elapsed. (Can. 919, §2)

> It does not matter when the binations or trinations occur. E.g., a priest who celebrates the Eucharist in the morning and again in the evening is not bound to

fast for the second celebration even though it is later in the day.

G. Paschal Precept

All the faithful, after they have been initiated into the Eucharist, are obliged to receive Holy Communion at least once a year. This precept must be fulfilled in paschal time, but for a just cause it may be fulfilled at another time during the year. (Can. 920)

> Those bound to the paschal precept, or law of the Easter duty, are all who have been initiated into the Eucharist, i.e., those who have made their first Communion. They must receive Communion at least once a year during the Easter season, which in this context means from Passion (Palm) Sunday to Pentecost Sunday inclusive. In the United States, by special concession of the Holy See, the time for fulfilling one's Easter duty extends from the first Sunday of Lent to Trinity Sunday inclusive, unless the Ordinary restricts the time. (See Second Council of Baltimore, n. 257.) The paschal precept may be fulfilled at some other time during the year for a just cause, e.g., in a remote area when a minister is lacking to celebrate Mass or give Communion. Those in serious sin are also bound to go to confession at least once a year. (Can. 989)

H. Communion Twice a Day

Those who have already received the Holy Eucharist may receive it again on the same day but only during the Eucharistic celebration at which they are participating. Those in danger of death may receive Viaticum even outside Mass, even if they have already received Communion that day. (Cans. 917; 921, §2)

> In order to receive Communion a second time on the same day, one must receive it only during the Mass at which one is participating, i.e., *attending*. It is not sufficient simply to enter Mass at Communion time in order to receive a second time. One must be participating in the whole celebration. Those who are in danger of death may receive Viaticum during or outside Mass, even if they have already received Communion once or more that day.

I. Viaticum

1. The faithful who are in danger of death from any cause should be refreshed by Holy Communion in the form of Viaticum. Even if they have already received Holy Communion that same day, it is highly recommended that those who are in danger of death communicate again. As long as the danger of death lasts, it is recommended that Holy Communion be administered a number of times, but on separate days. Holy Viaticum should not be delayed too long. Those involved in pastoral care are to be especially vigilant that the dying receive Viaticum while fully conscious. (Cans. 921; 922)

> The cause for the danger of death must be proximate, not remote. For example, a person who is about to undergo open heart surgery is in proximate danger; a person taking an airplane trip is only in remote danger.

2. All baptized Christians who are able to receive Communion are bound to receive Viaticum by reason of the precept to receive Communion when in danger of death from any cause. (RA, 27)

> All the baptized who are eligible by law to receive Communion are obliged to receive Viaticum in danger of death. Children who have not reached the age of reason may receive Viaticum provided they can distinguish the body of Christ from ordinary food and receive Communion reverently. (Can. 913, §2) Even if a person has received Communion once or twice that day, Viaticum should still be received. Ideally, Viaticum should be received during Mass and under both species of bread and wine. Those who for medical reasons are unable to take the consecrated bread may receive Viaticum in the form of wine alone.

II. Ministries

A. The Celebrant

Note: The term "celebrant" in this work includes concelebrants as well as the presider unless the contrary is evident or is specified.

Within the community of believers, the presbyter is another [besides the bishop] who possesses the power of orders to offer sacrifice in the person of Christ. He therefore presides over the assembly and leads its prayer, proclaims the message of salvation, joins the people to himself in offering the sacrifice to the Father through Christ in the Spirit, gives them the bread of eternal life, and shares it with them. At the Eucharist he should, then, serve God and the people with dignity and humility; by his bearing and by the way he recites the words of the liturgy he should communicate to the faithful a sense of the living presence of Christ. (GIRM, 60)

> Only a validly ordained priest may bring about the sacrament of the Eucharist. (Can. 900, §1) If a lay person attempts the liturgical action of the Eucharistic sacrifice, he incurs automatically the penalty of interdict; if a deacon, the penalty of suspension. (Can. 1378, §2, 1°)

> Priests who have been deprived of their order by a penalty (cans. 1331, §1, 2°; 1332; 1333, §1, 1°; 1338, §2), or who have lost the clerical state (cans. 290; 292; 1336, §1, 5°), may not licitly celebrate (preside at or concelebrate) the Eucharist. It does not seem that a woman who pretends to celebrate the Eucharist can incur the penalty of interdict since the purpose of the law likely is to protect the faithful from impostors; and no one would be deceived into thinking that a Eucharist celebrated by a woman would be a sacrament recognized by the law as valid.

B. The Deacon

Among ministers, the deacon, whose order has been held in high honor since the early Church, has first place. At Mass he has his own functions [in addition to those during the Liturgy of the Word]: he assists the priest, gives communion to the people (in particular, ministering the chalice), and sometimes gives directions regarding the assembly's moving, standing, kneeling, or sitting. (GIRM, 61)

C. The Acolyte

1. The acolyte is instituted to serve at the altar and to assist the priest and deacon. In particular it is for him to prepare the altar and the vessels and, as a special minister of the Eucharist, to give Communion to the Faithful. (GIRM, 65)

2. Lay men who are of the age and who possess the qualities specified by decree of the episcopal conference are able to assume on a stable basis the ministry of acolyte by the prescribed liturgical rite. However, the conferral of this ministry does not give the acolyte a right to support or remuneration from the Church. (Can. 230, §1)

> It is not customary in many countries, including the United States, to make wide use of acolytes who are permanently instituted for this ministry by the rite prescribed in the Roman Pontifical. More common is the use of altar servers. Under the revised Code, the use of altar servers is optional, and they are not explicitly restricted to males as in the former Code. It seems that particular law or custom is the best indicator whether females may function at Mass as altar servers. (See J. Huels, "Female Altar Servers: The Legal Issues," *Worship* 57 (1983) 513-525.)

D. Eucharistic Ministers

The ordinary minister of Holy Communion is a bishop, presbyter, or deacon. When ordinary ministers are lacking and the needs of the Church require it, an acolyte or other deputed lay person may serve as a special minister of Holy Communion. (See cans. 909 and 230, §3.)

> In virtue of their liturgical institution, acolytes are commissioned special ministers of the Eucharist on a permanent basis. Other special ministers are commissioned for a set period by the local Ordinary or his delegate according to the *Rite of Commissioning Special Ministers of Holy Communion*. Local Ordinaries also have the faculty to permit individual priests to appoint a qualified person to distribute Communion for a specific occasion when there is genuine need, e.g., when a priest determines that there will not be sufficient Eucharistic ministers to handle the number of communicants for a specific Mass. In such a case, the person designated by the priest to distribute Communion comes to the altar during the breaking of the bread and the commingling. After the "Lamb of God" is sung, the priest blesses him or her, saying: "Today you

are to distribute the body and blood of Christ to your brothers and sisters. May the Lord bless you, N." (See *Rite of Commissioning a Special Minister to Distribute Holy Communion on a Single Occasion*.) In case of an unforeseen necessity, the permission of the local Ordinary to use this single occasion commissioning may often be presumed.

E. Ministers of Viaticum

1. The administration of Viaticum is a function especially committed to the pastor. (See can. 530, 3°.) Pastors, parochial vicars, and chaplains have the duty and right to bring Viaticum to the dying. In the house of a clerical religious institute or society of apostolic life, this duty and right belongs to the superior of the house who may exercise it on behalf of all staying in the house. (See can. 911, §1.) In case of need or with at least the presumed permission of the pastor, chaplain, or superior, any priest or other minister of Holy Communion must give Viaticum and notify the proper authority afterwards. (Can. 911, §2)

2. Whenever possible Viaticum should be given during Mass and under both species of bread and wine. If Mass is not celebrated in the presence of the dying person, the blood of the Lord should be kept in a properly covered chalice which is placed in the tabernacle after Mass. It should be carried in a vessel which is closed in such a way as to eliminate all danger of spilling. All who take part in the celebration may receive Communion under both kinds. (RA, 26, 95, 96)

3. A priest or deacon administers Communion or Viaticum to the sick in the manner prescribed by the *Rite of Anointing and Pastoral Care of the Sick*. When an acolyte or a special minister gives Communion to the sick or Viaticum to the dying, he or she uses the *Rite of Holy Communion and Worship of the Eucharistic Mystery Outside Mass* under the title, "Administration of Communion and Viaticum to the Sick by a Special Minister." (HCW, 54)

F. Other Ministries.

See pp. 75-77 on the Liturgy of the Word, and GIRM, nn. 68-69.

III. Different Forms of Celebration

A. Mass With a Congregation

Mass with a congregation means a Mass celebrated with the people taking part. As far as possible, and especially on Sundays and holy days of obligation, this Mass should be celebrated with song and with a suitable number of ministers. But it may be celebrated without music and with only one minister. (GIRM, 77)

B. Concelebration

1. *Occasions for concelebration.*
a) Concelebration is *required* at the ordination of bishops and priests and at the Chrism Mass.
b) It is *recommended*, unless the good of the faithful should require or suggest otherwise, at:
   i) the evening Mass of Holy Thursday;
   ii) the Mass for councils, meetings of bishops, and synods;
   iii) the Mass for the blessing of an abbot;
   iv) the conventual Mass and the principal Mass in churches and oratories;
   v) the Mass of any kind of meeting of priests, whether secular or religious. (GIRM, 153)
c) Concelebration is also *optional* at other times. It may take place provided the needs of the faithful do not require or suggest individual celebration. It is forbidden to have an individual celebration of the Eucharist in the same church or oratory during a concelebration. (See can. 902.)

2. *General discipline of concelebration.*
a) Where there is a large number of priests, the authorized superior may permit concelebration several times on the same day, but either at different times or in different places. (GIRM, 154)
b) No one is ever to be admitted into a concelebration once Mass has already begun. (GIRM, 156)

> This law means that *no priest* may join the ranks of the concelebrants once Mass has begun in order to ensure proper decorum. The Mass begins with the initial sign of the cross and greeting; hence, it is not re-

89

quired that all the concelebrants be in the entrance procession.

c) In the sacristy or other suitable place, the concelebrants put on the vestments usual for individual celebrants. For a good reason, however, as when there are more concelebrants than vestments, the concelebrants may omit the chasuble and simply wear the stole over the alb; but the principal celebrant always wears the chasuble. (GIRM, 161)

> In some regions, including the United States and Canada, the chasuble-alb may be worn at concelebrations. The stole is worn over the chasuble-alb and should be the color appropriate to the Mass being celebrated. (CLD 8:528)

d) Ordinarily, whoever concelebrates may not preside at or concelebrate another Mass on the same day. (See can. 905, §1.) Exceptions to this rule are given below under *bination*.
e) Each concelebrant may accept a Mass offering. (See can. 945, §1.)

3. *Regulation of concelebration.*
    The right to regulate, in accord with the law, the discipline for concelebration in his diocese, even in churches and oratories of exempt religious, belongs to the bishop. (GIRM, 155)

> The bishop may establish rules governing the external conduct of concelebration held in his diocese. This is merely an application and recognition of the general right and duty of the bishop to moderate the liturgy in his diocese. (See can. 838, §1.)

4. *Interritual concelebration.*
    Catholic priests are prohibited from concelebrating the Eucharist with priests or ministers of churches or ecclesial communities which do not have full communion with the Catholic Church. (Can. 908)

> This canon excludes interdenominational concelebration, but not concelebration with Catholics of other rites. Permission for interritual concelebration can be obtained from the papal legate. Such permission is necessary in view of canon 846, §2 which states that ministers are to celebrate the sacraments according to

their own rite. On the other hand, it is an accepted custom that no permission is needed for interritual concelebration on an occasional basis. (See Pospishil/Faris, 35.) At such concelebrations only one rite, that of the host church, can be followed, and incompatible elements from another rite are not permitted. The concelebrants may retain the vestments and insignia of their own rites, as well as other elements which will not offend the unity of the concelebration or amount to a confusion of rituals. (*The Jurist* 42 (1982) 168)

C. Mass with Elderly, Infirm or Blind Celebrant

1. A priest who is infirm or elderly and is unable to stand may celebrate the Eucharistic sacrifice while seated, observing the liturgical laws. He may not celebrate in this way before the people unless he has the permission of the local Ordinary.

2. A blind priest or one who has some other infirmity may lawfully celebrate the Eucharistic sacrifice using the text of any approved Mass. If need be, he should have the assistance of another priest or deacon or even a properly instructed lay person. (Can. 930)

D. Mass Without a Congregation

The priest should not celebrate the Eucharist without the participation of a server or at least some member of the faithful except for a just and reasonable cause. (See GIRM, 211 and can. 906.) By their very nature liturgical actions are communal celebrations and when possible should be celebrated with the presence and active participation of the faithful. (See can. 837, §2.)

> The presence of a server is not required, but ordinarily there must be at least some, i.e., at least one member of the faithful present to respond to the priest and represent the Christian people who celebrate sacraments as a community.

> A just and reasonable cause for celebrating alone would be demonstrated whenever a member of the faithful is unavailable and when the priest is unable to participate in a communal celebration, e.g., as a result of illness, infirmity, or travel. The mere convenience of

the priest or his preference for celebrating alone would not be sufficient cause.

The liturgical law governing such a celebration is found in GIRM, 209-231 and the *Order of Mass Without a Congregation* in the *Roman Missal*.

N.B. On Holy Thursday Mass without a congregation is prohibited.

IV.   Rites and Ceremonies

A.   Eucharistic Bread and Wine

1. *The bread* must be merely wheat and recently made so that there is no danger of corruption. (Can. 924, §2)

> For *validity*, the bread must be made substantially of wheat flour. If there are any additives in it, they cannot be such that the bread would no longer be considered wheat bread *according to the common estimation*. (SCSacr, instr, Mar. 26, 1929, CLD 1: 355) The judgment concerning the validity of the substance to be used as Eucharistic bread must be based on the bread's contents, not on its appearance. Thus, knowing the composition of the bread, if the common estimation of persons would judge that it is wheat bread it would be valid matter even if there are other additives. However, the use of any additives at all other than wheat flour and water is illicit. Likewise, if the bread has become so corrupt that its nature is substantially altered and can no longer be considered bread, it constitutes invalid matter.

2. In accord with the ancient tradition of the Latin church, the priest should use *unleavened* bread for the Eucharistic celebration whenever he offers Mass. (Can. 926) The nature of the sign demands that the material for the Eucharistic celebration truly have the appearance of food. Accordingly, even though unleavened and baked in the traditional shape, the Eucharistic bread should be made in such a way that in a Mass with a congregation the priest is able actually to break the host into parts and distribute them to at least some of the faithful. (When, however, the number of communicants is large or other pastoral needs require it, small hosts are in no way

ruled out.) (GIRM, 283) It is most desirable that the faithful receive the Lord's body from hosts consecrated at the same Mass. . . . (GIRM, 56, h.)

> All the requirements in the above paragraph are for liceity only.

3. *The wine* must be natural from the fruit of the grape and not corrupt. (Can. 924, §3)

> Wine made from any other kind of fruit than grapes is invalid matter, as is wine which is made chemically, although it have the color of wine and may be said in a sense to contain its elements, or wine to which water has been added in a greater or equal quantity. (SCSacr, instr, Mar. 25, 1929, CLD 1:355) The criterion for what constitutes natural wine is the common estimation of persons. The wine must be a natural product from the juice of grapes and not an artificial product of chemical synthesis. Wine would be altered or corrupted when it has lost those qualities by which the common estimation of people identify wine.

> Care must be taken so that the wine does not turn to vinegar. (See GIRM, 285.) If it is so sour that the common estimation of persons would regard it as vinegar rather than wine, it is invalid matter. Or if other substances are added, such as water, to such an extent that it loses the qualities of wine, it is likewise invalid.

> The wine for the Eucharist must be from the fruit of the vine (see Lk 22:18), natural, and pure, that is not mixed with any foreign substance. (GIRM, 284) This latter requirement is for liceity only provided the additives do not substantially alter the nature of the wine such that it could no longer be considered wine in the common estimation, in which case the additives would render it invalid.

4. *A small amount of water* is to be mixed with the wine. (Can. 924, §1)

> The ritual mixing of water and wine by the deacon or celebrant at the preparation of the gifts is for liceity only. It need be observed only for the principal vessel in order to preserve the symbol of the one cup. Other

cups should be kept on a separate table until Communion time when they are filled with the consecrated wine. (BCL, *Environment and Art in Catholic Worship*, (Washington, D.C.: NCCB, (1978), n. 96)

5. *Alcoholic priests* who are unable to consume wine may receive by intinction when concelebrating or, when celebrating alone, again by intinction but leaving it to an assistant to consume the consecrated wine. (SCDF, letter, Sept. 12, 1983) Those who concelebrate need no further permission to receive by intinction. Those who celebrate alone must receive permission from the local Ordinary to receive by intinction. (SCDF, response, Oct. 29, 1982, AAS 74 (1982) 1298) Alcoholic priests who wish to use grape juice instead of wine, or receive the consecrated bread alone when concelebrating, must individually petition for an indult from the Apostolic See.

> Those desiring the indult to use grape juice instead of wine when they preside, or to receive the consecrated bread alone when they concelebrate, must petition for an indult. The practice of the Holy See has been for the priest's proper superior (the bishop or superior general) to send the petition of the alcoholic priest. The petition should in a discrete manner explain the circumstances of the case and provide testimony from the priest's doctor (insofar as possible) who should explain the progress of the infirmity and the means used to cure it. (See SCDF, Sept. 22, 1981, *Commentarium pro Religiosis et Missionariis* 63 (1982) 167–70.)

> In 1974 the Congregation for the Doctrine of the Faith had granted general indults to Ordinaries in the United States and elsewhere allowing alcoholic priests who request permission to concelebrate without receiving from the cup or, when concelebration is not possible, to preside at the Eucharist using must, the unfermented juice of ripe grapes. Priests who received such a permission prior to the change in practice of the Holy See may continue to use it. After September 12, 1983, permission to use grape juice can be obtained only from the Apostolic See.

6. It is sinful, even in extreme necessity, to consecrate one element

without the other or even to consecrate both outside the Eucharistic celebration. (Can. 927)

B. Communion under Both Kinds

1. In the United States, Communion under both kinds may be given, in accordance with the judgment of the Ordinary:

a)   to other members of the faithful present on the special occasions enumerated in n. 242 of the General Instruction of the Roman Missal, as well as at funeral Masses and at Masses for a special family observance;

b)   at Masses on days of special religious or civil significance for the people of the United States;

c)   at Masses on Holy Thursday and at the Mass of the Easter Vigil;

d)   at weekday Masses;

e)   on Sundays and holy days of obligation if, in the judgment of the Ordinary, Communion may be given in an orderly and reverent manner. (*Appendix to the GIRM for the Dioceses of the U.S.*, n. 242)

> The occasions on which Communion under both kinds may be distributed are regulated by particular law as well as by the universal law found in the GIRM, n. 242. The conferences of bishops have the power to decide to what extent and under what considerations and conditions Ordinaries may allow Communion under both kinds on occasions that are of special significance in the spiritual life of any community or group of the faithful.

2. The liturgical rite to be observed in the distribution of Communion under both kinds recognizes four distinct methods of ministering the consecrated wine:

a)   the communicant *drinks* from the cup;

b)   Communion is given by *intinction*, i.e., part of the host is dipped in the consecrated wine and placed on the recipient's tongue;

c)   the Precious Blood is taken through a *tube*;

d)   the consecrated wine is given to the communicant by *spoon*. (GIRM, 244-251)

> The method of drinking from the cup is preferred

to the others. If other priests are present, or deacons, acolytes, or special ministers of the Eucharist, they should assist by presenting the cup to each communicant. (SCDW, instr, June 29, 1970, n. 6; cf. can. 230, §3.)

C. Communion under the Species of Wine Only

1. In a case of need, Holy Communion may be given even under the species of wine alone. (Can. 925)

> A case of need is demonstrated when a person is unable to consume the consecrated bread on account of medical or other reasons.

2. If Communion under the form of wine alone is given outside Mass, the blood of the Lord is kept after Mass in the tabernacle in a chalice which is properly covered. It is brought to the sick in a vessel sealed in such a way that there is no danger of spillage. (PCS, 95)

D. Communion in the Hand

In the dioceses of the United States, the local Ordinary may permit the faithful to have the *option* of receiving Communion in the hand. When Communion is distributed under both kinds by intinction, the host is not placed in the hands of communicants, nor may the communicant receive the host and then dip it into the chalice. Intinction should not be introduced as a means of circumventing the practice of Communion in the hand. Children have the option to receive Communion in the hand or on the tongue. (Appendix to the GIRM for the Dioceses of the U.S., n. 240)

> Episcopal conferences may decree that Communion may be given in their territories by placing the consecrated bread in the hands of the faithful provided there is no danger of irreverence or false opinions about the Eucharist. The decree requires the confirmation of the Apostolic See. (HCW, 21)

E. Language of the Eucharist

1. The Eucharist may be celebrated in Latin or another language provided the liturgical texts have been lawfully approved. (Can. 928)

Whether the Eucharist is celebrated in Latin or the vernacular, only the liturgical books approved by the Apostolic See may be used, in particular the 1970 Roman Missal of Paul VI.

The Tridentine Mass may be used only with the permission of the diocesan bishop by those who petition for the permission and in accord with the following conditions: (a) It must be proven without ambiguity, also publicly, that the priest and faithful who wish to do so have no part with those who call into doubt the legitimate force and doctrinal correctness of the 1970 Roman Missal. (b) The celebration should be done only for the advantage of those groups who have petitioned for it; only in those churches and oratories which the diocesan bishop has designated (but not in parishes, except when the bishop permits it in extraordinary cases); and on those days and under the conditions approved by the bishop himself, whether by way of custom or by act. (c) The celebration follows the 1962 Missal and is said in the Latin language. (d) There is to be no mixing of rites and texts of other Missals. (e) Each bishop should notify the Congregation for Divine Worship of the permissions he has given. (See SCDW, letter, Oct. 3, 1984, AAS 76 (1984) 1088–89.)

2. *Sign language*

Sign language may be used with and by deaf people throughout the liturgy whenever it is judged to be pastorally suitable. (Reply of Consilium, Dec. 10, 1965, CLD 6:552)

F. Vestments

1. The vestment common to ministers of every rank is the alb, tied at the waist with a cincture, unless it is made to fit without a cincture. An amice should be put on first if the alb does not completely cover the street clothing at the neck. A surplice may not be substituted for the alb when the chasuble or dalmatic is to be worn or when a stole is used instead of the chasuble or dalmatic. (GIRM, 298)

The GIRM, nn. 299-310, contains other norms governing vestments for Mass.

2. In several countries, including the United States and Canada,

the chasuble-alb may be used in concelebrations, in Masses for special groups, in celebrations which are carried on outside of a sacred place, and in similar cases in which considerations of place or persons advise it. The stole, which is worn over the chasuble-alb, is to be the color appropriate to the Mass being celebrated. (CLD 8:528)

3. In the United States the color of vestments for *funeral services* and at other offices and Masses for the dead is white, violet, or black. (Appendix to the GIRM for the Dioceses of the U.S., n. 308)

4. When a priest or deacon distributes Communion in a church or oratory, he wears an alb and stole, or a surplice and stole over a cassock or habit. Special ministers are to wear whatever is customary or approved by the Ordinary. For Communion outside a church or oratory, the vesture of the minister should be suitable and in accord with local circumstances. (HCW, 20)

V. Frequency, Time and Place of Celebration

A. Bination and Trination

1. A priest may not celebrate Mass licitly more than once a day except in those cases in which the law permits it. If there is a scarcity of priests, the local Ordinary may allow priests to celebrate Mass twice a day for a just cause; in pastoral necessity he can allow priests to celebrate Mass even three times on Sundays and holy days of obligation. (Can. 905)

> If he so desires, the local Ordinary can simply grant faculties to all the secular and religious priests in the diocese to binate on weekdays and trinate on Sundays and holy days. However, should he choose to extend the faculties only to the parish clergy, any priest who substitutes for the pastor or one of his parochial vicars could celebrate more than one Mass, because of the local character of the permission in this case. Even in case the local Ordinary should make no general grant of faculties to binate or trinate, permission could be presumed should an emergency arise when the local Ordinary cannot conveniently be contacted.
>
> A *just cause* is required for a priest to celebrate

two Masses on a weekday. Although canon 905 makes no mention of the good of the faithful, it seems that the just cause must have some relation to it. If a purely private reason of the priest would suffice (e.g., devotion), there would hardly be reason to require a scarcity of priests before the faculty could be used. Therefore the just cause must have some public character. Obviously, the just cause exists when there is question of weddings, funerals, renewal of the sacred species in houses of lay religious, Lent, etc. (Mathis/Bonner, 71)

In order for a priest to trinate on Sundays or holy days, there must be a genuine *pastoral necessity*. The mere convenience of the faithful would not be adequate reason to trinate unless a sufficient number of them could not otherwise attend Mass as, e.g., when a priest has the care of more than one church or when the church is unable to accommodate all the faithful who wish to attend. The Apostolic See discourages a priest from celebrating more Masses than necessary for the faithful because "the pastoral effort is weakened" by multiple Masses, i.e., the participation of the people in a scattered congregation is diminished and the effectiveness of overworked priests is reduced. (See Instruction on the Worship of the Eucharistic Mystery, May 25, 1967, n. 26, CLD 6:533.)

2. Ordinaries in the United States no longer have the general faculty to permit priests to celebrate Mass three times on Saturdays and days preceding holy days of obligation. In particular cases, the diocesan bishop can grant a dispensation to permit this. For general permission for all priests of a diocese, an indult should be sought from the Congregation for Divine Worship.

3. There are a number of occasions when the law itself permits a priest to preside at or concelebrate more than one Mass in a given day.

a) One who has celebrated or concelebrated the chrism Mass on Holy Thursday may also celebrate or concelebrate the evening Mass.

b) One who has celebrated or concelebrated the Mass of the Easter Vigil may celebrate or concelebrate the second Mass of Easter.

c) All priests may celebrate or concelebrate the three Masses of

Christmas, provided the Masses are at their proper times of day.

d) One who concelebrates with the bishop or his delegate at a synod or pastoral visitation, or concelebrates on the occasion of a meeting of priests, may celebrate another Mass for the benefit of the people. This holds also, in analogous circumstances, for gatherings of religious. (GIRM, 158)

> Priests who have permission to trinate on holy days need not observe the requirement that the three Masses on Christmas be at the proper times of day. On Christmas the Mass offerings may be kept by the priest for all three Masses. The All Souls Day trination has been abrogated by the revised Code. (See CLSA Comm., 647.)

B. Time of Celebration

1. *Ordinarily*, the celebration of the Eucharist and the distribution of Communion can take place on any day and at any hour. (See can. 931.)

2. *Anticipated evening Masses* on days before a day of precept may be held only in the evening. (See can. 1248, §1.)

> The evening is generally considered to include the late afternoon not earlier than 4:00. It is unlikely that a Mass held before this time would satisfy the precept to attend Mass for the Sunday or holy day of obligation.

3. *During Holy Week* there are additional regulations for the time for the Eucharist, as follows:

a) *The Mass of the Lord's Supper* is to be celebrated in the evening at a convenient hour. Where true pastoral reasons require it, the local Ordinary may permit another Mass in churches or oratories and, in case of true necessity, even in the morning, but only for the faithful who find it impossible to participate in the evening Mass. Such Masses must not be celebrated for the advantage of private persons or prejudice the principal evening Mass. Holy Communion may be distributed only during Mass, except for the sick. (*Roman Missal*, for the Evening Mass of the Lord's Supper)

b) On *Good Friday* Holy Communion is distributed only during the celebration of the passion of the Lord which takes place at 3:00 in the afternoon, unless for a pastoral reason a later hour is selected. For the sick who are unable to participate in this celebration, it may be given at any hour of the day. (*Roman Missal* for the Celebration of the Lord's Passion, n. 3)

c) The *Easter Vigil* takes place at night. It should not begin before nightfall and should end before daybreak. It is never permitted to anticipate the Mass of Easter before the Easter Vigil or celebrate more than one Easter Vigil service in the same church. In the United States, for pastoral reasons the local Ordinary may permit an additional anticipated Mass of Easter after the Easter Vigil. (*The Sacramentary*, Introd. to the Easter Vigil, n. 3) On *Holy Saturday*, Holy Communion may be given only as Viaticum for those in danger of death. (*Roman Missal* for Holy Saturday)

C. Place of Celebration

1. The Eucharist should be celebrated in a sacred place, unless in a particular case necessity requires otherwise. In such a case, the celebration must occur in a decent place. (Can. 932, §1)

> A particular case includes not only a single occasion but also an individual priest who must celebrate outside a sacred place on a regular basis. Cases of necessity include sickness, old age, distance from a church, and pastoral advantage such as Masses for children and other particular groups. A decent place is principally one that would not unduly hinder the participation of the people as a result of undesirable distractions.

2. The Eucharistic sacrifice should take place on a dedicated or blessed altar. Outside a sacred place a suitable table may be used, always with a cloth and corporal. (Can. 932, §2)

3. *In a non-Catholic church.* For a just cause and with the express permission of the local Ordinary, a priest may celebrate the Eucharist in the place of worship of some church or ecclesial community which does not have full communion with the Catholic Church, provided there is no scandal. (Can. 933)

> The local Ordinary's permission is not needed to celebrate the Eucharist in an interdenominational chapel, such as at a hospital, prison, or military installation, since the canon refers only to the place of worship of some Christian denomination which is not in

full communion with the Catholic Church, such as a Protestant or Orthodox church.

4. *In a church where the celebrant is unknown.* A priest should be allowed to celebrate the Eucharist even if he is unknown to the rector of a church provided he has a letter of recommendation from his Ordinary or his superior which is dated at least within the year. If he lacks such a letter he can still be allowed to celebrate if it is prudently thought that he should not be prevented. (Can. 903)

This is the law of the *celebret*. A celebret is a letter from a priest's local Ordinary or religious superior, including local superior, which testifies that the priest is in good standing so that he might celebrate the Eucharist in places where he is not known. The letter must have been dated at least within a year of its presentation to the rector, namely, the pastor, superior, or other person in charge of the church. The celebret is not absolutely required; the rector of a church can safely admit a visiting priest provided there is no reason for suspicion.

CHAPTER III
Reservation and Veneration of the Holy Eucharist

I.   Reservation

A.   Purpose of Reservation

The primary and original reason for reservation of the Eucharist outside Mass is the administration of Viaticum. The secondary ends are the giving of Communion and the adoration of our Lord Jesus Christ present in the sacrament. (HCW, 5)

B.   Communion Outside Mass

1.   It is strongly recommended that the faithful receive Communion during the Eucharistic celebration. Nevertheless, if they ask for it for a just reason, it should be administered to them outside Mass, observing the liturgical rites. (Can. 918)

2.   It is fitting that those who are impeded from partaking in the community's celebration of the Eucharist should be refreshed with the sacrament. . . . Pastoral ministers should see to it that an opportunity to receive the Eucharist frequently is given to the sick and aged, even those not gravely sick or in imminent danger of death, and to receive it even daily, insofar as possible, especially during the Easter season. It is lawful to give Communion under the species of wine alone to those who are unable to receive it under the species of bread. (HCW, 14)

> Ordinarily Communion is administered during Mass but, by exception, it can be given outside Mass for a just cause, e.g., for the sick, elderly, or those who lack a priest to celebrate the Eucharist. The minis-

ter of Communion follows the *Rite of Distributing Holy Communion Outside Mass* from the Roman Ritual. There are two forms, a long rite and a short rite, both with a celebration of the Word. The short rite is used when the longer form is unsuitable, especially when there are only one or two communicants and a truly communal celebration is impossible. (HCW, 42) The vesture appropriate for ministering Communion outside Mass is described above in the section on "Rites and Ceremonies of the Eucharist."

C. Place of Reservation

1. The Holy Eucharist *must* be reserved in a cathedral church or its equivalent, in every parish church, and in the church or oratory attached to the house of a religious institute or society of apostolic life. (Can. 934, §1, 1°)

> In the house of a religious institute or some other pious house, the Holy Eucharist is reserved only in the church or principal oratory connected with the house. Nevertheless, for a just cause the Ordinary may permit it to be reserved in some other oratory of the same house. (Can. 936) An example of a just cause would be when there is more than one distinct community living under the same roof; each may have its own oratory with the reserved Blessed Sacrament.

2. The Holy Eucharist *may* be reserved in a bishop's chapel and, with the permission of the local Ordinary, in other churches, oratories, and chapels. (Can. 934, §1, 2°)

3. In sacred places where the Holy Eucharist is reserved, there must always be someone who cares for it and, as far as possible, a priest who celebrates Mass there at least twice a month. (Can. 934, §2)

> No one may have personal possession of the Eucharist or take it on a journey unless there is urgent pastoral necessity and the regulations of the diocesan bishop are observed. (Can. 935)

4. Unless there is a serious reason, the church in which the Holy Eucharist is reserved should be open for at least some hours every

day so that the faithful may pray before the Blessed Sacrament. (Can. 937)

> An example of a serious reason for not opening the church each day would be the unavailability of someone to guard it together with a reasonable fear of burglary or vandalism.

D. The Tabernacle

1. The Holy Eucharist should be reserved on a regular basis in only one tabernacle in a church or oratory. (Can. 938, §1)

2. Every encouragement should be given to the practice of Eucharistic reservation in a chapel suited to the faithful's private adoration and prayer. If this is impossible because of the structure of the church, the sacrament should be reserved at an altar or elsewhere, in keeping with local custom, and in a part of the church that is worthy and properly adorned. (GIRM, 276; HCW, 9)

> Further regulations on the tabernacle are found in canon 938, §§2–5, the *Rite of Holy Communion and Worship of the Eucharistic Mystery Outside Mass,* nn. 10–11, and the *General Instruction of the Roman Missal,* n. 277.

E. The Lamp

Before the tabernacle in which the Holy Eucharist is reserved there should be a special lamp continually lit which indicates and honors the presence of Christ. (Can. 940) According to traditional custom, an oil lamp or a lamp with a wax candle is to be used as far as possible. (HCW, 11)

> Although the law prefers the traditional oil lamp or wax candle *as far as possible*, other kinds of lamps are not excluded if there is a just cause for using them.

F. Renewal of the Sacred Species

Consecrated hosts in sufficient quantity for the needs of the faithful should be kept in a pyx or ciborium. They are to be renewed frequently, with the old ones being properly consumed. (Can. 939) A sufficient number of hosts is that required for the Communion of the sick and others outside Mass. (Cf. HCW, 7.)

It is most desirable that the faithful receive the Lord's body from hosts consecrated at the same Mass. . . . (GIRM, 56 h) Consequently, on the grounds of the sign value, it is more in keeping with the nature of the celebration that, through reservation of the sacrament in the tabernacle, Christ not be present eucharistically from the beginning on the altar where Mass is celebrated. That presence is the effect of the consecration and should appear as such. (HCW, 6)

II. Exposition of the Blessed Sacrament

A. General Norms

1. In churches or oratories in which it is permitted to reserve the Holy Eucharist, exposition may be done using a pyx or a monstrance, observing the norms of the liturgical books. The exposition of the holy sacrament should not be held in the same part of the church or oratory in which Mass is being celebrated. (Can. 941)

2. If exposition of the Blessed Sacrament goes on for a day or for several successive days, it should be interrupted during the celebration of Mass, unless it is celebrated in a chapel separate from the area of exposition and at least some of the faithful remain in adoration. (HCW, 83)

B. Lengthy Exposition

1. It is recommended that in churches and oratories that have the reserved Eucharist there be an annual solemn exposition of the Blessed Sacrament extended for a suitable period even if not continuous, so that the local community might more attentively meditate on and adore the Eucharistic mystery. However, such an exposition should take place only if it is foreseen that it will attract a suitable number of the faithful, and approved regulations are observed. (Can. 942)

2. For any serious and general need, the local Ordinary is empowered to order prayer before the Blessed Sacrament exposed for a

more extended period of time in those churches to which the faithful come in large numbers. (HCW, 87)

C. Brief Exposition

Shorter expositions of the Eucharist are to be arranged in such a way that the blessing with the Eucharist is preceded by a reasonable time for readings of the word of God, songs, prayers, and a period for silent prayer. Exposition merely for the purpose of giving benediction is prohibited. (HCW, 89)

D. Ministers of Exposition and Benediction

The priest or deacon is the minister of exposition and benediction. In particular circumstances and observing the norms of the diocesan bishop, an acolyte, special minister of Holy Communion, or other person deputed by the local Ordinary may be the minister of exposition and reposition, but not benediction. (Can. 943) Such ministers may open the tabernacle and also, as required, place the ciborium on the altar or place the host in the monstrance. At the end of the period of adoration, they replace the Blessed Sacrament in the tabernacle. It is not lawful, however, for them to give the blessing with the sacrament. (HCW, 91)

CHAPTER IV
Mass Intentions and Offerings

I. Mass Intentions

A. Application of Mass

1. Priests may apply Mass for anyone, whether living or dead. (Can. 901)

2. It is highly recommended that priests celebrate Mass for the intention of the faithful, especially of the poor, even if they receive no offering. (Can. 945, §2)

B. Missa pro populo

The diocesan bishop and the pastor have the duty of applying a Mass for their people on all Sundays and holy days. (See cans. 388 and 534.)

II. Mass Offerings (Stipends)

A. General Discipline

1. In accord with the approved custom of the Church, each priest, whether presider or concelebrant, may accept an offering to apply Mass for a certain intention. (Can. 945, §1)

2. Once the offerings are accepted, separate Masses are to be applied for the intentions of those who gave individual offerings, even though they be small in amount. (Can. 948)

The basic rule is stated here that there can be no

more than one offering conjoined with an intention accepted by each priest for a single Mass. The intention may, however, include more than one person.

Even the appearance of trafficking or commercialism in regard to Mass offerings is strictly prohibited. (See can. 947.) Whoever has the obligation to celebrate and apply a Mass for the intention of those who gave an offering is bound to fulfill this obligation even if without fault he has lost the offering. (Can. 949)

3.   No one is allowed to accept more Mass offerings to be applied by himself than he is able to satisfy within a year. (Can. 953)

If in certain churches or oratories the number of Masses requested to be celebrated is greater than can be celebrated there, the Masses may be celebrated elsewhere unless the donors shall have manifested expressly a contrary desire. (Can. 954) Whoever intends to commit to others the celebration of Masses to be applied should do so as soon as possible to priests of his own choice, provided he is certain that they are trustworthy. He must transmit the entire offering received unless it is certain that the excess of the amount established in the diocese was given to him personally. He is further bound to see that the Masses are celebrated until such time as he has received evidence that both the obligations were accepted and the offerings were received. The time within which a priest has to celebrate these Masses begins on the day on which he has received them, unless established otherwise. (Can. 955, §§1–2)

All administrators of pious causes or those in any way obliged to see to the celebration of Masses, whether cleric or lay, should send to their Ordinary, in the manner defined by him, all Mass obligations not satisfied within a year. (Can. 956)

B.   Additional Masses the Same Day

A priest who presides at more than one Mass on the same day may apply each one for an intention for which an offering is given. On Christmas a priest may keep offerings for three Masses celebrated. On all other days he may keep only one offering, and give the others to purposes prescribed by the Ordinary. However, some compensation by virtue of an extrinsic title is admissible. (Can. 951, §1)

An example of an extrinsic title is the compensation owed to a priest for his services in celebrating the Mass over and above the amount of the Mass offering. Those who must celebrate a Mass *pro populo* on Sundays and holy days may keep the offering from a second Mass that day.

2. A priest concelebrating another Mass on the same day may not accept an offering for it under any title. (Can. 951, §2)

Except on Christmas, a priest who is concelebrating may not accept an offering for that Mass unless it is the only Mass he is offering that day.

C.   Amount of Offering

1. The provincial council or the meeting of the bishops of a province is to define by decree the amount that is to be offered in the whole province for the celebration and application of Mass. A priest may not ask for an amount higher than this. However, a priest is free to accept an offering voluntarily given which is higher or lower than the established amount. In the absence of such a decree, the custom of the diocese is to be observed. Also the members of every kind of religious institute must observe the amount defined by the above-mentioned decree or custom. (Can. 952)

2. If a sum of money is offered for the application of Masses and there is no indication of the number of Masses to be celebrated, the number is reckoned on the basis of the amount of the offering established in the place where the donor lives, unless the donor's intentions must legitimately be presumed to have been otherwise. (Can. 950)

D.   Record and Supervision

1. Each priest must accurately record the Masses he has agreed to celebrate and those which he has satisfied. (Can. 955, §4)

Those who transfer to others Masses to be celebrated should record without delay in a book both the

Masses which were received and those which were given to others. The amount of the offerings is also to be noted. (Can. 955, §3)

2. The pastor or rector of some church or other pious place in which Mass offerings are customarily received should have a special book in which they accurately record the number of Masses to be celebrated, the intention, the offering received, and also the fact of their celebration. (Can. 958, §1)

3. The duty and right of ensuring that Mass obligations are satisfied belong to the local Ordinary in churches of the secular clergy and to superiors in churches of religious institutes or societies of apostolic life. (Can. 957)

The Ordinary is obliged either personally or through another to inspect every year the Mass offering books. (Can. 958, §2)

Penance

Part V

CHAPTER I
Celebration of the Sacrament

I. Forms of Celebration

The Roman Ritual provides three sacramental rites of penance and a non-sacramental penitential service. Among the former are two rites for individual confession of sins—the *Rite of Reconciliation of Individual Penitents* and the *Rite of Reconciliation of Several Penitents with Individual Confession and Absolution*—and a rite using general absolution—the *Rite for Reconciliation of Several Penitents with General Confession and Absolution*.

A. Individual Confession

1. Individual and integral confession and absolution constitute the only ordinary way by which the faithful who are conscious of serious sin are reconciled with God and the Church. Only physical or moral impossibility excuses from this kind of confession, in which case there also may be reconciliation in other ways. (Can. 960)

2. To obtain the saving remedy of the sacrament of penance, according to the plan of our merciful God, the faithful must confess to a priest each and every grave sin that they remember after an examination of conscience. (RPen, 7a)

> The Council of Trent solemnly taught that for complete and perfect remission of sins three acts are required on the part of the penitent as parts of the sacrament, namely, contrition, confession, and satisfaction. It also taught that absolution by a priest is a judicial act and that by divine law it is necessary to confess to a priest each and every mortal sin and the circumstances which change the species of the sin insofar

115

as the memory can recall them after a diligent examination of conscience. (SCDF, Pastoral Norms, *Sacramentum Paenitentiae*, June 16, 1972, CLD 7:668)

The ordinary way that sacramental reconciliation occurs is by individual and integral confession and absolution. The extraordinary ways are by general absolution and by an act of perfect contrition. An act of perfect contrition includes the intention to confess as soon as possible. (See can. 916)

Reconciliation with God and the Church for those in venial sin can also take place through other means, especially through the Eucharist as well as non-sacramental penance and contrition.

3. Shorter Rite of Individual Confession

When pastoral need dictates, the priest may omit or shorten some parts of the rite but must always retain in their entirety the penitent's confession of sins and acceptance of the act of penance, the invitation to contrition (RPen, 44), and the formularies of absolution and dismissal. In imminent danger of death, it is sufficient for the priest to say the essential words of the form of absolution, namely: I ABSOLVE YOU FROM YOUR SINS IN THE NAME OF THE FATHER, AND OF THE SON, AND OF THE HOLY SPIRIT. (RPen, 21)

Individual penance should be scheduled so that the complete rite may be used properly with all penitents without haste or delay. However, pastoral need, such as the great number of penitents, may sometimes suggest that the complete rite be shortened as indicated in the Ritual.

B. General Absolution

1. Absolution may not be imparted in a general fashion to many penitents at the same time without previous individual confession, unless: (a) danger of death is imminent and there is not time for the priest or priests to hear the confessions of each penitent; (b) there is a serious need such as when, due to the number of penitents, there are not enough confessors to hear properly the confessions of individuals within a suitable time such that the penitents, through no

fault of their own, would be forced to go for a long time without sacramental grace or Holy Communion. However, the need is not considered sufficient if confessors cannot be present for the sole reason of the great number of penitents such as may happen on some great feast or pilgrimage. (Can. 961, §1)

> The availability of a sufficient number of confessors is a relative matter depending on various circumstances, especially the period of time necessary for properly celebrating the individual rite. It could even involve a relatively small number of penitents in a remote area which might deny freedom of choice of confessors or desired anonymity to penitents. (McManus, 679)

> Another condition for the use of general absolution is that the faithful, through no fault of their own, would be *forced to go without sacramental grace or Holy Communion for a long time.* The sacramental grace refers to the grace of the sacrament of penance. This applies to those in venial sin as well as mortal sin who may wish to have the sacramental grace, even though it is not required to have venial sins absolved by the sacrament. The "long time" must be understood relatively; even if it is only one day, it may be a long time for some people to go without the grace of the sacrament.

> It pertains to the diocesan bishop to make the judgment whether the conditions for the use of general absolution under b above are fulfilled. He may establish such cases of need in view of criteria agreed upon with other members of the episcopal conference. (See can. 961, §2.) In the absence of such criteria, the diocesan bishop can act on his own authority.

2. That the faithful may receive a valid absolution given to many at the same time it is required not only that they be properly disposed but likewise have the intention in due time to confess individually their serious sins which at present they are unable to confess. The faithful are to be taught this requirement insofar as possible, even on the occasion of the reception of general absolution. There is to be an exhortation preceding general absolution that each person is to make an act of contrition, even in the case of danger of death if there is time. (Can. 962)

Insofar as the faithful are concerned, in order that they may take advantage of sacramental absolution granted to many at one and the same time, it is absolutely required that they be properly disposed, that is, that they be sorry for their sins and that they propose to abstain from sins, that they resolve to make reparation for scandal and harm done, if any, and at the same time intend in due time to confess individually the serious sins which they cannot at present thus confess. (SCDF, *Sacramentum Paenitentiae,* June 16, 1972, n. VI, CLD 7:670)

The law requires, for validity of the general absolution, that anyone in serious sin must not only be suitably disposed but also intend to confess individually those serious sins *in due time.* This due time is explained in canon 963 as meaning "as soon as possible when there is the opportunity." Minimally, this must be before another general absolution, unless there is a just reason, or within a year from one's last confession. (See can. 989.)

Those persons who actually are a source of scandal to the faithful and are sincerely penitent and seriously intend to remove the scandal can, to be sure, receive sacramental absolution along with the others; nevertheless, they should not receive Holy Communion until after they shall have removed the scandal in accord with the judgment of the confessor to whom they should first of all personally have recourse. With regard to remission of censures, the norms of the current law should be observed with the computation of time of recourse starting from the next individual confession. (See *Sacramentum Paenitentiae*, n. XI, CLD 7:672.)

3. Unless a just cause prevents it, one whose serious sins are remitted by a general absolution should go to individual confession as soon as possible when there is the opportunity before receiving another general absolution. The obligation of can. 989 remains in force. (Can. 963)

Can. 989 is the precept to confess serious sins annually. Thus, since those who receive a general absolution are bound to confess their serious sins individually *as soon as there is opportunity before they receive a second general absolution*, this could well be even before they would be required to confess their mortal sins annually. They are excused from this requirement if they are impeded by a just cause. An example of a just cause would be serious inconvenience to the penitent or the confessor. Hence, if the penitent is unable to approach individual confession at a regularly scheduled time at a church in the area, this would be sufficient cause to excuse from this requirement. Another example is the case of a remote area where sufficient confessors are not available to guarantee desired anonymity or freedom of choice of confessors.

On the other hand, only physical or moral impossibility would excuse from the requirement to confess mortal sins annually. (See RPen, 34.) Examples would include physical illness; lack of a confessor; a psychological reason, such as a deep fear of confessing individually.

II. Time and Place of Celebration

A. Time of Celebration

The reconciliation of penitents may be celebrated in all liturgical seasons and on any day. But it is right that the faithful be informed of the day and hours at which the priest is available for this ministry. They should be encouraged to approach the sacrament of penance at times when Mass is not being celebrated and preferably at the scheduled hours. Lent is the season most appropriate for celebrating the sacrament of penance. (RPen, 13)

> All to whom the care of souls is committed by virtue of office are obliged to provide for the hearing of the confessions of the faithful entrusted to them when the faithful reasonably request it. They are to provide for the faithful the opportunity for individual confession at days and hours established for the faithful's convenience. In urgent necessity any confessor is obliged to hear the confessions of the faithful, and in danger of death any priest. (Can. 986)

> Thus, there must be regularly scheduled times for the celebration of the sacrament. It is not sufficient

119

simply to allow penitents to come whenever they wish, or by appointment.

B. Place of Celebration

1. The proper place for hearing sacramental confession is a church or oratory.
2. Confessions should not be heard outside the confessional except for a just cause. (Can. 964, §§ 1 and 3)

> The episcopal conference should establish norms governing the confessional, but ensuring that the confessionals, which the faithful who so desire may freely use, are always located in an accessible place and have a fixed grille between the penitent and the confessor. (Can. 964, §2)

> In the United States, a reconciliation chapel or room is permitted, which must allow the option for the penitent's kneeling at a fixed grille. (NCCB, decree, *BCL Newsletter 1965–1975* (Dec., 1974) 450. See also *Environment and Art in Catholic Worship* (Washington, D.C.: NCCB, 1978), n. 81.)

CHAPTER II
Roles and Ministries

I. The Community

The whole Church, as a priestly people, acts in different ways in the work of reconciliation that has been entrusted to it by the Lord. Not only does the Church call sinners to repentance by preaching the word of God, but it also intercedes for them and helps penitents with a maternal care and solicitude to acknowledge and confess their sins and to obtain the mercy of God, who alone can forgive sins. (See RPen, 8.)

II. The Minister

Only a priest is the minister of the sacrament of penance. (Can. 965) For the valid absolution of sin it is required that the minister, besides having the power of order, also have the faculty to exercise the power on behalf of the faithful to whom he gives absolution (Can. 966, §1)

> When one attempts to impart a sacramental absolution or hear a sacramental confession when one is unable validly to do so, one automatically incurs an interdict if a layperson or a suspension if a cleric. (Can. 1378, §2, 2°)

A. Faculty by Law

The following possess the faculty to hear confessions in virtue of the law itself:

1. The pope and cardinals for anywhere in the world (See can. 967, §1.)

2. All bishops anywhere in the world, unless a local Ordinary has denied this in a particular case. (See can. 967, §2.)

3. In virtue of their office, within the limits of their jurisdiction, local Ordinaries, canons penitentiary, pastors, and those who take the place of pastors unless a local Ordinary denies it in a particular case. (See cans. 968, §1 and 967, §2.)

> The one who takes the place of the pastor is the administrator or the parochial vicar when the parish is vacant or the pastor is impeded. (See cans. 540–541.)

> If a local Ordinary denies an outside priest the faculty in a particular case, that priest may not validly absolve in that territory except in danger of death.

4. In virtue of their office, superiors of religious institutes or societies of apostolic life—if they are clerical and of pontifical right, and if the superiors have executive power of governance according to the Constitutions—for their own subjects and others who live in the house day and night; they use this faculty licitly unless a major superior denies this in a particular case for his own subjects. (See cans. 968, §2 and 967, §3.)

> Superiors include local superiors, provided they have executive power of governance according to the Constitutions. Ordinarily the Constitutions will not explicitly state this power is possessed by the local superior, but it is implicit in virtue of the kinds of acts that the local superior can perform, e.g., dispensing members in certain cases. If even implicit indications are lacking, but there are no contrary indications that the local superior does not possess this power, the superior may safely hear the confessions of his subjects and others who live in the house in virtue of the faculty supplied in the case of a doubt of law. (See can. 144.)

> A major superior can deny a local superior, or another major superior subject to him, permission to hear the confessions of his subjects and those who live in the house, but this affects liceity only.

5. All priests, even if they lack the faculty, for those in danger of death, absolving from all sins and censures, even if an approved priest may be present. (See can. 976)

For cases of common error of fact or of law and also in positive and probable doubt of law or fact, see below, section C. (See can. 144.)

B. Delegated Faculty

1. The faculty to hear confessions should not be granted except to presbyters whose suitability has been demonstrated by examination or by some other means. (Can. 970)

> The faculty may be granted for a determinate or indeterminate period. (See can. 972.) The faculty for hearing confessions habitually should be granted in writing. (Can. 973) A habitual faculty granted verbally would be valid but illicit.

2. *From the local Ordinary.* Only the local Ordinary is competent to grant to any presbyter at all the faculty for hearing confessions of any of the faithful. Presbyters who are members of religious institutes are not to use the faculty without at least the presumed permission of their superior. (Can. 969, §1) The local Ordinary should not grant the faculty for hearing confessions habitually to a presbyter, even one having domicile or quasi-domicile in his jurisdiction, unless he has first consulted that presbyter's Ordinary insofar as possible. (Can. 971)

> The presumed permission of the superior means that a religious priest may hear confessions with a faculty granted by a local Ordinary unless the superior forbids it. If the superior forbids it, the priest hears confessions validly but illicitly.

The habitual faculty from the local Ordinary is not limited by the territory of the diocese and can be exercised everywhere the priest travels unless a local Ordinary denies it in a particular case. (See can. 967, §2.)

3. *From the superior.* The superior of a religious institute or society of apostolic life who enjoys executive power of governance according to the Constitutions is competent to grant to any presbyter at all the faculty for hearing confessions of the superior's subjects or others who reside day and night in the house. (Can. 969)

Even a local superior who has executive power of governance is competent to grant any priest—even one not of the institute—the faculty for hearing the confessions of his subjects and those who live in the house. (See commentary above under A, 4.) However, the local superior must be a priest because the concession of the faculty rests on the principle that the faculty depends upon a power residing in the grantor over those to whom or for whom the priest ministers the sacrament. (See McManus, 685.) One cannot delegate power that one does not have.

Presbyters who have this faculty use it licitly unless some major superior denies it in a particular case for his own subjects. (See can. 967, §3.)

For example, the provincial of province X grants the faculty to a member, but the provincial of province Y refuses to allow that priest to hear the confessions of the members of province Y. Such a prohibition affects liceity only. Only one's own major superior (general or provincial) can revoke the faculty. (See can. 974, §4.)

C. Supplied Faculty

1. *Inadvertence.* An act of delegated power, which is exercised only in the internal forum and which is placed through inadvertence after the elapse of the time for the grant, is valid. (Can. 142, §2)

Thus, e.g., a priest is given the faculty for confession to be valid during the time of the parish mission he is giving. The morning after the mission has closed and his faculty has expired because the time for which it was granted has run out, a woman approaches him for the sacrament of penance. Inadvertently, he hears her confession and absolves her, completely unaware that his faculty has expired. The absolution is valid, even if during the course of the celebration of the sacrament he should remember that the faculty had ceased.

2. *Common error.* In error that is common, about a fact or the law, the Church supplies executive power of governance for both the external and the internal forum. This norm also applies to the faculty for confessions. (See can. 144.)

The error here envisioned concerns the *existence of the faculty*; it is based upon a factual situation which gives rise to the belief that a person has the faculty to hear confessions, whereas he does not. *Common* error, as opposed to merely private error, affects some sort of community and is, in some manner, common to the people of a diocese, parish, religious community, etc. However, in order for common error to exist, it is not at all required that the majority of the persons in a place *actually elicit a false judgment* concerning the existence of a public fact which normally is capable of leading people into error. Rather, there exists a public circumstance from which all reasonable persons, without any error of law, would naturally conclude that the faculty exists. It is *not* necessary that a number of persons *actually err* concerning the existence of the faculty, provided that the circumstances are such that they would err.

Furthermore, the Church only supplies the faculty when the *common good* is at stake, not when merely the private good of one or several persons is in question. For example, a priest without the faculty is sitting in the confessional, or other place where the sacrament of penance is ordinarily celebrated. By this very set of circumstances, the community would erroneously conclude that the priest has the faculty, or else he would not be there. The Church supplies the faculty because the common good is at stake, namely, the potential invalidity of many absolutions. Even if only one person approaches that priest, the Church still supplies the faculty because the potential is there for harm to the common good.

In practice, the mere fact that a priest is actually in the confessional, or other place where penance is ordinarily celebrated, is sufficient to constitute the foundation for common error; people would commonly judge that any priest hearing confessions there has the faculty.

On the other hand, if a priest is hearing confession outside a place where penance is ordinarily celebrated, the Church would not supply the faculty because there would be no basis for the community to believe that such a priest should have the faculty. For example, a priest is approached by a passenger at the airport who asks to confess before boarding the plane. The Church would not supply the faculty on the basis of common error in such a case.

3. *In positive and probable doubt of law or of fact*, the Church supplies the executive power of governance both for the internal and the external forum. (See can. 144.)

A doubt is positive and probable when there is a good and serious reason to conclude that one has the power of governance, although there is also good reason to say that one has not. The mind, therefore, is unable to reach a certain judgment concerning the fact of possessing the power. A doubt of law regards the existence, the extent, or the meaning of the law. It must be an objective doubt, i.e., the law is interpreted variously even by the experts; the law itself is not clear. On the other hand, the Church does not supply power of governance for merely subjective doubt, which is ignorance. An example of a doubt of law would be a doubt whether the Constitutions of a religious institute grant local superiors executive power of governance.

A doubt of fact regards the existence of some circumstances which the law certainly requires in order that an act be included within its ambit; e.g., I doubt whether this particular person is really in danger of death, whether a given case meets all the requirements for an automatic censure, whether my one year faculty has elapsed, whether the faculties from my new diocese have been granted while I am in transit, etc. Again, the doubt must be positive and probable; there must be some objective basis for the doubt, not just ignorance of the facts. Note that in the last analysis, the doubt always comes back to this question: Do I have the power in this case? Once the situation of positive and probable doubt is verified, the Church supplies the power of governance to cover the case in question.

D. Loss of Faculty

1. In addition to revocation, the faculty for hearing confessions

126

habitually in virtue of one's office ceases by the loss of that office; the faculty for hearing confessions habitually in virtue of delegation by the local Ordinary or the Ordinary of incardination ceases by excardination or by loss of domicile. (See can. 975.)

Once one loses the habitual faculty by loss of office, excardination, or loss of domicile, it is lost everywhere until a new one is granted. The only exception is when a local Ordinary prohibits a priest in a particular case from hearing confessions only in his territory.

2. *Revocation.* The local Ordinary, and also the competent superior, should not revoke a faculty for hearing confessions habitually except for a serious reason. If the faculty is revoked by the local Ordinary of incardination or domicile who granted it, the presbyter loses that faculty everywhere; but if it is revoked by some other local Ordinary, he loses it only in the territory of the one who revoked it. (See can. 974, §§1–2.)

Serious reasons for revoking the faculty would include evidence of incompetence as a confessor, violation of the seal or related indiscretions which jeopardize the seal, and other abuses mentioned in the canons.

Any local Ordinary who has revoked the faculty of some presbyter shall notify the Ordinary proper to him by reason of incardination or, if it is a question of a member of a religious institute, of his competent superior. If the faculty is revoked by one's own major superior, the presbyter loses it for members of the institute everywhere; but if the faculty is revoked by some other competent superior he loses it only for those subjects under that superior's jurisdiction. (Can. 974, §§3–4)

The principle behind the law is this: the one who grants the faculty is able to revoke it. Hence, if one's own Ordinary grants the faculty and then revokes it, it is lost everywhere. If another Ordinary grants it for his own jurisdiction and then revokes it, it is lost only in that jurisdiction. For example, the bishop of a diocese grants the habitual faculty to a religious priest. The faculty is good everywhere in the world as long as the priest retains domicile in that diocese. The priest also has the faculty from his major superior to hear confessions of members of the institute. The bishop revokes the faculty, but the major superior does not. The priest may continue hearing the confessions of members of the institute and those who live in its houses, but not of any others.

The faculty is also revoked by the censure of excommunication or interdict or another penalty which specifies the loss of the faculty. This applies both to the faculty obtained by law and that obtained by delegation. (See cans. 1331–1333.)

> Any priest, even one who has been excommunicated, interdicted, suspended, laicized, or in any other way has lost the faculty, may hear confessions in danger of death. If a priest has incurred an automatic censure but it has not been declared, he may hear the confession of any of the faithful who requests it for any just cause. (See can. 1335.)

E. Seal of Confession

1. The sacramental seal is inviolable. Therefore it is absolutely forbidden for the confessor to betray the penitent either by words or by any other means for any reason whatsoever. Also bound to the observance of secrecy are the interpreter, if there is one, and all others who have gained knowledge in any way of a sinner's confession. (Can. 983)
2. The confessor who directly violates the sacramental seal incurs the penalty of automatic excommunication reserved to the Apostolic See. If he violates it only indirectly, he is to be punished in accordance with the gravity of the offense. An interpreter or any others who violate the secret are to be punished with a just penalty, not excluding excommunication. (Can. 1388)

> The *sacramental seal* is the obligation to keep secret all those things known through sacramental confession, the revelation of which would betray both the sin and the sinner.

> A *direct violation* of the seal consists in revealing both the person of the penitent and the sin of the penitent. A direct violation can occur not only by stating the penitent's name and the sin, but also by revealing circumstances by which this could be known.

An *indirect violation* is had when from the things the confessor says or does there arises a danger that others will come to know a sin confessed and the identity of the penitent. (Mathis/Bonner, 130)

Both direct and indirect violations of the seal are forbidden by canon 983, but only the direct violation by a confessor results in the automatic penalty of excommunication reserved to the Apostolic See.

F. Restrictions on Confessors

1. The confessor is totally prohibited from using knowledge acquired in confession to the detriment of the penitent, even when there is no danger of revelation. Anyone who has a position of authority may not in any way use for external governance knowledge of sins which he has gained at any time in confession. (Can. 984)

Any knowledge gained in the sacrament of penance, even if not of sins, may not be used by the confessor to the detriment of the penitent. For example, a confessor has reason to believe that a certain penitent, who is going to be ordained to the permanent diaconate, is psychologically unstable. He may not use this knowledge against the penitent if it was gained primarily from what the penitent said in confession.

Also, any knowledge of sins cannot be used by anyone in a position of authority for external governance, even if there is no danger that the sin will be revealed, or even if it could be of benefit to the penitent. For example, a confessor knows that a certain person is a compulsive thief. The confessor is later appointed pastor of a parish where that person is on the parish finance council. The pastor may not remove the person solely on the basis of the knowledge gained from the confession.

2. The master of novices and his assistant and the rector of the seminary or other educational institution should not hear the sacramental confessions of their students who are living in the same house unless the students in particular cases spontaneously request it. (Can. 985)

3. Except in danger of death, the absolution of an accomplice in a

129

sin against the Sixth Commandment is invalid. (Can. 977) A priest who acts contrary to this prescription incurs automatic excommunication reserved to the Apostolic See. (Can. 1378, §1)

> An accomplice is one who participates immediately with the priest in the same act of impurity which is a grave sin. It does not suffice that one cooperate, even proximately, in the sin of another, e.g., by advising one to commit sin, procuring the occasion, etc. Both must take part in the same action. It is required that the sin, on the part of both persons, be certain, external, and grave. If there is a doubt whether the sin was committed, or whether it was external and grave, the censure is not incurred. (Mathis/Bonner, 131–35)

4. If anyone confesses that he or she had falsely denounced to ecclesiastical authority a confessor innocent of the crime of solicitation to a sin against the Sixth Commandment, that person should not be absolved unless he or she first formally retracts the false denunciation and is prepared to make amends for damages, if there are any. (Can. 982)

> A priest who in the act or on the occasion or under the pretext of confession solicits a penitent to commit a sin against the Sixth Commandment is to be punished, in accord with the gravity of the offense, by suspension, prohibitions, privations and, in more serious cases, is to be dismissed from the clerical state. (Can. 1387)

> Anyone who before an ecclesiastical superior falsely denounces a confessor of commiting the crime of solicitation incurs automatically the penalty of interdict and, if he is a cleric, also suspension. (Can. 1390)

G. Confessors for Religious

Superiors should recognize the proper freedom of members concerning the sacrament of penance and the direction of conscience, without prejudice to the discipline of the institute. In accordance with their proper law, superiors should be solicitous to have available worthy confessors for their members so that they may confess frequently.

In monasteries of nuns, in houses of formation, and in the larger houses of lay religious there should be ordinary confessors approved by the local Ordinary, chosen in consultation with the community, but with no obligation on anyone's part of approaching them.

Superiors should not hear the confessions of their subjects unless the members themselves spontaneously request it. (Can. 630, §§1–4)

> The master of novices likewise may not hear the confessions of the novices or others living in the novitiate unless they ask him on their own initiative. (See can. 985.)

> Members of religious institutes should approach their superiors with trust, and they may freely and spontaneously be open with them. However, superiors are forbidden from inducing them in any way to make a manifestation of their conscience to them. (Can. 630, §5)

> Can. 630 also applies to societies of apostolic life. (Can. 734)

III. The Penitent

A. Disposition

In order that the faithful might receive the healing remedy of the sacrament of penance, they must be so disposed that they are converted to God by repudiating the sins which they committed and having the intention of reforming their lives. (Can. 987) If the confessor does not doubt the disposition of the penitent who seeks absolution, he should not deny or defer the absolution. (Can. 980)

B. Obligation to Confess

1. The faithful are bound by obligation to confess in kind and number all serious sins committed after baptism which have not yet been directly remitted by the keys of the Church and admitted in individual confession. They are to confess those serious sins of which they are conscious after a diligent examination of conscience. It is recommended that the faithful also confess their venial sins. (Can. 988)

> *Seminarians* are to be accustomed to approach the

sacrament of penance frequently. (See can. 246, §4.)

Clerics are to be solicitous in going to the sacrament of penance frequently. (See can. 276, §2, 5°.)

Members of religious and secular institutes are to frequently approach the sacrament of penance. (See cans. 664 and 719, §3.)

2.   All the faithful, after they have reached the age of discretion, are obliged to confess faithfully their serious sins at least once a year. (Can. 989)

3.   One who is conscious of a serious sin may not celebrate Mass or receive the body of the Lord without previous sacramental confession unless there is a grave reason and there is no opportunity for confessing. In such a case the person should be mindful of the obligation to elicit an act of perfect contrition, which includes the intention of confessing as soon as possible. (Can. 916)

C.   The Penance

The confessor should impose salutary and appropriate penances according to the kind and number of sins, keeping in mind the penitent's condition. The penitent is obliged personally to perform the penance. (Can. 981)

The refusal of the penitent to perform the penance would be sufficient reason for the confessor not to absolve in the case of serious sin. The penance may be in the form of prayer, self-denial, and especially service to neighbor and works of mercy, and it should correspond to the gravity and nature of the sins. (See RPen 18.)

D.   Choice of Confessors

All the faithful are free to confess their sins to a lawfully approved confessor of their own choice, even to one of another rite. (Can. 991)

In seminaries, besides the ordinary confessors, other confessors should regularly come to the seminary. Without prejudice to the discipline of the seminary, it is always the right of a student to go to any confessor either in or outside the seminary. (See can. 240, §1.)

E. Those Being Received into Full Communion with the Church

If the profession of faith and reception take place within Mass, the candidates, according to their own conscience, should confess their sins beforehand. They should first inform the confessor that they are about to be received into full communion. Any confessor who is lawfully approved may hear such a confession. (*Rite of Receiving Baptized Christians into the Full Communion of the Catholic Church*, 9, RCIA, Appendix)

CHAPTER III
Remission of Censures by the Confessor

It is rare that a confessor encounters a penitent with an inflicted or declared penalty, neither of which may be remitted in the sacrament of penance by the typical confessor, except in danger of death. Thus, the treatment of penal law here will focus mainly on automatic (*latae sententiae*) penalties.

I. Automatic (Latae Sententiae) Censures

A. Excommunication

The law states that the penalty of excommunication is incurred automatically upon commission of any of the following crimes:
1. apostasy, heresy, schism (can. 1364, §1);
2. violation of the consecrated species (can. 1367);
3. physical attack on the pope (can. 1370, §1);
4. absolution of an accomplice in a sin against the Sixth Commandment (can. 1378);
5. unauthorized ordination of a bishop (can. 1382);
6. direct violation by a confessor of the seal of confession (can. 1388);
7. procuring an abortion (can. 1398).

N.B. The remission of the crimes in nn. 2–6 is reserved to the Apostolic See.

B. Interdict

Commission of any of the following crimes results in the penalty of automatic interdict:
1. physical attack on a bishop (can. 1370, §2);
2. pretended celebration of the Eucharist by a non-priest (can.

1378, §2, 1°);

3. attempt to impart sacramental absolution or hear confession by one who cannot do so validly (can. 1378, §2, 2°);

4. false accusation of the crime of solicitation in the confessional (can. 1390, §1);

5. attempted marriage, even civil, by a religious in perpetual vows (can. 1394, §2).

N.B. The crimes mentioned in nn. 2 and 3 result in automatic suspension, rather than interdict, if the offender is a cleric. The crimes in nn. 1 and 4 result in both automatic interdict and suspension if the offender is a cleric.

C. Suspension

In addition to those who commit the crimes mentioned in nn. 1–4 above under interdict, the following also incur automatic suspension:

1. a cleric who attempts marriage, even civil (can. 1394, §1);

2. a cleric who is ordained by a bishop who does not have legitimate dimissorial letters. The suspension affects only the order received illicitly, not a prior order received lawfully. (See can. 1383.)

II. Effects of Automatic Censures

A. Excommunication

The excommunicate is prohibited from:

1. having any ministerial participation in the celebration of the Eucharist or any other ceremonies of worship;

2. celebrating the sacraments or sacramentals and receiving the sacraments;

3. exercising any ecclesiastical offices, ministries, or functions, or placing acts of governance. (Can. 1331, §1)

B. Interdict

The interdicted is prohibited from nn. 1 and 2 under A. (Can. 1332)

C. Suspension

Suspension, which affects only clerics, prohibits:

1. all acts of the power of order;
2. all acts of the power of governance;
3. the exercise of all rights or functions connected with an office.
(Can. 1334, §2)

> N.B. The cleric who is automatically suspended as a result of illicit ordination by a bishop lacking legitimate dimissorial letters (can. 1383) is prohibited only from exercising that order, not a lower order licitly received or acts of the power of governance or rights or functions connected with an office.

D. Exceptions to Observance of Censures

1. *If a censure prohibits the celebration of sacraments or sacramentals or placing an act of governance*, the prohibition is suspended whenever it is necessary to provide for the faithful who are in danger of death. If it is an automatic censure which has not been declared, the prohibition is moreover suspended whenever the faithful request a sacrament or sacramental or an act of governance. They may make this request for any just reason at all. (Can. 1335)

2. *If the penalty forbids the reception of the sacraments or sacramentals*, the prohibition is suspended as long as the person in question is in danger of death. The obligation of observing an automatic penalty, which has not been declared and is not notorious in the place where the offender is living, is suspended totally or partially insofar as the offender is unable to observe it without the danger of grave scandal or infamy. (Can. 1352)

III. Those Subject to Penalties

A. General Principles

1. In general, those subject to the law are subject to a penalty if they break the law, with the exceptions noted below. A penalty binds personally, not territorially, and therefore remains in effect wherever one goes until it is remitted.

2. A penalty cannot be incurred or inflicted unless the delict be perfectly executed according to the strict letter of the law. Laws

which establish a penalty are subject to strict interpretation. (See can. 18.)

> Whoever does or omits anything in attempting to commit a crime but, contrary to his or her desire, has not completed the crime, is not bound to the penalty attached by law to the completed crime, unless a law or precept should state otherwise. (Can. 1328, §1; see also can. 1328, §2.)

3. No one is punished unless the external violation of the law or precept committed by that person is gravely imputable to him or her by reason of malice or culpability. One is bound to the penalty established by a law or precept if that person deliberately violates the law or precept. If the violation occurs as a result of a lack of due diligence the person is not punished, unless the law or precept states otherwise. If the violation is external, imputability is presumed, unless it should appear otherwise. (Can. 1321)

4. Those who habitually lack the use of reason, even if they seem to have been of sound mind when they violated a law or precept, are considered incapable of committing a crime. (Can. 1322)

5. If a law has changed after a crime is committed, that law is to be applied, whether the earlier or later, which is the more favorable to the offender. If the later law abolishes the earlier one, or at least the penalty connected with it, the penalty ceases immediately. (Can. 1313)

6. *Accomplices* who are not named in a law or precept incur an automatic penalty connected with an offense if the offense would not have been committed without their efforts and the penalty is of such a nature that it is able to affect them. Otherwise they can be punished by inflicted penalties. (Can. 1329, §2)

B. Those Exempt from All Penalties

1. Anyone under 16.
2. Anyone inculpably ignorant of the law; also inadvertence to or error of the law.
3. One who acts under physical force or in virtue of a mere acci-

dent which either could not be foreseen or could not be prevented.

4. One who violates the law out of grave fear, even if only relatively grave, or out of necessity or serious inconvenience, unless the offense is intrinsically evil or brings harm to souls.

5. One who acts with due moderation in legitimate self-defense or defense of another against an unjust aggressor.

6. One lacking the use of reason.

7. A person who without fault thought that any of the circumstances in nn. 4 or 5 were present. (Can. 1323)

C. Those Exempt from Automatic Penalties

1. A person having only the imperfect use of reason.

2. One lacking the use of reason due to drunkenness or another similar mental disturbance which was culpable.

3. Someone in a serious heat of passion, which nevertheless did not precede or impede all deliberation of the mind and consent of the will, provided the passion was not voluntarily excited or fostered.

4. Minors (under 18).

5. Anyone who was forced, out of serious fear—even though only relatively serious—or out of necessity or serious inconvenience, if the offense was intrinsically evil or tends to be harmful to souls.

6. One who for the sake of the legitimate protection of oneself or another acted against an unjust aggressor but did not observe due moderation.

7. One who acted against another who gravely or unjustly provoked it.

8. One who through error or culpability thought that any of the circumstances in can. 1323, nn. 4 or 5 were present.

9. One who without fault did not know that there was a penalty attached to the law or precept.

10. One who acted without full imputability, provided it remained serious. (Can. 1324, §1)

> Crass, supine, or affected ignorance can never be considered in applying the prescriptions of cans. 1323 and 1324. Likewise not exempting are drunkenness or other disturbances of the mind, if they are deliberately induced to perpetrate the crime or excuse it, or passion which is willfully excited or fostered. (Can. 1325)

IV. Remission of Penalties

A. Automatic Penalties Not Reserved

Automatic penalties not reserved to the Apostolic See, including abortion, can be remitted by any of the following persons, provided the penalties have not been declared, i.e., the competent ecclesiastical authority has not made any public declaration that the offender has incurred a penalty automatically upon the commission of some delict:

1. All Ordinaries for their subjects; and all local Ordinaries for their subjects and those in their territory or those who committed an offense there. (Can. 1355, §2)

2. All bishops in the act of sacramental confession. (Can. 1355, §2)

3. Canons penitentiary (or their equivalent) in the sacramental forum. (Can. 508)

4. Chaplains in hospitals, prisons, and on ships on voyages. (Can. 567, §2)

5. Any confessor in the internal sacramental forum if it would be hard on the penitent to remain in a state of serious sin for the duration necessary for the competent superior to provide the remission. This applies only to automatic excommunications and interdicts, but not suspensions. In granting the remission the confessor should enjoin the penitent with the burden of having recourse within one month to, and obeying the mandates of, any of the authorities in nn. 1–3 above, under pain of reincidence of the penalty. Meanwhile he should impose an appropriate penance and, to the extent indicated, should impose the repair of scandal and harm. However, recourse can also be taken by the confessor without mentioning any names. (Can. 1357, §§1–2)

> The confessor may presume that anyone who comes to confession is finding it hard to remain in serious sin. According to the traditional commentators, even if the penitent finds it hard to remain in serious sin for one day, the above provisions may be used by the confessor. (See Green, 917.)

6. Any priest, even one without the faculty to hear confessions, may absolve from all penalties if the penitent is in danger of death, even if an approved priest is present. (Can. 976) Should the penitent recover, recourse is not necessary unless the censure is reserved to the Apostolic See.

B. Automatic Penalties Reserved to Apostolic See

The following can remit penalties reserved to the Apostolic See:

1. The Apostolic See. Recourse is had by the penitent or the confessor to the Apostolic Penitentiary.

2. Any confessor in the internal sacramental forum if it would be hard on the penitent to remain in a state of serious sin during the time necessary to receive a remission from the Apostolic See. The conditions of can. 1357 are to be observed as described above at A. 4, with the Apostolic See being the competent authority to which recourse is made.

3. Any priest, even one without the faculty to hear confessions, may absolve from all penalties if the person is in danger of death. If the person recovers, recourse must be made to the Apostolic See. (Cans. 976, 1357, §3)

V. Formula of Remission

When a priest, in accord with the norm of law, remits an automatic censure in the sacramental forum, the formula of absolution is not to be changed. It suffices that he intend to remit the censure as well as absolve the sins. Nevertheless, the confessor can remit the censure before he absolves the sins by using the formula given below for use outside the sacrament of penance. (See RPen, Appendix I, n. 1.)

When a priest, according to the norm of law, remits a censure outside the sacrament of penance, the following formula is used: **By the power granted to me, I absolve you from the bond of excommunication (suspension, interdict). In the name of the Father, and of the Son, + and of the Holy Spirit.** The penitent answers: **Amen.** (See ibid., n. 2.)

The remission of a penalty is a separate act from the absolution of sin. However, it suffices that a confessor who has the power to remit the penalty *intend to do so* at the same time he absolves from sin. With this intention, by reciting the formula of absolution the confessor simultaneously remits the penalty and absolves from the sins. A second option would be to remit the censure using the special formula above before giving absolution.

VI. Remission of Penalty for Abortion

Abortion, which results in automatic excommunication, is likely the crime most often encountered in the sacrament of penance, and so it is a practical example to demonstrate how a confessor should handle automatic censures. In this discussion the typical case will be assumed, i.e., not the danger of death situation and not a priest who has power to remit censures as discussed above (bishops, Ordinaries, canons penitentiary). When the priest hears the sin of abortion confessed, he must determine whether a crime was truly committed by ascertaining certain facts from the penitent. If the answer is yes to any of the following questions, then the crime was not committed and the sin can be handled as usual.

1. Was it only an attempted abortion that did not succeed, or was it indirect?

> An example of an indirect abortion would be a hysterectomy when the intention was not to abort the fetus but only to remove a diseased uterus.

2. If the penitent was an accomplice to the abortion, would the crime have been committed without the accomplice's action or advice?

> For example, the doctor who directly procures the abortion might well incur the penalty; on the other hand, the assistance rendered by a nurse may not be so direct and decisive as to incur the penalty. Or a parent who advises the abortion may have incurred the penalty if the daughter would not have acted without such advice.

3. Was the penitent ignorant, through no fault of his or her own,

that a penalty was attached to the law forbidding abortion?

> It is not enough to know that abortion is a mortal sin. One must also know that a penalty is incurred, although precise knowledge about the nature of the penalty is not required to incur it.

4. Was the penitent under 18 at the time the crime was committed?

5. Was there inadvertence to or error of the law?

> Had the penitent acted without recalling that this was an offense which resulted in a penalty? Did the penitent make a mistake about the law, e.g., thinking it applied only to the person having the abortion and not accomplices?

6. Was it accidental and not intentional?

> If the mother, e.g., intended to get an abortion, but accidentally had a fall which resulted in an abortion, she would not have incurred the penalty. It must be intentional with the result that an inviable fetus is aborted.

7. Did the penitent have an imperfect use of reason?

> E.g., borderline mentally retarded, psychological disturbance, etc.

8. Had the penitent acted out of serious fear, even if only relatively serious, or through necessity or serious inconvenience?

> Was there, e.g., a serious fear about parental or societal reaction to a pregnancy? Was it a necessity? e.g., a doctor who performs an abortion to save the life of the mother.

9. Did the penitent erroneously believe that one of the circumstances in n. 8 above was verified?

> E.g. Did she think that having a child was a serious enough inconvenience in her circumstances to warrant an abortion when objectively it is not?

10. Did the penitent erroneously believe that the abortion was done in self-defense and therefore was justifiable?

> E.g., if her life was in danger, did she think an abortion was an acceptable alternative?

11. Did the person procure the abortion while lacking the use of reason due to drunkenness or another mental disturbance which was culpable but not deliberately induced to commit or excuse the offense?

12. Was the abortion induced by a person in the serious heat of passion which was not voluntarily excited or fostered?

If the answer is no to all of the above questions, then the person has likely incurred an automatic excommunication. If that is the case, only a bishop, an Ordinary, or a canon penitentiary (or his equivalent) can absolve the censure. However, if it would be hard on the penitent to remain in a state of serious sin during the time necessary for the competent superior to provide a remission, any confessor can remit the censure.

A good way to proceed is for the confessor to arrange for the penitent to return to him at an agreed upon time within the next month, notifying the penitent of the reason for this, namely, that he has the power only to absolve the censure temporarily but he must have recourse to someone who has the power for definitive remission. (The penitent can return either in confession or outside of it, although if he or she confesses behind the grille it should be presumed that anonymity is desired.) Before the penitent returns the confessor should request a remission from the local Ordinary, and if the confessor knows the penitent's identity, it should not be mentioned. When the penitent returns, the confessor informs the penitent of the remission.

N.B. In some dioceses all confessors have the delegated faculty to remit the censure of abortion without recourse.

Anointing of the Sick

Part VI

I. The Celebration of the Anointing of the Sick

A. The Liturgical Books

The anointing of the sick is conferred on seriously ill persons by anointing them with oil using the words prescribed in the liturgical books. (See can. 998.) In the dioceses of the United States, the approved liturgical rites are found in *Pastoral Care of the Sick: Rites of Anointing and Viaticum* (PCS), the use of which became mandatory on November 27, 1983. However, the *editio typica*, the 1972 *Rite of Anointing of the Sick* (RA), will be cited except when the PCS text is not found in the RA.

B. Matter and Form

The celebration of this sacrament consists especially in the laying on of hands by the priests of the Church, the offering of the prayer of faith, and the anointing of the sick with oil made holy by God's blessing. (RA, 5)

1. *The sacramental form* for the anointing of the sick in the Latin rite is: THROUGH THIS HOLY ANOINTING MAY THE LORD IN HIS LOVE AND MERCY HELP YOU WITH THE GRACE OF THE HOLY SPIRIT. MAY THE LORD WHO FREES YOU FROM SIN SAVE YOU AND RAISE YOU UP. (RA, 25)

> The sick person is anointed on the forehead and on the hands. It is appropriate to divide the sacramental form so that the first part is said while the forehead is anointed, the latter part while the hands are anointed. (RA, 23)

2. *The matter.* The minister must use olive oil or some other plant

oil which has been recently blessed by the bishop; he may not use old oil except in necessity. The pastor should obtain the sacred oils from his own bishop and keep them in a suitable place. (See can. 847.) Priests should make sure that the oil remains fit for use and should replenish it from time to time, either yearly when the bishop blesses the oil on Holy Thursday or more frequently if necessary. (RA, 22) Every priest may carry blessed oil with him so that, in case of necessity, he may administer the sacrament of anointing. (Can. 1003, §3)

> The oil used for the anointing is the oil of the sick (*oleum infirmorum*). For the lawful administration of the sacrament it is required that it be recently blessed, i.e., at the Chrism Mass most recently celebrated. However, if the new oils are not at hand, it is licit to use the old oils.

> After obtaining the new oils each year, the old oils are to be absorbed in cotton and burned.

C. Blessing of Oil

The oil of the sick ordinarily is blessed by the bishop at the Chrism Mass on Holy Thursday. Besides a bishop, those who can bless the oil to be used in the anointing of the sick are: (1) those who are equated in law with the diocesan bishop; and (2) any presbyter in case of necessity provided it is blessed during the celebration of the sacrament itself. (See can. 999; RA, 21.)

> A case of necessity for a presbyter to bless the oil would be, e.g., whenever a presbyter is celebrating the sacrament and oil blessed by the bishop cannot be conveniently had.

D. The Anointings

1. The anointings are to be carefully administered in accord with the words, order, and manner prescribed in the liturgical books. The sick person is anointed on the forehead and on the hands. It is appropriate to divide the sacramental form so that the first part is said while the forehead is anointed, the latter part while the hands are anointed.

2. In case of necessity, it suffices that there be one anointing on the forehead or even on some other part of the body, while the entire sacramental form is said. (Can. 1000, §1; RA, 23)

> A case of necessity would mainly involve the fear of contagion from the hands or forehead; or it may be lack of time due to the large number of persons to be anointed, in which case a single anointing on the forehead would suffice.

3. Depending upon the culture and traditions of the place, as well as the condition of the sick person, the priest may also anoint additional parts of the body, for example, the area of pain or injury. He does not repeat the sacramental form. (PCS, 124; RA, 24)

> If the anointing is to be an effective sacramental symbol, there should be a generous use of oil so that it will be seen and felt by the sick person as a sign of the Spirit's healing and strengthening presence. For the same reason, it is not desirable to wipe off the oil after the anointing. (PCS, 107)

4. The minister performs the anointings with his own hand, but for a serious reason he may use an instrument. (Can. 1000, §2)

> The anointings are made with the thumb in the form of a cross. In case of danger of contagion, extreme repugnance, or some other serious reason, the minister may use some instrument such as a ball of cotton attached to a small stick.

5. When two or more priests are present for the anointing of a sick person, one of them may say the prayers and carry out the anointings, saying the sacramental form. The others may take the remaining parts, such as the introductory rites, readings, invocations, or instructions. Each priest may lay hands on the sick person. (RA, 19. See also PCS, 108–110.)

E. Communal Celebrations

The communal celebration of anointing for a number of the sick at the same time may be held in accord with the prescriptions of the diocesan bishop. Those to be anointed must be suitably prepared and rightly disposed. (Can. 1002)

The practice of indiscriminately anointing numbers of people on these occasions simply because they are ill or have reached an advanced age is to be avoided. Only those whose health is seriously impaired by sickness or old age are proper subjects for the sacrament. (PCS, 108)

F. Place of Celebration

Ordinarily the anointing of the sick is celebrated in church, at home, or in a hospital or other institution. In necessity it can be celebrated in any fitting place. *Pastoral Care of the Sick* contains three rites for these circumstances: anointing outside Mass, anointing within Mass, and anointing in a hospital or institution.

When the state of the sick person permits it, and especially when he or she is going to receive Holy Communion, the anointing may be conferred within Mass, either in church or even, with the consent of the Ordinary, in some suitable place in the home of the sick person or in the hospital. (RA, 80)

> In light of can. 932, §1 which states that in necessity the Eucharist may be celebrated outside a sacred place, the permission of the Ordinary usually would not be necessary in this case. If the seriously sick person is unable to come to church for Mass, this in itself constitutes a case of necessity which would allow Mass to be celebrated outside a sacred place without further permission.

II. Roles and Ministries

A. The Community

It is especially fitting that all baptized Christians share in this ministry of mutual charity within the Body of Christ by doing all that they can to help the sick return to health, by showing love for the sick, and by celebrating the sacraments with them. Like the other sacraments, these too have a community aspect, which should be brought out as much as possible when they are celebrated. (RA, 33)

> Because of its very nature as a sign, the sacrament of the anointing of the sick should be celebrated with

members of the family and other representatives of the Christian community whenever this is possible. (PCS, 99)

B. Family and Friends

The family and friends of the sick and those who take care of them in any way have a special share in this ministry of comfort. . . . If the sickness grows worse, the family and friends of the sick and those who take care of them have the responsibility of informing the pastor and by their kind words of prudently disposing the sick for the reception of the sacraments at the proper time. (RA, 34; see also can. 1001.)

C. The Minister

Any priest, and only a priest, validly administers the anointing of the sick. All priests who are entrusted with the care of souls have the duty and right to administer the anointing of the sick to the faithful committed to their pastoral office. This duty is ordinarily exercised by bishops, pastors and parochial vicars, chaplains, seminary rectors, and superiors in clerical institutes. For a reasonable cause, any other priest can administer this sacrament with at least the presumed consent of the proper priest mentioned above. Every priest may carry blessed oil with him so that, in case of necessity, he may administer the sacrament of the anointing of the sick. (See cans. 1003; 262; 530, 3°; 566; RA 16.)

The priest should ensure that the abuse of delaying the reception of the sacrament does not occur, and that the celebration takes place while the sick person is capable of active participation. (PCS, 99)

III. Recipient of Anointing

A. Eligibility for Reception

1. The anointing of the sick may be administered to the faithful who have the use of reason and begin to fall into danger as a result of illness or old age. Great care and concern should be taken to see that those of the faithful whose health is seriously impaired by sick-

ness or old age receive this sacrament. (Can. 1004, §1; RA, 8)

Among those who may be anointed, the Ritual mentions in particular: those undergoing surgery whenever a serious illness is the reason for the surgery; elderly people if they have become notably weakened even though no serious illness is present; sick children if they have sufficient use of reason to be strengthened by this sacrament. (See RA, 10–12.)

A prudent or reasonably sure judgment, without scruple, is sufficient for deciding on the seriousness of an illness; if necessary a doctor may be consulted. (RA, 8)

The person must be seriously impaired by some *intrinsic* cause such as a disease, wound, accident, weakness of old age, etc. One who is in danger of death due to some *extrinsic* cause cannot be anointed, e.g., a soldier before battle, a criminal awaiting execution. (Mathis/Bonner, 174)

It is a serious mistake to wait too long, perhaps until the advanced stages of a disease, to anoint a sick person. As soon as the sick person *begins* to be in danger is the fitting time for the anointing.

In public and private catechesis, the faithful should be educated to ask for the sacrament of anointing and, as soon as the right time comes, to receive it with full faith and devotion. They should not follow the wrongful practice of delaying the reception of the sacrament. (RA, 13)

2. The anointing may be administered to sick persons who at least implicitly asked for it when they were in control of their faculties. (Can. 1006)

Implicit requests for anointing include the cases of those who ask that a priest be summoned, or declare that they wish to die as a Christian, or give some other sign of repentance. They very likely *would have asked* for the sacrament, if in life they had faithfully fulfilled the duties of a Christian, or even if they had not always been faithful in these duties, nevertheless, did not altogether neglect them. In practice, the intention of receiving the sacrament of anointing of the sick is presupposed in all Catholics until the contrary is proven. (Genicot, II, n. 427)

On the other hand, those who have neglected their religion entirely and have refused the ministration of the priest, if they gave no sign of repentance before becoming unconscious, they cannot be anointed because they lack the intention which is requisite for the validity of the sacrament. (Ibid.)

3. The anointing of the sick should not be administered to those who obstinately persist in manifest serious sin. (Can. 1007)

A manifest sin is one that is publicly known, even if only by a few. Obstinate persistence implies that the person neglects to heed the teachings of the Church or the warnings of ecclesiastical authority. The clearest case of such obstinate persistence in manifest serious sin is the person with an imposed or declared censure who refuses reconciliation by having the censure remitted. If such persons are unconscious and have given no previous sign of repentance, they may not be anointed. If they are conscious and ask for the sacrament, they may not be anointed unless the censure is remitted. In danger of death, all censures may be remitted by means of the sacrament of penance. (Can. 976)

Another case is a notorious criminal or other public sinner who refuses reconciliation and gives no sign of repentance. Such persons may not be anointed.

One reason for the requirement of this law is the necessity of the recipient having the proper disposition for the sacrament. Ordinarily one should not presume that a person who is divorced and remarried does not have the proper disposition or had given no sign of repentance. Often the divorced and remarried may have repented of past sins but are unable to quit the second invalid union due to moral obligations to spouse and children. In their conscience and in fact, they may not be in serious sin at all.

B. Doubt about Eligibility

If there is doubt whether the sick person has the use of reason, is seriously ill, or is dead, the sacrament may be administered. (Can.

1005) N.B. There is no longer a provision for conditional anointing; the sacrament is to be administered with the usual form.

> A person who once had the use of reason but lost it due to sickness, old age, or other reason may always be anointed, even if there is no doubt that they lack the use of reason. The requirement of the use of reason applies only to infants and others who have never had the use of reason. (McManus, 710)

> When a priest has been called to attend a person who is already dead, he should pray for the dead person, asking that God forgive his or her sins and graciously receive him/her into his kingdom. The priest is not to administer the sacrament of anointing. (RA, 15) Thus, conditional anointing of dead persons is forbidden. Instead the priest or other minister should say the prayers for the dead found in *Pastoral Care of the Sick*.

C. Repetition of the Sacrament

The anointing of the sick may be repeated if the sick person has become better and again falls into a serious illness or, if during the same illness, a more serious crisis develops. (Can. 1004, §2)

> A person may be anointed again whenever there is a new serious illness after recovery from a previous serious illness, or if during a protracted illness the patient's condition appreciably worsens. If there is any doubt whether this worsening of condition constitutes a more serious crisis, the sacrament may be celebrated. The law excludes frequent anointings during the same illness even if the patient's condition is gradually deteriorating. Traditional canonical opinion holds that in such cases the person should not be anointed again unless a notable time has elapsed. (Noldin, III, n. 448) In view of this canon, however, this does not mean that the sacrament should be administered on some regular basis, such as monthly, to the ill person, without any reference to the progress of the illness. (McManus, 710)

Marriage

Part VII

CHAPTER I
Introduction

I. Jurisdiction over Marriage

A. Marriage of Catholics

The marriage of Catholics, even if only one party is Catholic, is regulated not only by divine law, but also by canon law, without prejudice to the competence of the civil authority concerning the merely civil effects of the marriage. (Can. 1059)

The Church claims authority over the *marriage of a Catholic and a non-Catholic*, even a non-sacramental marriage involving a non-baptized spouse. Thus, whenever at least one party is Catholic, the Catholic canon law must be followed. To be *sacramental*, or *ratified*, both parties must be *baptized*, whether Catholic or non-Catholic.

B. Inter-ecclesial (inter-ritual) marriages

Inter-ecclesial (inter-ritual) marriages involving two Catholics of different ritual churches (e.g., a Latin Catholic and a Ukrainian Catholic) are governed by the law of both churches. Both parties must be free of all diriment impediments (whether relative or absolute) as specified by the law of *both* ritual churches before the parties can marry validly. (Pospishil/Faris, 27)

C. The Marriage of Non-Catholics

The marriage of two *non-Catholics* is also governed by the civil law, which canon law recognizes provided it is not contrary to the divine law or unless canon law has provided something else. (See can. 22.) Hence, a marriage between two non-Catholics that is invalid according to civil law would likewise not be recognized as valid by canon law.

D. The Marriage of Baptized Non-Catholics

In addition to being bound by divine law and the civil law, the marriage of two *baptized non-Catholics* has certain theological and canonical effects. Such marriages are *ipso facto* sacramental when they are valid. Therefore, for the validity of their marriage, baptized non-Catholics may not, by a positive act of the will, exclude from their marriage consent the sacramental dignity of marriage. (Cf. cans. 1099, 1101.)

E. The Marriage with One Baptized Spouse

Although not stated in this canon, the Church also claims some authority over *any marriage in which at least one spouse is baptized*. As a rule, baptized non-Catholics are not subject to canon law (cf. can. 11); but in the case of marriage there is an exception to this rule, as e.g., when a divorced non-Catholic wishes to marry a Catholic and seeks an annulment or dissolution of the previous marriage in accord with canon law.

With regard to the *doubtfully baptized*: If the validity of the baptism is doubtful there is a general presumption at least in the external forum in favor of the validity of baptism, except where the privilege of the faith is involved. (See can. 1150.)

II. Presumption in Favor of Marriage

1. Marriage enjoys the favor of law; therefore, when there is a doubt, the validity of a marriage is to be upheld until the contrary is proven. (Can. 1060)

When there is doubt concerning the validity of a marriage that was certainly celebrated, the marriage is considered valid until the contrary is proved with moral certainty. The presumption presupposes an "appearance of marriage," i.e., some wedding ceremony according to the canonical form for Catholics or some publicly recognized exchange of consent for non-Catholics. (Doyle, 744) If the very fact of the celebration of the marriage is doubtful, but it is favored by the fact that the parties are in possession of a decent public reputation as husband and wife, the marriage is likewise considered as valid until the opposite is proved. (Mathis/Bonner, 197)

2. When there is a positive and insoluble doubt concerning the validity of a first marriage, a second marriage is to be declared invalid in virtue of canon 1060; the case is however to be handled according to the norms of law, i.e., not merely in a summary and administrative manner. (CodCom, reply, June 26, 1947, CLD 3:404) Hence a second marriage is to be declared invalid if it was celebrated at the time a former marriage existed that was doubtfully valid.

3. The presumption of canon 1060 holds not only for the marriages of Catholics but also of non-Catholics.

CHAPTER II
Preparation for the Celebration of Marriage

I. Catechetical and Spiritual Preparation

A. Duties of Pastoral Ministers

Pastoral ministers are bound to see to it that their own ecclesial community offers assistance to the faithful by which the married state is preserved in its Christian spirit and progresses toward perfection. This assistance should be offered especially by:

1. preaching and catechesis adapted to minors, young people, and adults, and also by the use of other means of communication, so that the faithful are instructed on the meaning of Christian marriage and on the duty of spouses and Christian parents;

2. personal preparation for entering marriage by which the couple is disposed for the holiness and duties of their new state;

3. a fruitful liturgical celebration of marriage, which brings out the fact that the spouses signify and participate in the mystery of unity and fruitful love between Christ and the Church;

4. help offered to married persons, that by faithfully observing and protecting the conjugal covenant, they may grow day by day toward a holier and fuller family life. (Can. 1063)

> Priests should first of all strengthen and nourish the faith of those about to be married, for the sacrament of marriage presupposes and demands faith. (RM, 7)

> The bridal couple should, if necessary, be given a review of these fundamentals of Christian doctrine

161

[found in RM, 1–4]; then the catechesis for marriage should include the teachings on marriage and the family, on the sacrament itself and its rites, prayers, and readings. In this way the bridegroom and the bride will receive far greater benefit from the celebration of the sacrament. (RM, 5)

B. Reception of Confirmation, Penance, Eucharist

1. Catholics who have not yet received the sacrament of confirmation should receive it before being admitted to marriage, if it can be done without serious inconvenience. (Can. 1065, §1)

> . . . if it is foreseen that the conditions for a fruitful reception of confirmation cannot be satisfied, the local Ordinary will judge whether it is better to defer confirmation until after marriage. (RConf, 12)

2. In order for the sacrament of marriage to be received fruitfully, it is highly recommended that the parties receive the sacraments of penance and the holy Eucharist. (Can. 1065, §2)

II. Pre-Marital Investigation

A. General Principles

1. All persons are able to contract marriage unless they are prohibited by law. (Can. 1058) Ordained ministers may not refuse the sacraments to those who ask for them under suitable circumstances, who are properly disposed, and who are not prohibited by law from receiving them. (Can. 843, §1)

> In virtue of these canons, as well as the general right of the faithful to receive the sacraments (can. 213), ministers should not deny a Catholic marriage celebration to a couple unless they have some legal basis for doing so, whether that basis exists in universal or particular law.

2. Before a marriage is celebrated, it must be evident that nothing prevents its valid or licit celebration. (Can. 1066) The one who assists at marriage acts illicitly unless he has established according to the norm of law the free status of the parties. (See can. 1114.)

The pastoral minister can best be assured of the validity and liceity of marriage celebrations by carefully following the pre-marital preparation programs and policies of the particular church as well as by observing the norms of universal law.

B. Duties of Faithful and Ministers

1. *The faithful*. Before the celebration of a marriage, all the faithful who know of any impediments are bound to reveal them to the pastor or local Ordinary. (Can. 1069)

2. *The one who assists*. If someone other than the pastor is to assist at the marriage and conducts the investigation, that person should notify the pastor of the results as soon as possible by means of an authentic document. (Can. 1070)

> The pastor is ultimately responsible for seeing that the pre-marital investigation is conducted even if he does not do it personally. When someone outside the parish handles the investigation or, for that matter, any other aspects of the preparation for marriage, the proper pastor should be notified by means of an authentic document, i.e., one that is signed, dated, and sealed if possible.

> The episcopal conference may establish regulations for the examination of the parties as well as for the marriage banns or other suitable means for carrying out the investigation which is necessary before marriage. After these regulations have been diligently followed, the pastor [or other official witness] may proceed to assist at the marriage. (Can. 1067)

> The universal law no longer requires *marriage banns*, but leaves such regulations to the episcopal conference. In the United States, the N.C.C.B. has left it to each diocese to make its own regulations governing marriage banns and the pre-marital investigations and preparation. (Plenary session, Nov., 1984) Hence, particular law must be followed in all of these matters.

> In danger of death, if other proofs are unavailable, it suffices, unless there are contrary indications, that the parties affirm, even under oath if the case calls for

it, that they are baptized and are not prevented by any impediment. (Can. 1068) Thus, in danger of death of one or both parties, the usual pre-marital preparation is not required. The danger of death refers to *probable* danger from either extrinsic causes (e.g., war, natural disasters, execution) or intrinsic causes (e.g. serious illness, wounds, etc.) on the part of either or both parties. (Doyle, 752)

C. Cases Requiring the Local Ordinary's Permission

In addition to the permission needed for mixed marriages, permission of the local Ordinary is needed to assist in seven other situations except in the case of necessity.

> A case of necessity would include danger of death or some other serious necessity according to the circumstances. Extra-marital pregnancy does not constitute a sufficient reason to proceed without the local Ordinary's permission, but rather is a circumstance calling for even greater preparation for marriage to ensure readiness for a lifetime commitment. The necessity for proceeding without permission must clearly outweigh the dangers that may arise in each case. (Doyle, 755–56)

The seven cases requiring the local Ordinary's permission for the liceity of the marriage celebration are:

1. *Vagi* (transients), i.e., those who have no domicile or quasi-domicile.

> If the parties have a month-long residence in the parish, it is not necessary to get the local Ordinary's permission. (Can. 1115) However, particular law in many places requires a specified period of preparation longer than one month. In such cases the permission of the diocesan bishop will be needed to dispense from the obligation of the particular law in question.

2. Those whose marriage cannot be recognized or celebrated according to the civil law.

> Among the impediments of many civil law jurisdictions are prior marriage, lack of minimum age, blood

164

relationship within specified degrees, severe mental disorder, adoptive relationship, and venereal disease. Ordinarily, such civilly prohibited marriages should not be celebrated by the Church until the impediment ceases or the marriage is allowed by court order. (Doyle, 753–54) In any case, the local Ordinary's permission is always required for such marriages except in necessity.

3. Those bound by natural obligations towards another party or towards children from a previous union.

> Natural obligations toward a former spouse would include a serious illness or financial destitution that may impose some moral obligation to assist the former spouse. There also may be legal obligations such as the payment of alimony and child support. The minister conducting the pre-marital investigation should inquire about this matter whenever the party's prior marriage had been invalid or was dissolved and the former spouse is still living or the children of the previous union are not yet raised.

4. A person who has notoriously rejected the Catholic faith. The local Ordinary should not grant permission to assist at the marriage of one who has notoriously rejected the Catholic faith unless the regulations of canon 1125 are observed, making appropriate adaptations. (Can. 1071)

> Notorious rejection of the faith means public rejection, namely, the case either of a person who has formally joined another religion or has publicly declared that he or she is no longer Catholic. Such a person is no longer considered Catholic by the law, and the marriage to a Catholic is considered a mixed marriage. The declaration and promise on the part of the Catholic party and the other requirements of can. 1125 are to be observed as given below. N.B. Permission of the local Ordinary is not necessary in the case of a person who has not practiced the Catholic faith without notoriously rejecting it; however, special pastoral attention, such as additional catechesis, may be necessary for such persons.

5. A person who is bound by a censure.

Those bound by the censures of excommunication and interdict are prohibited from celebrating or receiving the sacraments and sacramentals. (See cans. 1331, §1, 2° and 1332.) Therefore, in the case of a sacramental marriage involving two baptized persons, the local Ordinary could not give permission for such a marriage until the censure is remitted. Even in the case of the marriage of a non-baptized person with a Catholic who has a declared or inflicted censure, it seems highly inappropriate for the local Ordinary to grant permission for such a marriage until the censure has been remitted. The requirement of the local Ordinary's permission, therefore, is best seen as a provision of the law to ensure that the necessary steps are taken to have the censure remitted before the celebration of the marriage.

6.   A minor [under 18] when the parents are unaware of the marriage or are reasonably opposed to it. Pastoral ministers should see to it that young people are prevented from marrying before the age which is customary in the region. (Can. 1072)

A boy under 16 or a girl under 14 may not marry validly. However, even older persons should be dissuaded from marrying if they are younger than the usual age in the region. The civil law should also be consulted, for many civil jurisdictions require the permission of the parents for the marriage of minors. Particular law should also be observed since episcopal conferences can establish a higher age for liceity. (See can. 1083, §2.)

Except in necessity, no minister without the permission of the local Ordinary may perform the marriage ceremony of a person under 18 whose parents are unaware of it or opposed to it. Even if only one party is a minor, such a case must be referred to the local Ordinary. The pastor or other minister should interview the parents of the minor party when they are opposed to the marriage to determine what their reasons are, and should make a recommendation to the local Ordinary who determines whether the marriage can proceed or should be delayed. Although not required by universal law, it is wise to seek the judgment of the local Ordinary in all marriages where the minister doubts the maturity of one or both parties, even when the parents do not oppose the marriage. Many particular churches have marriage preparation programs that detect such immaturity, and policies that should be followed, including counselling and the delay of marriage.

7.   A proxy as provided in canon 1105.

A proxy marriage is one in which one or both parties are represented by someone else who has been mandated in accord with canon 1105. Since proxies should only be allowed in extraordinary circumstances, the permission of the local Ordinary for such marriages is necessary except in necessity such as danger of death.

III.   Mixed Marriages

In the strict sense of the term, a mixed marriage is one between a Catholic and a baptized non-Catholic. In the broad sense, it includes marriages between a Catholic and a non-baptized. The former require permission of the competent authority for the liceity of the celebration. The latter require a dispensation from the impediment of disparity of cult for the validity of the marriage.

A.   Permission Needed to Marry a Baptized Non-Catholic

A marriage between two baptized persons, one who was baptized in the Catholic Church or was received into it after baptism and who has not left it by a formal act, and the other who belongs to a church or ecclesial community which does not have full communion with the Catholic Church, is prohibited without the express permission of the competent authority. (Can. 1124)

In brief, a mixed marriage (in the strict sense) is one between a Catholic and a baptized non-Catholic. Such marriages require the *permission* of the local Ordinary, but not for validity as is the case for a marriage between a Catholic and a non-baptized person which requires a *dispensation* from the impediment of disparity of cult.

The local Ordinary is the competent authority to grant permission. It may be the local Ordinary of the Catholic party or of the place where the marriage is being celebrated. It could even be the local Ordinary of the place where the Catholic party is staying temporarily. The local Ordinary may also delegate others, even habitually, to grant this permission. Some dioceses, as part of the diocesan faculties, routinely allow the pastor or the priest or deacon who assists at marriage to grant this permission.

B. Declaration and Promise of Catholic Party

The local Ordinary can grant permission for a mixed marriage if there is a just and reasonable cause.

A just and reasonable cause includes negative reasons, such as the danger of a civil marriage or defection from the faith, and also positive reasons such as the couple's awareness of the responsibilities of a sacramental marriage, their commitment to their respective churches, their maturity and other strengths. (Doyle, 802) Particular churches often provide convenient forms so that the minister need only check the appropriate reason or reasons. Despite the routine granting of such permission, the minister should see to it that the couple have considered the implications for their marriage of their different faiths, and take account of any disagreements or conflicts. If such disagreements are serious and cannot be resolved, the minister should not proceed with the marriage, or recommend that the permission of the local Ordinary not be granted.

The local Ordinary should not grant permission for a mixed marriage, or grant a dispensation from a disparity of cult marriage (cf. can. 1086, §2), unless the following conditions are fulfilled:

1. The Catholic party declares that he or she is prepared to remove dangers of falling away from the faith and makes a sincere promise to do all in his or her power to have all the children baptized and brought up in the Catholic Church. (Can. 1125, 1°)

Broad interpretation of this requirement is necessary because the permission for a mixed marriage should be considered as a favor which protects the natural right to marry the person of one's choosing. Hence, it may be necessary, as when the Catholic is re-

168

luctant to make the promise, to explain to the parties
the broad meaning of the phrase, *to do all in one's
power*. In fact, there may be times when the Catholic
party is not able to have the children baptized and
raised Catholics. Perhaps the faith of the non-Catholic
is stronger; or perhaps the insistence that all the children be baptized and raised Catholic will be disruptive
to the marriage. In such cases one is required to do
only what is in one's power to do, even if the children
in the end may not be baptized and raised Catholic.

The declaration and promise are made in the presence of a priest or deacon either orally or in writing as
the Catholic prefers. The promise must be sincerely
made. If the priest or deacon has reason to doubt the
sincerity of the promise made by the Catholic, he may
not recommend the request for the permission or dispensation and should submit the matter to the local Ordinary. (NCCB, *Statement on the Implementation of
the Apostolic Letter on Mixed Marriages*, Jan. 1, 1971)

The episcopal conference may establish regulations
governing the manner in which these declarations and
promises, which are always required, are to be made,
and it may define the way in which they are to be
proven in the external forum and made known to the
non-Catholic party. (Can. 1126)

2. The other party is to be informed at a suitable time of the
Catholic party's promises so that it is clear that the non-Catholic is
truly conscious of the promise and obligation of the Catholic party.
(Can. 1125, 2°)

The suitable time for informing the non-Catholic
party of the Catholic's promise is to be determined by
the circumstances, but it should be done before the
marriage so that any problems it may cause can be discussed and resolved ahead of time. Frequently it is best
to discuss the requirements of canon 1125 and the implications of a mixed marriage with both parties together so that an attitude of openness and dialogue on
the important subject of religion are there from the beginning.

3. Both parties are to be instructed on the ends and essential prop-

erties of marriage which are not to be excluded by either party. (Can. 1125, 3°)

This requirement can be taken care of for the most part by observing the preparation program of the particular church. It is important to note that the non-Catholic party does not have to *believe* in the Church's doctrine on the ends and essential properties of marriage, but may not exclude them by a positive act of the will. For example, the non-Catholic may believe that divorce and remarriage are acceptable, but he must *intend* to enter *this* marriage with *this* Catholic woman for life.

CHAPTER III
Impediments

I. Impediments in General

A diriment impediment renders a person incapable of contracting marriage validly. (Can. 1073) N.B.: There are no longer any impedient impediments; hence all impediments affect the validity of marriage.

> Since the canon law of the Eastern Catholic ritual churches is not revised at the present time, there are impedient impediments in Eastern canon law which affect only the liceity of marriage. (See Mp, cans. 48–56.)

A. Division

1. Impediments are of *divine law* or of *ecclesiastical law*. Only the supreme authority of the Church may declare authentically when divine law prohibits or nullifies marriage. (Can. 1075, §1) Prior bond and impotence are certainly considered impediments of the divine law, and consanguinity in the direct line and second degree collateral are at least treated as if they were of the divine law because they are never dispensed. Divine law impediments bind everyone and cannot be dispensed; ecclesiastical impediments bind only Catholic marriages, even marriages involving only one Catholic. Canon law also recognizes the binding force for the marriage of non-Catholics of civil law impediments. N.B.: Before November 27, 1983, when the revised Code took effect, even baptized non-Catholics were bound to canon law, and thus subject to ecclesiastical impediments. Marriages which were contracted before this date are subject to the former law.

Canon 1075, §2 states that the supreme authority

may establish ecclesiastical impediments for the baptized. While the Church therefore has the power to establish impediments for all the baptized, in keeping with the principle of canon 11 which states that merely ecclesiastical laws bind only Catholics, the "baptized" here should be understood as referring in practice to baptized Catholics.

2. Impediments are said to be *absolute* if they prohibit marriage with any person (e.g., age) and *relative* if they prohibit marriage with some particular person only (e.g., consanguinity).

3. A *public* impediment is one that can be proved in the external forum; otherwise it is an *occult* impediment. (Can. 1074)

> Possibility of proof in the external forum is had when the impediment can be proved by an authentic document or by two witnesses giving concordant testimony of things of which they have personal knowledge, or by the testimony of an official in reference to matters pertaining to his office, e.g., a pastor asserting he assisted at a certain marriage; also by the testimony of experts or by the confession of the party made in court. Note however that proof in the external forum must be possible not theoretically only but also practically, i.e., in the concrete case the impediment can be proved. (V.C., II, 297)

> A case is to be considered occult if the impediment is by nature public but is in fact occult. (CodCom, Dec. 28, 1927) Thus an impediment which is public by nature (because it arises from a fact which is in itself public), e.g., consanguinity, age, holy orders, affinity, etc., can be occult in fact because it is not known and not likely to become known. A public case is one in which the impediment is known or very likely will become known. In the granting of dispensations a local Ordinary may accept this distinction of public and occult or the distinction given in canon 1074. (Gasparri, I, n. 210)

B. Establishment of Impediments and Prohibitions

1. *Impediments.* Only the supreme authority of the Church may authentically declare when the divine law prohibits or nullifies marriage. Also only the supreme authority has the right to establish

other impediments for the baptized. (can. 1075)

2. *Prohibitions.* The local Ordinary can prohibit marriage in a particular case but only temporarily for a serious reason and only while that reason exists. He may do this for his own subjects anywhere they are staying and for anyone actually in his territory. Only the supreme authority of the Church may add an invalidating clause to the prohibition. (Can. 1077)

> The local Ordinary therefore can forbid a marriage for a time and because of a serious reason, but his prohibition affects only the liceity and not the validity of the marriage. Some serious reasons for such a prohibition may be: grave immaturity, a hasty engagement due to an unexpected pregnancy, psychological problems and, in general, any serious doubt whether either party, for whatever reason, is able or intends to consent validly to marriage.

C. Dispensations

1. *Competent authority.* The local Ordinary may dispense from all impediments of ecclesiastical law except those whose dispensation is reserved to the Apostolic See. He may dispense his own subjects everywhere they are staying and everyone actually in his territory. (Can. 1078, §1)

> The local Ordinary may not dispense from the impediments of prior bond, impotence, consanguinity in the direct line and second degree collateral, and from impediments which are reserved to the Apostolic See. The dispensation may be given by the Ordinary of the place where the marriage is celebrated or the Ordinary of the place where either party, if Catholic, or the Catholic party in a mixed marriage, have domicile or quasi-domicile.

> *Eastern Catholics.* The Latin local Ordinary may also dispense Eastern Catholics subject to him, but not Eastern Catholics who have their own Ordinary unless one of the parties to the marriage is from the Latin Church. At the present time the following Eastern Catholics have their own Ordinaries in the United States and Canada: Ukrainians, Ruthenians, Maronites, Melkites, Armenians, Slovaks, Chaldeans, and Roma-

nians. (Pospishil/Faris, 14–15)

A dispensation is given in the external forum if the impediment is public; in the internal forum if the impediment is occult. If both a public and occult impediment occur in the same case, the dispensations may be asked for separately: that from the public impediment from the diocesan chancery or, if the impediment is reserved, from the Apostolic See, without mentioning the other impediment; the dispensation from the occult impediment should be obtained from the chancery (or from the Apostolic Penitentiary if the impediment is reserved) without endangering the sacramental seal. (Bouscaren-Ellis, 483)

Note: Whenever the impediment is public, a dispensation should be obtained in the external forum. If the case is *de facto occult*, even if the impediment is public by nature and even though it is public according to the definition given in canon 1074, one may still petition for the dispensation in the internal forum.

Necessity of reason for dispensation. No dispensation from an ecclesiastical law can be granted without a just and reasonable cause proportionate to the gravity of the law from which a dispensation is given; otherwise the dispensation from a universal law given by the local Ordinary is invalid. (See can. 91, §1.) Therefore the one applying for the dispensation must give a reason which is true. If the cause is false the dispensation will ordinarily be invalid.

When there is doubt about the sufficiency of the reason, the dispensation may be licitly asked for and licitly and validly granted. (See can. 90, §2.) According to the common opinion, the same rule applies when there is doubt as to the very existence of the reason; and if after the dispensation is granted it should become evident that the reason for the dispensation was not sufficient or was non-existent, it is probable that the dispensation is still valid, provided that all concerned acted in good faith. (Coronata, I, n. 115)

2. *Reserved impediments.* A dispensation from the following impediments is reserved to the Apostolic See: (a) the impediment arising

from holy orders or from a public perpetual vow of chastity in a religious institute of pontifical right; (b) the impediment of crime treated in canon 1090. (Can. 1078, §2)

Clerics in any grade of holy orders may not marry without a dispensation from the pope. (See can. 291.) This includes married permanent deacons who may not remarry (when their wife dies or their marriage is annulled or dissolved) without this dispensation. A dispensation from the impediment of a public perpetual vow of chastity in a religious institute is ordinarily not dispensed. Rather, the vow itself can be dispensed, either by the Apostolic See in the case of a religious in an institute of pontifical right, or by the diocesan bishop in the case of a religious in an institute of diocesan right.

The impediment of crime, rarely encountered in pastoral ministry, will typically be occult. The competent tribunal to grant the dispensation is the Apostolic Penitentiary. If the impediment was revealed in the sacrament of penance, the confessor should write to the Apostolic Penitentiary for the dispensation, describing the case without mentioning the name of the penitent or otherwise violating or endangering the sacramental seal.

3. *Impediments never dispensed.* Besides the impediments of prior bond and impotence, a dispensation is never given from the impediment of consanguinity in the direct line or in the second degree of the collateral line. (See can. 1078, §3.)

The practice of the Holy See has also been never to dispense from the order of episcopate and from the impediment of crime when it is public; it rarely dispenses from affinity in the first degree of the direct line after the marriage from which affinity arose has been consummated, or from the presbyterate. (V.C., II, n. 310) Regarding the latter, the general practice is to obtain a dispensation from the obligations of celibacy rather than a dispensation from the impediment of holy orders. Once the dispensation from celibacy has been obtained from the pope, the impediment to marriage ceases.

D. Dispensation In Danger of Death.

1. *Powers of the local Ordinary.* In danger of death, the local Ordinary may dispense from the form to be observed in celebrating marriage and from each and every impediment of ecclesiastical law whether public or occult, except for the impediment arising from the order of the presbyterate. He may dispense his own subjects wherever they are staying and everyone actually in his territory. (Can. 1079, §1)

> The local Ordinary's power is ordinary power and hence may be delegated to others, even habitually; it may be used even if recourse to the Holy See is possible; it may be used on one's subjects everywhere and on non-subjects when in the local Ordinary's territory; it extends to all impediments that are certainly of ecclesiastical law only, with the exception of the one mentioned; it extends to impediments from which the Holy See only rarely dispenses, e.g., crime; it does not extend to impediments which are certainly or most probably of divine law, i.e., consanguinity in the direct line and in the second degree collateral line, previous bond, certain impotence; it extends to the form of marriage, but not to the renewal of consent. (V.C., II, n. 307)

> For the valid use of the power to dispense in danger of death, it is necessary that the danger probably exists; it need not be *articulum mortis*, i.e., the last moment, but the "danger" of death suffices, provided that the danger is certain or seriously probable; the danger may affect only one of the parties, the party directly dispensed or the other party, the Catholic or the non-Catholic party; the danger may arise from intrinsic causes (e.g., sickness) or extrinsic causes (e.g., floods, impending serious surgery, war, proximate execution, etc.).

> There must be some reason for the dispensation, such as the quieting of conscience or the legitimation of the children.

2. *Powers of the pastor, assisting minister, confessor.* In the same circumstances mentioned in canon 1079, §1, but only for cases in which the local Ordinary cannot be reached, the same power to dis-

pense in danger of death is enjoyed by the pastor, the ordained minister who is properly delegated to assist at marriage, and the priest or deacon who assists at a marriage celebrated according to the norm of canon 1116, §2. The local Ordinary is not considered as being able to be reached if this can be done only by means of the telegraph or telephone. The pastor or priest or deacon should immediately notify the local Ordinary of a dispensation granted for the external forum, and it should be recorded in the marriage register. In danger of death the confessor enjoys the power to dispense from occult impediments for the internal forum whether within or outside the sacrament of penance. (See cans. 1079, §§2–4, 1081.)

> Hence, in danger of death, for the purpose of peace of conscience or of legitimation of children or some other reason, the above-mentioned ordained ministers may dispense from the form (but not from renewal of consent) and from impediments of ecclesiastical law as above, D, 1. The local Ordinary is also considered out of reach if he cannot be approached without danger of violating the sacramental seal or a secret. (Genicot, II, n. 593)

E. Dispensation in Urgent Cases

1. *Powers of the local Ordinary.* The local Ordinary may dispense from all impediments of ecclesiastical law, public as well as occult, except the impediments arising from holy orders or from a public perpetual vow of chastity in a religious institute of pontifical right, whenever the impediment is discovered only when everything is already prepared for the wedding and the wedding cannot, without probable danger of grave harm, be deferred until a dispensation is obtained from the Holy See. They may dispense their own subjects wherever they may be staying, and all others actually staying in their territory.

This power also holds for the convalidation of a marriage already contracted, if there is the same danger in delay and there is not sufficient time for recourse to the Apostolic See. (See can. 1080.)

> a. For the use of this power it is required that there be probable danger of grave harm in delay. Examples are scandal, danger of a merely civil marriage, notable financial loss. (Matthis/Bonner, 245) The possible loss

of money already invested in the wedding preparations or the fear of temporary embarassment are not sufficient reasons to dispense from an impediment if it appears that the relationship is not secure and will be imperiled. (See Doyle, 763–64.)

The time required for obtaining a dispensation from the Apostolic See can be taken as from six to eight weeks. Means such as telegraph or telephone need not be used, since these are considered extraordinary in law.

b. It is required that preparations have already been made for the marriage. This condition is usually verified as soon as the proclamation of the banns has begun even though not all the material preparations have been completed. The fact that the invitations have not been issued does not necessarily exclude the use of the power. (SRR, case, May 25, 1925)

c. The existence of the impediment is discovered only after preparations have been made and it is too late to defer the marriage; that is, it is only then that the impediment is discovered by the minister or the local Ordinary, even though the parties may have known it beforehand (see CodCom, Mar. 1, 1921), so that to avoid grave harm the wedding must be celebrated within a shorter time than that which is required to obtain a dispensation from the Apostolic See.

d. When the local Ordinary uses canon 1080 to convalidate a marriage already contracted, it is not necessary that the impediment be just now discovered. Danger in delay is had if the parties cannot be separated without grave harm (e.g., because all think them to be husband and wife, because there are children to care for, etc.).

e. By virtue of canon 87, §2 the Ordinary can dispense from the above-mentioned impediments if recourse is difficult and there is a danger of grave harm even if all the preparations for the wedding have not been made, provided it is a dispensation which the Holy See is accustomed to grant, namely, the impediment of crime in occult cases.

2. *Powers of the Pastor, Assisting Minister, Confessor.* In the same circumstances of canon 1080, §1 given as above for the local Ordinary, *but only for occult cases*, the same power to dispense when everything is prepared for the wedding is enjoyed by the pastor, the properly delegated ordained minister, or the priest or deacon who assists at marriage in accord with canon 1116, §2, and the confessor (but the latter only for the internal forum whether within or outside the sacrament of penance). (See can. 1080, §1.) This power can be used only for occult cases when the local Ordinary cannot be reached or when he cannot be reached without the danger of the violation of a secret. Hence, this power can be used only:

a. if preparations have been made for the marriage and there is probable danger of grave harm in delay (see commentary above, E, 1);

b. if the local Ordinary or Apostolic See (in the case of crime) cannot be reached by the ordinary means of the mail in time to avoid the danger of grave harm, or cannot be reached without the danger of the violation of a secret, including any professional secret as well as the secret of the seal of confession;

c. to dispense from all impediments of ecclesiastical law, with the exceptions noted above;

d. for occult cases, i.e., not only impediments which are occult by nature but also those occult in fact, namely, that they are not publicly known;

If there is danger of harm in delaying until a dispensation can be obtained from the competent authority, the power may be used also for the convalidation of an invalid marriage. (See can. 1080, §2.)

> If the dispensation was granted in the external forum, the pastor or priest or deacon should immediately notify the local Ordinary and the dispensation should be recorded in the marriage register. (Can. 1081)

> Unless a rescript from the Penitentiary stipulates otherwise, a dispensation in the internal non-sacramental forum for an occult impediment should be recorded in a book reserved in the secret archives of the diocesan curia. Another dispensation for the external forum is unnecessary should the occult impediment later become public. (Can. 1082)

II. Impediments in Particular

The treatment of each impediment will cover the Latin rite law from the 1983 Code and, where significant, the Eastern canon law, the civil law, and the law from the 1917 Code. The Eastern law and the Latin rite law must both be observed in marriages involving a Latin Catholic and an Eastern Catholic. (The Eastern law is given only when it is at variance with the Latin law.) N.B.: THE LAW GIVEN HERE FOR THE EASTERN CATHOLIC CHURCHES IS FROM THE 1949 *MOTU PROPRIO, CREBRAE ALLATAE*, since the Oriental Code of Canon Law is not promulgated as of this writing. However, even after the Oriental Code is published, it will still be useful to have available the law of *Crebrae allatae* because the validity of all marriages involving a Catholic of the Eastern rite will be judged according to this law if it was in force at the time the marriage was contracted.

The civil law is recognized by canon law as applicable to the marriages of non-Catholics, and therefore if a marriage contracted between two non-Catholics is invalid in the civil law, it is also invalid according to canon law. The former law from the 1917 Code can also be important for annulment cases, because the marriages of the baptized contracted before November 27, 1983, were subject to the laws of the former Code.

Unless noted otherwise, dispensations from any impediment can be given by the local Ordinary, or by the others mentioned in canons 1079 and 1080 in danger of death and *omnia parata* cases.

A. Age

1. A man before he has completed his sixteenth year and a woman before the completion of her fourteenth year are not able to marry validly. The episcopal conference may establish a higher age for the licit celebration of marriage. (Can. 1083)

Pastoral ministers should see to it that young people are diverted from marrying before the customary age of the region. (Can. 1072) Except in a case of necessity, no one without the permission of the local Ordinary may assist at the marriage of a minor child (under 18) whose parents are unaware of it or reasonably opposed to it. (Can. 1071, §1, 6°)

> The impediment consists of the ages of 16 for males and 14 for females, and marriage by a Catholic

party under these ages is invalid. Any higher age specified in particular law is for liceity only. Note that the day of birth is not computed in the age and hence one completes the sixteenth or fourteenth year at the close of the day on which the birthday is celebrated. (Can. 203) Furthermore, a marriage contracted invalidly by reason of lack of age is not convalidated by the mere running of time, but the consent must be renewed. (Cans. 1156–1158) The law states the canonical age irrespective of actual puberty; hence the marriage is valid even if the parties are not yet physically adolescent and capable of the marriage act. (Genicot, II, n. 548)

2. *Civil law*. Practically all the states of the union have the impediment of nonage; however, there is variation as to its effect. One must consult the laws of the state in which the marriage takes place, for the impediment may or may not be civilly invalidating. In some states the marriage may be validated upon the cessation of the impediment by mere cohabitation freely accepted and granted. In some states the judge or other public official is authorized to grant a dispensation from the impediment especially in cases of pregnancy. Practically all the states have, besides the age at which the impediment of nonage is established, another and higher age under which parental consent is required. This latter form of impediment however is usually only a conditional prohibition in reference to the issuance of the marriage license and does not affect the validity of the marriage. (See Abbo/Hannan, II, n. 1067.)

Knowledge of the impediments of civil law is important for the minister who is faced with the necessity of investigating the validity of marriages contracted by two non-Catholics.

B. Impotence

1. Antecedent and perpetual impotence for intercourse, whether on the part of the man or the woman, whether absolute or relative, by its very nature renders marriage invalid. (Can. 1084, §1)

Impotence is the incapacity for intercourse which is in itself suitable for generation. Impotence is the impossibility of having normal sexual intercourse. Impotence in the male is verified if he fails to achieve erection, penetration of the vagina, and ejaculation, though the ejaculation need not be true semen capable of conception. Hence, in the case of a man with a double vasectomy, marriage is not to be impeded or declared null. (SCDF, decr, May 13, 1977) For the female to be impotent means that she is incapable of receiving the erect penis of the husband.

Impotence may be organic or functional. In either case it constitutes an impediment. Organic impotence is due to some physical cause. In the male it may be the lack of a penis or an abnormally sized penis which prohibits vaginal insertion. Female organic impotence occurs when a woman lacks a vagina, either natural or artificial, of sufficient length and width to receive the erect penis. Functional impotence can result from physical or psychic causes. Paraplegia can cause functional organic impotence. It is a paralysis of the lower extremities of the body resulting from disease or injury to the central nervous system. About 10% of paraplegics are capable of ejaculation but 70% are capable of erection. There are three kinds of male psychic impotence: (1) the inability to obtain or sustain an erection; (2) an excessive excitability resulting in premature ejaculation; (3) ejaculatory incompetence, namely, the inability to ejaculate during intercourse. A female can be functionally impotent when she suffers from vaginismus. Vaginismus is the painful spasm of all the muscles surrounding and supporting the vagina which happens when intercourse is attempted or even when the area is merely touched and which renders intercourse impossible. Not all forms of vaginismus, however, constitute impotence. (See Wrenn, *Annulments*, 8–17.)

Impotence can be either absolute or relative. Absolute impotence prevents marital intercourse with all persons; relative impotence prevents it with a certain person or persons. Relative impotence is an impediment only in regard to the persons with whom the person affected cannot have intercourse.

To be invalidating the impotence must be both antecedent (before the marriage is celebrated) and perpetual, i.e., incapable of being cured by ordinary means. Extraordinary means include a miracle, illicit means, danger to one's life, serious harm to health, or doubtfully successful means.

2. If the impediment of impotence is doubtful, whether it be a doubt of law or of fact, marriage is not to be impeded nor, while the doubt persists, declared null. (Can. 1084, §2)

The reason for this rule is the extreme difficulty of directly solving doubts of law or fact regarding this impediment. To settle the consciences of the faithful in these cases, the Church declares that in all probable and prudent doubts, the natural right to marry prevails, even though the impediment is of the divine natural law.

If the doubt exists before marriage, the marriage cannot be licitly celebrated until there is an investigation of the facts that create the doubt. If the doubt remains, marriage may be celebrated provided the other party is informed. If the impotence is detected after the marriage the presumption of canon 1060 in favor of the validity of the marriage holds until the contrary is proven before an ecclesiastical tribunal.

3. Sterility neither prohibits nor invalidates marriage, without prejudice to canon 1098. (Can. 1084, §3)

Sterility is the incapacity for generation. People who are sterile are capable of having intercourse (*capaces coeundi*) but are not capable of propagating offspring. Thus, the sterile include young people before they attain puberty, old people, women after they have reached menopause and ovulation ceases, women who have no ovaries, no uterus, who have suffered a double fallectomy, etc. Sterility does not affect the validity or the liceity of a marriage because the couple does not exchange the right to have children but the right to acts which are per se apt for the generation of children. Whatever hinders the *human* act of generation (intercourse) constitutes impotence; whatever hinders the *natural* process of generation constitutes sterility.

Canon 1098 refers to one who fraudulently marries another. Hence, while sterility itself does not prohibit marriage, the fraudulent concealment of one's sterility in order to obtain the consent of the other party might be invalidating.

C. Prior Bond

1. Anyone who is held by a prior bond of marriage, even if not consummated, invalidly attempts marriage. (Can. 1085, §1)

> This impediment is of divine law and also binds non-Catholics. Thus, the prior marriages of non-Catholics as well as Catholics must be annulled by a competent tribunal or dissolved by the competent ecclesiastical authority before a new marriage with a Catholic can be celebrated.

2. Even though a former marriage be invalid or dissolved for any reason whatever, it is not therefore allowed to contract another marriage until the nullity or dissolution of the former shall have been legally and certainly established. (Can. 1085, §2)

> a. *Death of a former spouse* can be proved from an authentic document, either ecclesiastical or civil, stating the fact of this person's death. If the death can be proved by an authentic document, the minister may allow the living spouse to enter a new marriage. If such a document is not available, there must be a declaration of presumed death of the spouse made by the diocesan bishop in accord with canon 1707 before a new marriage can be celebrated.

> b. *A lack of form case*, in which a Catholic marries without observing the canonical form or being dispensed from it, does not require an annulment from the tribunal. Such a person can remarry in the Church provided it is certain that the canonical form was not observed in the prior marriage. However, canon 1071, §1, 3° requires the permission of the local Ordinary for a marriage when either party has natural obligations to a former spouse or the children of a previous marriage. In some dioceses the priests have been delegated by the local Ordinary to grant this permission.

> Proof of the lack of form requires the following: baptismal certificate or certificate of reception into full communion of the Catholic Church or other proof of

being Catholic (see can. 876); civil marriage record (obtained from the county clerk); civil divorce record (obtained from the clerk of the circuit court); sworn statement that the marriage has never been celebrated in the form prescribed by the Church, and that the party had not left the Catholic Church by a formal act prior to the celebration of the previous marriage.

c. *Other cases* require an annulment of the previous marriage by the competent tribunal or its dissolution by the competent ecclesiastical authority.

D. Disparity of Cult

1. A marriage between two persons, one of whom was baptized in the Catholic Church or received into it and who has not left it by a formal act and the other of whom is not baptized, is invalid. (Can. 1086, §1)

Thus, the marriage of a Catholic and a non-baptized is invalid without a dispensation from the impediment. Considered to be Catholics by baptism, provided they have not left the Church by a formal act, are:

a) Adults who are baptized (seven and older with the use of reason) in the Catholic Church or who are received into it;

b) All infants (under seven or lacking the use of reason) whose parents or guardians have them baptized with the intention of aggregating them to the Catholic Church;

c) All infants or adults who are unconscious who are baptized by a Catholic minister in danger of death;

d) Infants baptized by a Catholic minister in the case where the parents do not wish or are not able to exercise parental rights over the child.

Reception into the Catholic Church occurs when a baptized non-Catholic makes a profession of faith and is received into full communion according to the *Rite of Reception of Baptized Christians into Full Communion with the Catholic Church.*

Those not considered to be Catholic include:

a) All adults baptized in a non-Catholic Church;

b) Infants whose non-Catholic parents or guardians have them baptized with the intention of aggregating them to their own church or ecclesial community;

c) Infants who are baptized by a non-Catholic minister with the intention of aggregating them to his church or ecclesial community, the parents not objecting when it is possible for them to do so. (V.C., II, n. 344)

Also not Catholic are those who have left the Church by a formal act, e.g., by joining another religion, or publicly declaring or signing a document attesting that they are no longer Catholic. Regular attendance at the worship services and other participation in the activities of that church, together with non-practice of the Catholic faith, could indicate an intention to leave the Catholic Church. However, mere non-practice of the faith does not constitute loss of membership in the Catholic Church. Even one baptized a Catholic in infancy, but who has never been brought up in the faith, is still Catholic unless there was some formal act taken to leave the Church.

Not bound to the impediment are children of non-Catholic parents who were baptized in infancy by a Catholic minister when there was not a founded hope that they would be brought up in the Catholic religion. On the other hand, anyone baptized in danger of death by a Catholic minister is considered Catholic and is bound by the impediment. (Doyle, 768)

2. The impediment of disparity of cult should not be dispensed unless the conditions mentioned in canons 1125 and 1126 are fulfilled. (Can. 1086, §2)

These canons were treated above in Chapter II, section III on preparations for mixed marriages. A dispensation granted without the fulfillment of these conditions would be invalid. (See can. 39.)

3. If a party at the time the marriage was celebrated was commonly held to be baptized or his or her baptism was doubtful, the validity of the marriage, in accord with canon 1060, is to be presumed, un-

less it is proven with certainty that one party was baptized and the other was not. (Can. 1086, §3)

> If doubt arises about the fact or validity of baptism before the marriage is celebrated, the case should be handled according to the norm of canon 869. See the commentary above in Part II on the sacrament of baptism. If the doubt arises after the marriage, the presumption of the law is in favor of the validity of the marriage. If it can be proved with moral certainty that one person was baptized and the baptism of the other was invalid, the presumption falls and the marriage is held as invalid if no dispensation from the impediment of disparity of cult had been obtained.

> Among the churches and ecclesial communities recognized as having valid baptism are: all Eastern non-Catholics (Orthodox), Adventists, African Methodist Episcopal, Amish, Anglican, Assembly of God, Baptists, Evangelical United Brethren, Church of the Brethren, Church of God, Congregational Church, Disciples and Christians, Episcopalians, Evangelical Churches, Lutherans, Methodists, Liberal Catholic Church, Old Catholics, Old Roman Catholics, Church of the Nazarene, Polish National Church, Presbyterian Church, Reformed Churches, United Church of Christ, Latter Day Saints (Mormons).

> Among the denominations without valid baptism are: Apostolic Church, Bohemian Free Thinkers, Christian and Missionary Alliance, Christian Scientists, Church of the Divine Science, Masons, Peoples Church of Chicago, Quakers, Salvation Army, Pentecostal Churches, Christadelphians, Jehovah's Witnesses, Unitarians.

4. *Eastern canon law.* The prescriptions of the Latin Code regarding the impediment of disparity of cult are found also in the Eastern legislation (Mp, canons 60, 61), with one notable difference, namely, the form of the impediment reads: *the marriage contracted by an unbaptized person with a baptized person is null.* (Mp, can. 60 §1) Hence, although the Latin Code exempts non-Catholic baptized persons from the impediment, the Eastern legislation does not. The impediment is therefore more comprehensive than in the Latin Code, insofar as Eastern non-Catholics are included under its terms.

The reason for this difference is that since Eastern non-Catholics retain the impediment of disparity of cult, it would have been imprudent to exempt them from the impediment; hence the impediment is retained according to the ancient discipline.

Eastern non-Catholics are therefore bound by the impediment of disparity of cult. The Holy Office declared in two private decisions (May 18, 1949; Apr. 17, 1950), that a marriage can be declared null on the ground of disparity of cult if it can be juridically proven that one party is not baptized and the other party is validly baptized in an Eastern non-Catholic church. (See CLD 3:422–24; 427.)

5. *1917 Code.* Under the former law, baptized non-Catholics were not bound to this impediment, the same as under the present law.

E. Holy Orders

1. One who has received holy orders invalidly attempts marriage. (Can. 1087)

Three conditions must be fulfilled before the impediment is incurred: (a) the cleric must be validly ordained; (b) he must be ordained with full knowledge of the obligations assumed; and (c) he must be ordained freely without grave force or fear being inflicted upon him. (Cappello, 437, 420; Doyle, 769)

The impediment binds deacons, including permanent deacons, presbyters, and bishops. Thus, a permanent deacon may not marry after ordination, even if his wife should die, although a dispensation from celibacy is sometimes given by the pope in such cases. In order for a cleric to marry validly, he must receive a dispensation from the obligation of celibacy which is granted by the pope alone. (Can. 291) Bishops are never dispensed from celibacy.

A cleric who attempts marriage, even if only civil marriage, is *ipso facto* removed from any ecclesiastical office. (Can. 194, §1, 3°) Moreover, he incurs an automatic suspension; and if he has been warned and has not reformed and continues to give scandal, he can be further punished with deprivations and even dismissal from the clerical state. (Can. 1394, §1)

In danger of death, deacons can be dispensed in accord with canon 1079, as treated above under I, D. Presbyters, however, may only be dispensed by the Apostolic See even in danger of death. No cleric may be dispensed by the local Ordinary in urgent cases when everything is prepared (*omnia parata*) for the wedding (can. 1080).

2. *Eastern canon law.* Clerics in major orders or in the subdiaconate attempt marriage invalidly. (Mp, can. 62) The particular laws of the various ritual churches should be consulted to determine if the subdiaconate remains an impediment. (See Vatican II, Decree on the Eastern Churches, n. 17.)

3. *1917 Code.* The order of subdeacon, abolished in 1972, was also an impediment to marriage. Those who were ordained subdeacons are still bound to the impediment and must be dispensed from celibacy before they can marry validly, except for the dispensation given in danger of death.

F. Public Perpetual Vow of Chastity in a Religious Institute

1. Those who are bound by a public perpetual vow of chastity in a religious institute invalidly attempt marriage. (Canon 1088)

The impediment binds perpetually professed members of either clerical or lay institutes, whether they are of pontifical or diocesan right. The perpetual vow may be either solemn or simple. Not bound by the impediment are religious in temporary vows, or members of secular institutes or societies of apostolic life.

A member of a religious institute who contracts marriage or attempts it, even only civilly, is *ipso facto* dismissed from the institute. (Can. 694, §1, 2°) Moreover, a religious in perpetual vows who is not a cleric incurs an automatic interdict. (Can. 1394, §2)

In danger of death, the local Ordinary, pastor, other priest or deacon, or confessor, in accord with canon 1079, may dispense from the impediment. However, for a dispensation in an urgent case (*omnia parata*) when everything is prepared for the wedding, only those in an institute of diocesan right may be dispensed by the local Ordinary.

2. *Eastern canon law.* Religious bound by solemn or major profession, as well as those who have taken the vow of chastity outside of major profession with which is connected the power of invalidating marriage by a special prescription of the Holy See, attempt marriage invalidly. (Mp, can. 63)

3. *1917 Code.* Only attempted marriages by persons in solemn vows were invalid under the former law. The only exception were members of the Society of Jesus whose simple vows also invalidated the contracting of marriage.

G. Abduction

There can be no marriage between a man and a woman who was abducted or at least detained for the purpose of marrying, unless the woman later has been separated from her abductor and while in a safe and free place willingly chooses marriage. (Can. 1089)

> The impediment applies only to the abduction or detention of a woman by a man, and not vice-versa. However, if a woman abducted a man and compelled him to marry, it could be invalid on the grounds of force or fear (can. 1103).

H. Crime

1. One invalidly attempts marriage who, in view of marrying a certain person, has brought about the death of the person's spouse or one's own spouse. They also marry each other invalidly who have brought about the death of the spouse of either of them through physical or moral cooperation. (Can. 1090)

> There are two degrees of crime which create the impediment: (a) a person who, with a view to marrying another, kills his or her own spouse or the spouse of the other; and (b) when two persons conspire and bring about the death of the spouse of either even without an intention of marrying each other. In either case the murder must be actually committed for the impediment

to be incurred, whether it be committed by the man or woman or both, or by someone else acting in the service of either or both, such as a hired killer.

The dispensation from the impediment is reserved to the Apostolic See. It is not given in public cases. A dispensation for the internal forum is sought from the Apostolic Penitentiary without mentioning any names if it is the internal sacramental forum, i.e., if the crime was revealed in the sacrament of penance. It may be dispensed in danger of death and *omnia parata* cases in accord with canons 1079–1082.

2. *Eastern canon law.* There is a third species of crime which creates an invalidating impediment to marriage, namely, those who, during the term of the same lawful marriage, commit adultery with each other and give each other a mutual promise of marriage or actually attempt marriage, even though by a merely civil act. (Mp, can. 65)

3. *1917 Code.* The same third species of the impediment existed as in Eastern canon law.

I. Consanguinity

1. In the direct line of consanguinity marriage is invalid between all ancestors and descendants both legitimate and natural. In the collateral line it is invalid up to the fourth degree inclusive. (Can. 1091, §§1, 2)

Direct line consanguinity is the blood relationship between direct ancestors and descendants, e.g., grandfather, mother, son, granddaughter, etc. Collateral consanguinity is the blood relationship when two persons have a common ancestor, but neither is the direct ancestor of the other, e.g., brother and sister, uncle and niece, first cousins, second cousins, etc. The impediment invalidates any marriages between persons related in the direct line and, on the collateral line, between brothers and sisters (second degree), aunt and nephew or uncle and niece (third degree), first cousins (fourth degree) and great aunt and grandnephew or great uncle and grandniece (fourth degree). On the computation of degrees of consanguinity, see Part I above, page 25.

191

N.B. The way consanguinity and other relationships is computed in the 1983 Code is different from that of the 1917 Code.

Since carnal generation is the basis of consanguinity, the relationship arises from both legitimate and illegitimate generation.

Consanguinity is of the full blood if the parties related have two common ancestors; of the half blood if they have only one ancestor in common. Thus, brothers who have the same mother but not the same father are relations of the half blood. Canonically there is no practical difference between relationship of full blood and half blood.

2. Marriage is never permitted if there is any doubt whether the parties are related by blood in any degree of the direct line or in the second degree of the collateral line. (Can. 1091, §4)

In the direct line, consanguinity is an impediment of the divine law certainly in the first degree, more probably in the other degrees; in the collateral line it is more probably an impediment of divine law in the second degree, although some authors doubt it; in all other degrees of the collateral line it is certainly an impediment of ecclesiastical law only.

Non-Catholics are not bound by the impediment in the degrees in which it is certainly of ecclesiastical law only. If the impediment exists in a degree in which it is not certainly an impediment by divine law, the marriage is to be considered valid. However, the unbaptized are bound by the impediment of consanguinity established by the civil law and hence the validity of the marriage must be judged according to the civil laws under which the marriage was contracted. (Mathis/Bonner, 232–33)

A dispensation is never given from the impediment of consanguinity in the direct line or in the second degree of the collateral line. (Can. 1078, §3) Third and fourth degree collateral consanguinity can be dispensed by the local Ordinary. The practice of the Holy See in the past has been to dispense third degree consanguinity very rarely and only for extraordinarily grave reasons and fourth degree rarely and only for grave reasons. (Doyle, 772)

3. *Civil law*. In almost all of the states the impediment of consanguinity is an invalidating one and it extends to all degrees of the direct line and to the third degree of the collateral line. In over half the states the impediment extends to first cousins; in a few states it extends to the fifth degree; in Oklahoma, to second cousins (sixth degree). (Alford, nn. 135–145)

> The following states permit marriages of first cousins: Alabama, California, Connecticut, District of Columbia, Florida, Georgia, Kentucky, Maine, Maryland, Massachusetts, New Jersey, New York, Rhode Island, South Carolina, Texas, Vermont, Virginia. (Doyle, 772)

4. *Eastern canon law*.

In the direct line of consanguinity, marriage is invalid between all in the ascending and the descending line, whether of legitimate birth or not. In the collateral line marriage is invalid to the sixth degree inclusively, and the impediment is multiplied as often as the common ancestor is multiplied. Marriage shall never be permitted as long as some doubt remains whether the parties are blood relatives in any degree of the direct line or in the second degree of the collateral line. (Mp, can. 66)

Note: When one party to a marriage is a Latin and the other party a member of an Eastern Catholic Church, they must be free to marry according to *both* the Latin and the Oriental legislation. This holds not only for consanguinity, but is a general principle applicable to all points of marriage legislation.

5. *1917 Code*. Besides the direct line, the impediment extended to what formerly was called the third degree of the collateral line. Second cousins could not validly marry under the former law without a dispensation. The impediment could also be multiplied as often as the common ancestor was multiplied. (See CIC, can. 1076.)

J. Affinity

1. Affinity in the direct line in any degree at all invalidates marriage. (Can. 1092)

Affinity arises from valid marriage, even if not consummated. It exists between the husband and the blood relatives of the wife, and between the wife and the blood relatives of the husband. For further discussion, see page 26.

Affinity arises from any valid marriage, and affinity contracted when one is a non-Catholic becomes an impediment when one is baptized a Catholic or received into the Church. (SCOf, response, Jan. 31, 1957)

2. *Civil law.* In more than half the states of the union the impediment of affinity does not exist in the civil law. In states where the impediment exists one must study the laws of the respective state to ascertain whether it is a diriment (invalidating) impediment or impedient impediment which is not invalidating. In some states the impediment ceases upon the death of one's spouse. Only in a few states does it extend to the collateral line, for usually the impediment is restricted to the direct line and extends to the mother- and father-in-law, the daughter- and son-in-law, the stepmother or stepfather, the stepson or stepdaughter. (See Alford, nn. 151–160 for details.)

3. *Eastern canon law.* In Eastern Catholic law affinity, which arises from any valid marriage, invalidates marriage in all degrees of the direct line, to the fourth degree inclusive of the collateral line. (Mp, canons 67, §1, 1°; 67, §2; 68, §1)

By particular law other types of affinity exist among the Chaldeans, Melkites, Rumanians, Bulgarians, Russians, Greeks from Greece and Turkey, Ethiopians, and among various Eastern non-Catholics. In some churches the impediment extends to a second species (between the blood relations of one spouse and the blood relations of the other), and even to a third species (when two persons contracted marriage with the same third person, after the previous marriage had been dissolved, with one after the other, or with two persons who were blood relations). (Pospishil/Faris, 30)

4. *1917 Code.* The impediment invalidated marriage in all degrees of the direct line and in what was formerly called the second degree of the collateral line (first cousins). The impediment was multiplied as often as the impediment of consanguinity on which it is based was

194

multiplied, or through a subsequent marriage with a blood relative of one's deceased spouse. (See CIC, can. 1077.)

K. Public Propriety

1. The impediment of public propriety arises from an invalid marriage after common life has been established or from notorious or public concubinage; it invalidates marriage in the first degree of the direct line between the man and the blood relatives of the woman, and vice-versa. (Can. 1093)

> An invalid marriage is one which has at least the appearance of marriage but is invalid for some reason. The impediment only exists once the couple begins to live together in the invalid union.

> Concubinage is had when two persons live as husband and wife for the purpose of habitually having sexual intercourse, the union however not having even the appearance of marriage. For the impediment to arise it is necessary that the concubinage be notorious or public, i.e., well known to the community.

> The impediment is of itself perpetual and hence even if the invalid marriage or concubinage has been dissolved, the impediment still exists and must be dispensed from. Whether or not the impediment remains or is rather absorbed by the impediment of affinity in case the invalid marriage is validated or those living in concubinage contract marriage, is doubtful; a dispensation should be obtained *ad cautelam*.

2. *Eastern canon law*. The impediment extends to the second degree of the direct line. (Mp, can. 69)

3. *1917 Code*. The impediment included the second degree of the direct line.

L. Legal Relationship

1. They are unable validly to contract marriage between themselves who are related in the direct line or in the second degree of the collateral line by the legal relationship arising from adoption. (Can. 1094)

> Canon law relies on the civil law to determine
> what constitutes legal adoption. The impediment arises
> only if the adoption is legal in accord with the civil law.

2. *Eastern canon law and 1917 Code.* Those who are disqualified
for marriage by the civil law because of legal relationship arising
from adoption, cannot validly marry under canon law either. (Mp,
can. 71; 1917 CIC, can. 1080)

3. *Civil law.* An invalidating impediment because of adoption exists
in Puerto Rico. Massachusetts prohibits marriages between adoptive
parents and children. Mississippi prohibits marriages between a
father and his adoptive daughter. (Doyle, 774) Persons who come to
the United States from other countries, if they intend to stay here
only temporarily, still remain subject to the laws of their own country.

> According to a general principle of law, a contract
> is governed by the laws of the place where the contract
> is made; however, some exceptions may be made to
> this principle for the matrimonial contract. Some states
> demand that the stranger be qualified to marry by the
> laws of his own country or of his own state; likewise
> that residents of the state intending to remain residents
> may not marry in another state if their marriage would
> be illegal in the home state. Other states recognize the
> general principle of contracts, i.e., if the contract is
> valid in the place where it was made, it is valid
> everywhere, and if invalid in the place where made, it
> is invalid everywhere. (Woywood, n. 1038)

M. Spiritual Relationship

1. The impediment binds only Eastern Catholics and those Latin
Catholics who married before the revised Code went into effect on
November 27, 1983.

2. *Eastern canon law.* In Eastern canon law the godparent at baptism contracts a spiritual relationship with the person baptized and
that person's parents. Spiritual relationship does not arise between
the minister and the person baptized. When baptism is repeated
conditionally, the godparent does not contract spiritual relationship,

unless the same godparent is employed for both baptisms. Spiritual relationship as just described is a diriment impediment. (See Mp, can. 70.)

3. *1917 Code.* Only spiritual relationship arising from baptism invalidates marriage. This relationship exists between the one baptizing and the person baptized as well as between the godparents and the person baptized. (CIC, cans. 1079; 768)

N. Guardianship

1. The impediment exists only in Eastern Canon Law, and therefore is binding also for marriages between an Eastern Catholic and a Latin Catholic.

2. *Eastern canon law.* Those who are disqualified for marriage by the civil law because they are guardians cannot validly marry under canon law either. (See Mp, can. 71.)

CHAPTER IV
Matrimonial Consent

I. Nature of Matrimonial Consent

A. Definition and Effect

Matrimonial consent is an act of the will by which a man and a woman mutually give and accept each other in an irrevocable covenant for the purpose of establishing marriage. (Can. 1057, §2) Marriage is made by the parties' consent legitimately manifested between persons who are legally capable, and no human power can substitute for this consent. (Can. 1057, §)

B. Perseverance

Even though a marriage was entered invalidly because of an impediment or lack of form, the consent which has been given is presumed to persevere until its revocation shall have been proved. (Can. 1107)

> The most important application of the presumption stated in this canon takes place in a radical sanation where an invalid marriage is convalidated without the renewal of consent. Consent must exist at the time when the sanation takes place, but the presumption of this canon is sufficient to show that the consent once given still exists, unless it can be proved that it was revoked.

II. Defective Consent

A. Lack of Sufficient Use of Reason

They are incapable of contracting marriage who lack sufficient use of reason. (Can. 1095, 1°)

The use of reason required for marriage is not the simple use of reason that the law presumes is attained by age seven, but "sufficient" use of reason to understand that marriage is a community of conjugal life for the good of the spouses and the generation and education of children. (Can. 1055, §1) Such use of reason could be lacking by reason of a transitory disturbance such as alcoholic intoxication or an epileptic ictal twilight state, or it could be lacking by a habitual disorder such as schizophrenia or profound mental retardation. Such persons cannot give consent, and it is consent which makes the marriage. (Can. 1057; see Wrenn, *Annulments*, 18–19.)

B. Lack of Due Discretion

They are incapable of contracting marriage who suffer from some serious defect of discretion of judgment concerning the essential matrimonial rights and duties which must be mutually given and accepted. (Can. 1095, 2°)

This differs from lack of sufficient reason because lack of due discretion involves the will and not just the intellect. Due discretion for marriage requires that the intellect make a mature judgment and that the will consent freely. One's decision to marry should be rational and informed. Moreover, a person must be able to make at least "a rudimentary assessment of the capacities of himself and his spouse, and to decide freely that he wishes to establish a perpetual and exclusive community of life with this person, a community that will involve a lifetime of fundamentally faithful caring and sharing." (Wrenn, *Annulments*, 22) Sufficient discretion for marriage involves the ability to evaluate critically the decision to marry in light of consequent obligations and responsibilities, one's own motivation for marriage, one's strengths and weaknesses as well as those of the other party, and one's abilities to live up to the demands of marriage. (Doyle, 776)

To have sufficient discretion for marriage, it is necessary not only to have some general appreciation of the fact that marriage is a permanent, heterosexual partnership, but that marriage involves obligations to

200

another person, including being truthful and self-revelatory with the spouse, understanding and appreciating the spouse as a separate person, and caring for the spouse's welfare. (Wrenn, *Annulments*, 23)

Those lacking in due discretion are frequently young and/or immature, or they may have an identity disorder or personality disorder of at least moderate degree. At times there are certain extrinsic factors connected with lack of due discretion including: premarital pregnancy or abortion; unhappy, burdensome life with the parents with a desire to escape; a brief courtship; belated reluctance to marry together with family pressure or fear of embarassment. (Ibid.)

C. Lack of Due Competence

They are incapable of contracting marriage who, for reasons of a psychic nature, are not able to assume essential marital obligations. (Can. 1095, 3°)

With lack of due discretion, one is incapable of consenting to marriage because one does not fully understand and appreciate the responsibilities that marriage entails, and therefore one cannot make a correct judgment about what one is undertaking and freely choose it. With lack of due competence, one may well understand and appreciate what marriage entails, but still not validly consent because one is incapable of assuming and fulfilling those obligations. The consent is defective because the person is not able to undertake that which is being consented to, namely, the essential obligations of marriage.

One of the essential obligations of marriage is the capacity for sexual intercourse. (See can. 1055, §1) When this is lacking a marriage is invalid due to the impediment of impotence (can. 1084). The other essential obligations involve "personalist" aspects of marriage, arising from the definition of the marriage covenant as a "partnership of the whole of life which by its nature is ordered toward the good of the spouses and the procreation and education of children." (See can. 1055, §1.) In particular, these obligations include self-revelation, understanding, and caring, both regarding the spouse and the children. Self-revelation is the ability to see oneself as a fairly consistent person, have a reasonable degree of respect for the spouse, and convey a knowledge of oneself to the spouse. Understanding is the ability to see the spouse as a separate person, and appreciate the spouse's way of thinking without distorting it excessively. Caring is the ability to pledge oneself with reasonable maturity to a lifelong communion with the spouse not out of a need to possess the other but out of a desire to share one's life with the other in mutual respect and affection. (See Wrenn, *Annulments*, 38–40)

In short, this personalist dimension of marriage involves the capacity for an interpersonal relationship. The spouses must be able to give and accept each other as distinct persons, relating to each other in a way that is distinct to marriage. They must be "other-oriented." More than just a physical reality, a covenant marriage involves "a true intertwining of the personalities," which presupposes the development of an adult personality. (See Doyle, 777.)

The "psychic reasons" behind lack of due competence could be many; it is a broad term that can include personality disorders, anxiety disorders, schizophrenic disorders, major affective disorders, alcoholism, and homosexuality. (See Wrenn, *Annulments*, 45–74.) Lack of due competence can also arise from "emotional immaturity," not the normal chronological immaturity of youth, but a permanent psychological condition which affects the ability to make judgments, control one's actions, and relate to others. (Doyle, 778)

Note that homosexuality is not classified as a psychological disorder, but it may give rise to an inability to establish the heterosexual "partnership of the whole of life" that is an essential element of marriage.

In proving the existence of lack of due competence, one looks to four areas: severity, antecedence, perpetuity, and relativity. The psychic reason for lack of due competence first of all must be severe, not just a mild disturbance. It also must be antecedent, i.e., at the time consent was given. For example, alcoholism which develops a number of years after the marriage and cannot be proved to have existed before marriage is not grounds for nullity. Perpetuity refers to the fact that a person lacking due competence does not have the capacity to assume the essential obligations on a permanent basis; it is not enough to be able to assume them for a few years, because marriage is a permanent partnership of the whole of life. Finally, the psychic cause in question can be either absolute and affect any marriage or relative, affecting only this marriage or marriages with certain kinds of people. (See Wrenn, *Annulments*, 41–42.)

D. Ignorance

In order for matrimonial consent to be possible, it is necessary that the parties at least not be ignorant of the fact that marriage is a permanent partnership between a man and a woman for the procreation of children by means of some sexual cooperation. This ignorance is not presumed after puberty. (Can. 1096)

For a valid matrimonial consent the parties must know at least:

a. That marriage is a partnership of the whole of life. Thus, there must be some realization of the personalist element in marriage, including the knowledge of some mutual cooperation, support, and companionship. (Doyle, 779) If a man, e.g., regarded marriage as simply a convenience to enable him to have a housekeeper or secretary, or a servant for his children, he would be ignorant of the personalist dimension of marriage. (See Wrenn, *Annulments*, 75.)

b. That marriage involves some sexual cooperation for the purpose of procreation. The person does not have to know precisely how the sexual organs of the opposite sex function, provided there is knowledge that the marital act involves some physical coming together of the sex organs for the purpose of generation.

Ignorance can arise as a result of societal and cultural values that conflict with the Catholic understanding of marriage, and people can come to adulthood and still be lacking an understanding of marriage as a permanent commitment ordered to the good of the spouse and the children. The principal difference between ignorance and the grounds for defective consent in canon 1095 is that ignorance does not necessarily involve a person who has subnormal intelligence, or is immature, or has some psychological problem or other condition rendering it impossible to assume marital obligations. Rather, the person could be completely normal, but simply lacks basic knowledge about what marriage minimally entails.

E. Error

1. *Error regarding the person* renders a marriage invalid. (Can. 1097, §1)

> Such error would be mistaken identity. One believes one is consenting to marry a certain person, but in reality is marrying someone else. There is little or no practical application of this rule.

2. *Error regarding a quality of a person*, even if it is the cause of the contract, does not render a marriage invalid, unless this quality was directly and principally intended. (Can. 1097, §2)

> A quality of a person may be defined as "some aspect of the person that contributes to the shaping of the overall personality." (Doyle, 780) It could be moral, physical, social, religious, or legal in nature, e.g., honesty, good health, wealth, occupation, marital status, education, religious convictions, etc. If one makes a mistake about some quality, it has no effect on the validity of the consent unless that quality was directly and principally intended. That quality, and not the person, must be the primary reason for marrying. For example, a woman always wanted to marry only a rich man, and thought her fiance was rich because he had expensive clothes and a nice car, charged gifts and dinners on his credit cards, etc. After marriage she discovers he is deeply in debt, and this revelation leads to the breakup of the marriage. In this example, the woman directly and principally intended to marry only a man with the quality of wealth, and did not give consent to a poor man. On the other hand, if she thought she were marry-

ing a wealthy man and she later discovered he was poor but accepted him anyway, the error would not be invalidating because the quality was not directly and principally intended.

In tribunal cases nullity has been decided on the fact that the quality, whether or not it was common to many, was truly significant, discovered after the marriage, and when discovered resulted in a serious disruption of marital life. (See Doyle, 780.)

3. *Error due to fraud.* One invalidly contracts marriage when one enters it deceived by fraud, perpetrated to obtain consent, concerning some quality of the other party which of its very nature can seriously disturb the partnership of the conjugal life. (Can. 1098)

This grounds for nullity is related to error regarding a quality of a person, in that the person contracting invalidly makes a mistake about some significant quality of the other party which can seriously disturb the marriage. The difference is that here the mistaken spouse was deceived in order to obtain consent to marry. Note that the deceiver does not have to be the other spouse, although that is the usual case.

For example, a woman wishes to marry only a doctor. Her fiance is aware of this desire and, after failing his medical exams, tells her he passed so that she will marry him. When the fraud is later discovered, the marriage breaks up.

Fraud or deceit is "a deliberate act of deception by which one person hides a significant fact from another to achieve a given end." (Doyle, 781) Certain essential elements must be proved in nullity cases on the grounds of fraud: (a) the fraud is deliberately perpetrated in order to obtain consent; (b) the quality is real, grave, and present (or absent) at the time of consent; (c) the quality must be unknown to the other party; and (d) the discovery of the absence or presence of the quality must precipitate the end of the marriage. (Ibid.)

Examples of such qualities that might be grave enough to nullify marriage when concealed are: homosexuality, alcoholism, drug addiction, sexual dysfunction, previous marriage, prior criminal record, mental illness, sterility, a serious or contagious disease. Qualities might also be subjectively grave as, e.g., a woman who always said she would never marry a man who smoked cigarettes, and her fiance concealed his addiction to tobacco in order to obtain her consent. Smoking is not an objectively grave quality, but for this particular woman it is grave enough to vitiate her consent to marry a man who smokes.

4. *Error regarding the essential properties of marriage.* Error concerning the unity or indissolubility or sacramental dignity of marriage, provided it does not determine the will, does not vitiate matrimonial consent. (Can. 1099)

Error concerning the unity of marriage would be to regard polygamy or marital infidelity as legitimate options. Error concerning indissolubility would be the belief that civil divorce can end a marriage or that there is no permanent marital bond which exists even after the spouses have separated and even after they remarried. Error concerning the sacramental dignity of marriage is the belief that marriage between two baptized is not *ipso facto* a sacrament (see can. 1055, §2), or that the marriage of the baptized is purely a secular affair. As long as this error does not affect the will, it does not invalidate marital consent.

Error is called "simple" if it remains in the mind without passing over to the will. It exists when error in the mind remains speculative and is not actually incorporated in the choice made by the will. Despite this error concerning indissolubility, unity, or sacramental dignity of the marriage, the will wishes to contract a marriage that is valid, a marriage as it has been instituted by the law of nature. The fact that one would not have chosen marriage in the absence of the error is a hypothetical fact; the *actual* fact is that the will has chosen marriage, without making any explicit modification or reservation.

For example, a person may erroneously believe that divorce and remarriage are possible, or that there is no sacrament of marriage. But if this error is only in the mind, it does not affect the consent which is an act of the will. On the other hand, if the person were to marry while reserving the right to divorce if things do not work out, or deliberately refusing to accept the sacramentality of marriage but embracing only a civil union, then the error passes over to the will and the marriage is invalid. Likewise, if someone were to marry with the belief that infidelity is not contrary to the nature of marriage, and was even theoretically open to the possibility of an occasional extra-marital affair, the consent would be valid because these erroneous notions remain only in the mind. However, if that person were to marry actually intending to have an affair with one or more other persons, then that mistaken belief has passed over to the will and the consent is invalid.

If the error modifies the act of the will, so that the consent is explicitly directed to a dissoluble marriage, or a non-sacramental marriage, or a polygamous or adulterous marriage, it is no longer simple error. It is then an error explicitly incorporated as a condition or reservation in the contract and hence the matrimonial consent is vitiated. (See Vlaming, 385.) It is one thing, e.g., to contract a marriage which one thinks is soluble, or even to contract *because* one thinks it is soluble, and another thing not to intend to contract *unless* it is soluble. Thus, if one wishes to contract a trial marriage the consent is invalid because indissolubility is positively excluded.

5. *Error regarding the validity of the marriage.* The knowledge or belief that the marriage is null does not necessarily exclude matrimonial consent. (Can. 1100)

The reason for this is that together with the knowledge or the opinion of nullity there can exist a will to enter marriage insofar as one can; true matrimonial consent can easily exist even though the marriage itself is invalid. For example, a couple can truly consent to marry each other, even though they know the marriage is invalid due to a prior bond. Or one may think the marriage is null when it is not, e.g., a Catholic woman marrying a non-baptized who thinks she does not have a dispensation when in fact she does. In either case, the consent is valid. Whether the marriage is valid depends on whether the impediment or dispensation exists or not.

F. Simulation

The internal consent of the mind is presumed to be in conformity with the words or signs used in the marriage celebration. But if either party or both parties by a positive act of the will should exclude marriage itself, or some essential element of marriage, or some essential property, they contract invalidly. (Can. 1101)

> The essential elements of marriage are the personalist (the partnership of the whole of life for the good of the spouses) and the procreational. (See can. 1055, §1.) The essential properties are unity and indissolubility. (See can. 1056.) Total simulation is the exclusion of the marriage itself, or the personalist element. Partial simulation is the exclusion of the procreational element (intention against children), or the property of unity (intention against fidelity), or the property of indissolubility (intention against perpetuity). (See Wrenn, *Annulments*, 81–82.)

> *A positive act of the will* can be either explicit or implicit, i.e., one can consciously exclude marriage or some essential element or property, or this exclusion can be implicitly revealed by the circumstances. In either case, the exclusion is an act of the will, something chosen by the party at the time the marriage was outwardly consented to, and not the result of extraneous or later events.

1. *Total simulation* is had when one does not have the intention to contract marriage even though he or she goes through the formalities, i.e., where the person does not intend any union at all with the other, or does not intend to enter a partnership of the whole of life for the good of the spouse. This simulation invalidates marriage since matrimonial consent is lacking. There is no intention to contract a marriage, as marriage is understood by the law of nature. (See can. 1055, §1.) However, simulation must be proved, since "the internal consent of the mind is presumed to be in conformity with the words or signs used in the marriage celebration." (Can. 1101, §1)

> The exclusion of marital consent in total simulation does not have to be explicit to be invalidating. There are three principal ways in which the partnership of the whole of life may be implicitly excluded: (a) by perma-

208

nently excluding the right to cohabitation; (b) by going through a marriage ceremony solely for an extraneous reason, e.g., a man who marries a foreigner so that he can legally emigrate to another country; (c) by substituting for true marriage one's own idea of marriage, e.g., a man who thinks a wife is only a housekeeper and a governess but not an equal partner (see can. 1135). (Wrenn, *Annulments*, 84–85)

2. *Partial simulation*

There are three kinds of partial simulation: intention against children (*contra bonum prolis*), intention against fidelity (*contra bonum fidei*), and intention against perpetuity (*contra bonum sacramenti*). Each of them vitiates marital consent. In cases of partial simulation one must be careful to distinguish *the intention not to grant the right or not to assume the obligation* from *the intention merely of not fulfilling the obligations* imposed by the marriage covenant. Thus if a person enters a marriage by a consent which excludes the right or obligation to normal intercourse, to perpetuity of the bond, or of fidelity, the marriage is invalid. On the other hand, if one acknowledges the rights in question but merely desires to abuse the right, consent is valid. For example, a couple enter marriage planning to practice birth control, but do not deny each other the right to have children when one of them wishes. That would not be an intention against children.

a. *Intention against children.* When a person enters marriage excluding the right to acts which are per se apt for the generation of children, the consent is invalid. Hence, it is not the exclusion of children that is invalidating, but the exclusion of sexual intercourse which is open to procreation. The actual procreation of children is not a requirement of marriage, as evidenced in canon 1084, §3 which permits marriage by those who are sterile. Likewise, it is not the absence of sexual intercourse that invalidates, but the intention to deny the *right* of the other party to the conjugal act.

> Thus, e.g., if a man and a woman agree to practice birth control for five years before having children, the marriage is not invalid. They are simply agreeing not to use their right to have sexual intercourse which is per se apt for generation. On the other hand, if after two years the wife decided it was time to have children,

and the husband adamantly refused, this could be an indication that he had intended from the beginning not to acknowledge his wife's right to have intercourse that is open to procreation. The intention to deny the *right* to the procreative act, even for a limited time, is invalidating. On the other hand, the *premarital, mutual agreement not to exercise the right* is not invalidating.

b. *Intention against fidelity.* One essential property of marriage is unity (see can. 1056), which means there can be but one partner in marriage, i.e., no polygamy. Although fidelity is different from unity in the strict sense, it is related. Fidelity means that the married person can have only one's spouse as a sex partner, that there can be no adultery. This is also indicated in canon 1134 which states that the marriage bond is "exclusive." If fidelity is excluded by a positive act of the will by either or both parties, the marriage is null. (See can. 1101, §2.) A marriage is invalid not, however, because one has engaged in adultery, but only if one intends to be unfaithful when consenting to the marriage. It must be proven that this intention existed from the moment the marriage was contracted.

> Wrenn explains this intention *contra bonum fidei* as follows: "In order to result in invalidity, fidelity must be excluded as part of the marriage covenant. It may happen, for example, that in entering marriage a man foresees and even intends that he will have an extramarital affair should he have the opportunity. If, however, this remains casual and incidental, his intention does not invade, and therefore does not vitiate, the covenant. If, on the other hand, his intention is so intense and important to him that it actually becomes part of his central agreement or exchange of rights, with the result that he would regard his wife's demands that he be hers alone as an undue extension of the agreement he entered, then such a man excludes the very right to fidelity." (*Annulments*, 95)

c. *Intention against perpetuity.* A second essential property of marriage is indissolubility. (See can. 1056.) A "perpetual bond" arises from a valid marriage. (See can. 1134.) If, at the time consent is given, indissolubility is excluded by a positive act of the will, the marriage is invalid. (See can. 1101, §2.)

> Perpetuity is an essential property of marriage by

the law of nature, and therefore one consenting to anything less than a perpetual marriage is not consenting to marriage at all.

Canon 1099 states in part that error concerning the indissolubility of marriage does not vitiate marital consent provided it does not determine the will. Thus, one can erroneously believe that a marriage can end by civil divorce, yet still marry validly. A person may believe that divorce, in general, is a viable option, yet still choose to marry perpetually *this person*. On the other hand, if the error concerning indissolubility affects the will such that one intends to enter a union that can be dissolved, then the consent is invalid.

The intention *contra bonum sacramenti* is often placed hypothetically, as, e.g., "I marry you till death do us part as long as everything works out all right." Nor does the intention against perpetuity have to be explicit. It can be implicit when "the circumstances are so unusual and compelling that the only reasonable conclusion that can be drawn from them is that indissolubility was excluded." (Wrenn, *Annulments*, 99.) For example, a person who believes in the possibility of divorce marries someone he does not love, divorces soon after the marriage, and attempts marriage with another. The person had not made a conscious and explicit decision against perpetuity, but the intention was there implicitly as demonstrated by subsequent circumstances.

G. Conditional Consent

1. *Future condition.* A marriage cannot be validly contracted on the basis of a condition regarding the future. (Can. 1102, §1)

A condition is a circumstance attached to a legal agreement on which the validity of the agreement depends. A future condition suspends the validity of the marriage until it is fulfilled. For example, "I marry you on the condition that I will find happiness with you." Such a marriage is invalid, because marriage is made by consent given in the present; it cannot be suspended until some future circumstance is realized. (Note: future licit conditions were possible under the 1917 Code, can. 1092, 3°; such marriages became valid only when the condition was fulfilled.)

A true future condition that invalidates marriage is one whose fulfillment is regarded as being more important than the marriage itself. Some examples: I marry you provided you make me happy; provided I am fulfilled; provided you do not want to have children. For a circumstance to be a true condition, ordinarily it must have real and objective importance and be related to the marital relationship. (Doyle, 787) On the other hand, a condition can sometimes be so important subjectively that there is no consent unless that condition is fulfilled. A woman, e.g., who was raised by alcoholic parents, insists she will never marry a heavy drinker; five years after marriage her husband begins drinking heavily and the marriage breaks up. If her consent was truly based on the future condition that her husband never become a heavy drinker, it was invalid.

Conditions are usually not explicitly placed and, even when implicit, future conditions invalidate consent. In the example above, the woman who would never marry a heavy drinker would not have to place this condition explicitly and consciously; it can be demonstrated to exist implicitly by the circumstances: her childhood experience, her aversion to people who drink heavily, the disruption of the marriage and her departure caused directly by the heavy drinking, etc.

2. *Past and present conditions.* A marriage, entered into on the basis of a condition regarding the past or the present, is valid or not depending on whether the basis for the condition exists or not. Such a condition may not be placed licitly without the written permission of the local Ordinary. (Can. 1102 §§2–3)

A past condition is based on a circumstance that occurred or existed before consent was given, e.g., "I marry you provided you have not had sexual intercourse with another." A present condition is based on a circumstance that occurs or exists at the time consent is given, e.g., "I marry you provided you do not have venereal disease." If the condition is not met, the marriage is invalid; if it is met, it is valid. The general remarks on condition under "future condition" above are also applicable to past and present conditions.

For liceity, the written permission of the local Ordinary is required to place a past or present condition. This has little practical importance because conditions are usually placed implicitly and, even if explicit, most Catholics are unaware of this requirement.

H.   Force and Fear

A marriage is invalid when entered into by force or grave fear from without, even if not inflicted intentionally, such that, in order to be freed from it, the person is forced to choose marriage. (Can. 1103)

Force is a physical or moral coercion from outside the person which the person cannot resist. Any legal act is invalid when it is placed as a result of extrinsic force brought to bear on a person who is not able to resist it. (See can. 125, §1.) Since marriage is made by the free consent of the parties, a marriage that is forced against one's will is invalid.

Fear comes from within the person. In order to be invalidiating it must be grave, inflicted from without, and causative of the marriage in order to be freed from the fear. *Grave* fear can be objectively serious and imminent, e.g., fear of loss of life or physical harm; or it can be subjectively grave, being perceived by one person as serious and imminent but not so by others. For example, an immature and impressionable nineteen year old girl, who has strict parents, may feel grave fear when she discovers an unwanted pregnancy and feel compelled to choose marriage so as not to displease her parents. On the other hand, a thirty year old woman who becomes pregnant may not have the same reaction.

The fear must also be inspired *from without*, that is, by another person. Reverential fear may be internal to oneself and not at all inspired by one's parents, for it may arise from one's imagination rather than from the action of the parents. However, the fear can even result from an external source who did not intend it. For example, the parents may have given past warnings about disowning their daughter if she ever became pregnant out of wedlock, but would not actually do so in the real situation.

The fear must *force one to choose marriage in order to be free of it*. The person feels no other choice but to enter the marriage in order to be free of the fear. Fear is the cause of the marriage which would not take place without it.

III.   Manifestation of Consent

A.   Presence

1.   In order that marriage be contracted validly, it is necessary that the contracting parties be present either in person or by proxy. (Can. 1104, §1)

> In virtue of this requirement marriage is not contracted validly if the parties are only morally present, i.e., by telephone, radio, letter, etc. (Vlaming, 377) This prescription is of ecclesiastical law only and does not bind marriages between non-Catholics.

2.   The parties must express matrimonial consent in words; but if they are unable to speak, in equivalent signs. (Can. 1104, §2)

> The use of speech by those who can speak, as well as the use of the words of the Roman Ritual, concern the liceity and not the validity of the marriage consent.

B.   Marriage by Proxy

1.   In order for a marriage to be validly contracted by proxy it is required that there be a special mandate to contract with a certain person, that the proxy be designated by the person giving the mandate, and that the proxy exercise this function in person. (Can. 1105, §1)

> For validity, the mandate must be signed by the one giving the mandate and also by the pastor or Ordinary of the place where the mandate is given, or by a priest delegated by either of them, or at least by two witnesses; or it must be drawn up by an authentic document in accordance with civil law. If the one mandating cannot write, this is to be noted in the mandate

itself and another witness should be added who also is to sign it, or else the mandate is invalid. (Can. 1105, §§2–3)

A special mandate is required, i.e., a written document for contracting marriage; it is not sufficient that one give a general mandate for the placing of all legal acts in one's name.

The mandate must be to contract marriage with a *specific* person; hence, one cannot give a mandate which would allow the proxy to choose a spouse and marry her in the name of the one giving the mandate.

The proxy must be designated by the one giving the mandate and this designation may not be committed to others. (SCOf, reply, May 31, 1948)

For liceity, the permission of the local Ordinary is necessary to allow a marriage to be celebrated with a proxy. (Can. 1071, §1, 7°) N.B. Many states do not allow proxy marriages. (See Doyle, 791.)

2. If the one mandating, before the proxy contracts marriage in that person's name, shall revoke the mandate or become insane, the marriage is invalid, even if the proxy or other contracting party does not know of this. (Can. 1105, §4)

C. Marriage Through an Interpreter

Marriage can be contracted through an interpreter. Nevertheless, the pastor should not assist at such a marriage unless he is convinced of the trustworthiness of the interpreter. (Can. 1106)

CHAPTER V
The Form of Marriage

I. The Canonical Form

A. The Minister and Two Witnesses

1. Only those marriages are valid which are contracted in the presence of the local Ordinary, the pastor, or the priest or deacon delegated by either of them, and in the presence of two witnesses, in accord with the regulations expressed in the canons which follow, and without prejudice to the exceptions in canons 144; 1112, §1, 1116; and 1127, §§2–3. (Can. 1108, §1)

> Assistance at marriage is not an act of governance nor an act of the power of order. It is very similar, however, to governance, for the right and power to assist at marriages is had by reason of one's office, or it can be delegated, and the act of assistance is requisite for the validity of the marriage.

> The exceptions to the canonical form are discussed below.

2. The one who assists at marriage is understood to be only the person who is present and asks for the manifestation of the consent of the parties and receives it in the name of the Church. (Can. 1108, §2)

> Hence, the minister who assists must do so *actively*. He must ask for and receive the consent of both parties, not only of one. (SCDF, Nov. 28, 1975, CLD 8:820–22) Mere passive assistance, e.g., when the minister allows the couple to give their consent without his asking for and receiving it, is invalid. The words for

this valid assistance are found in the *Rite of Marriage*, nn. 25–26.

The two witnesses who must assist at the marriage with the minister must be present physically, and indeed simultaneously with the minister. They must be present morally so that they can testify to what is taking place. They must be used as witnesses, but for validity it seems sufficient that they be implicitly designated by the parties, as they are whenever the parties in any way at all wish to contract in the presence of the persons who are watching the celebration of the marriage. (Genicot, II, n. 627) Anyone capable of being a witness by natural law acts as a valid witness in a Catholic marriage, whether the witness be a minor, a non-baptized, an excommunicated person, etc. Therefore, the witness must have the use of reason and be capable of understanding what is happening by the exchange of consent. The law presumes the use of reason is attained at age seven.

3. *Eastern canon law.* The form of marriage is the same as in the Latin Code, but with this difference: the marriage must be contracted with a sacred rite, i.e., with the blessing of the priest who witnesses the marriage. (Mp, can. 85) The sacred rite required for the validity of the marriage is not a certain liturgical rite, but a simple blessing; the orations and ceremonies are only for liceity. (Mathis/Bonner, 258–59)

Since the blessing of the priest is required in the Eastern churches, what of the validity of a marriage of an Eastern Catholic celebrated in the Latin rite before a deacon or a lay officiant (can. 1112)? Similarly, what of the case of an Eastern Catholic subject to a Latin priest when the Eastern Catholic marries a non-baptized and the Latin priest does not impart a blessing? Such marriages can be considered valid on the basis of the principle, *locus regit actum* (the place determines the act). (See Pospishil/Faris, 32–33.)

B. Those Bound to the Form

The above mentioned form must be observed if at least one of the parties to the marriage was baptized in the Catholic Church or was received into it and has not left it by a formal act, without prejudice to canon 1127, §2. (Can. 1117)

> In short, any marriage involving at least one Catholic requires the canonical form for validity in ordinary circumstances. All exceptions to this general rule are given below. For a discussion of who is considered a Catholic, see the commentary above, page 185.

C. Faculty in Virtue of Office

1 *The local Ordinary and the pastor*, unless they have been excommunicated or interdicted or suspended from office by a sentence or decree, or have been declared to be such, by virtue of their office and within their territory, validly assist at marriages not only of their subjects but also of non-subjects, provided at least one of them is of the Latin rite. (Can. 1109)

> Hence the pastor or local Ordinary cannot validly assist at marriages even of his own subjects outside of his territory; but within his territory he may validly assist at the marriages of people who are not his subjects, provided at least one of them is of the Latin rite. The territory of a parish is that within the parish boundaries, not simply the church property.

> *Eastern canon law.* At least one party must be of the same Eastern rite as the pastor or local hierarch who assists within his territory, unless the person's rite has been placed under the jurisdiction of the rite of the hierarch or pastor. (See Mp, can. 86.)

2. *Personal Ordinaries and pastors*, in virtue of their office and within the limits of their jurisdiction, validly assist only at those marriages in which at least one party is their subject. (Can. 1110)

> A personal Ordinary or pastor is one whose jurisdiction is not based on territory, but on a certain class of persons, e.g., members of a certain rite, nationality, language, profession, etc. It would include military chaplains, migrant chaplains, and others who may assist at marriages of special groups.

D. Delegated Faculty for Marriage

1. The local Ordinary and the pastor, as long as they validly hold office, can delegate the faculty, even a general one, to assist at marriage within their territory to priests and deacons. In order for the delegation of the faculty to assist at marriage to be valid, it must be expressly given to specified persons; if it is a question of special delegation, it must be given for a specific marriage; but if it is a question of general delegation, it must be granted in writing. (Can. 1111)

A pastor may validly delegate any priest or deacon to assist at marriages in his parish. General delegation must be given in writing, for the validity of the delegation. The following conditions also must be met for validity:

a) *A definite priest or deacon must be delegated*; the minister must be determined by name, or by office, etc. The priest or deacon is not sufficiently designated when the pastor notifies the superior of a monastery that he delegates as the priest to assist at a marriage whatever priest the superior shall select to send to the parish. (CodCom reply, May 20, 1923) However, several ministers may be delegated for one and the same marriage, provided that each is determined by name, or office, etc., i.e., is specifically designated. (Sipos, §134)

b) *The marriage must be determinate*; the marriage is specified by the names of the contracting parties, or by the hour and place of marriage, etc. However delegation can be given to one priest or deacon for several determinate marriages, provided each marriage is specifically designated (Capello, V, n. 674) This requirement applies only in the case of special delegation, not general delegation.

c) *The delegation must be express*; i.e., given explicitly by words or in writing, or implicitly by signs or other actions. A tacit or presumed delegation is invalid. Hence the mere silence of the pastor who knows another priest is assisting at a marriage in his parish is only tacit delegation and not sufficient; it is invalid.

d) *The marriage must take place in the territory of the delegating pastor.*

A personal pastor cannot delegate another priest or

deacon to witness a marriage in his church if neither of the parties is subject to him. (Doyle, 795)

2. *Subdelegation.*

a. One who has received general delegation for marriages can subdelegate another priest or deacon in individual cases. (See can. 137, §3.)

> Thus a parochial vicar or deacon who has received general delegation to assist at marriages from the pastor or local Ordinary, can subdelegate another priest or deacon to assist at a definite marriage. (CodCom, reply, Dec. 28, 1927)

b. One who has received a special delegation for a determinate marriage or marriages can subdelegate another priest or deacon to assist at the marriage only if this power of subdelegating is expressly conceded to him by the one delegating. (See can. 137, §3.)

> Thus a pastor or local Ordinary can delegate a certain priest or deacon to assist at a certain marriage and can also give him power to subdelegate another priest or deacon to assist at that marriage. (CodCom reply, Dec. 28, 1927) No subdelegated power can be subdelegated again unless it is expressly permitted by the one delegating. (Can. 137, §4) Thus, a parochial vicar who receives general delegation cannot grant his subdelegate the power to again subdelegate, unless this power was expressly granted to him by the pastor or Ordinary who delegated him.

3. Before special delegation is granted, everything must be done which the law requires to prove the freedom of the parties to marry. (Can. 1113)

> Hence, the one who grants the special delegation, not the one who receives it, is responsible for seeing that the pre-marital investigation is conducted and all other marriage preparation requirements of universal or particular law are observed.

E. Some Conditions for Licit Assistance

The one who assists at marriage acts illicitly unless he has first established the freedom of the parties to marry in accord with the law and, if possible, has the permission of the pastor whenever he assists in virtue of general delegation. (Can. 1114)

The one who assists can be assured of the parties' freedom to marry if he ascertains that all the marriage preparation requirements of universal and particular law have been fulfilled. The permission of the pastor by one who has general delegation can often be presumed. Since the assistance at marriages and the nuptial blessing are functions especially committed to the pastor by canon 530, 4°, the pastor may reserve any or all weddings in the parish to himself.

II. Exceptions to the Form

A. Marriage to an Eastern non-Catholic

The canonical form stated in canon 1108 is to be observed in mixed marriages; if, however, a Catholic contracts marriage with an Eastern non-Catholic party, the canonical form must be observed only for the liceity of the celebration; for validity, however, the intervention of the ordained minister is required, observing the other requirements of the law. (Can. 1127, §1)

If a Catholic wishes to marry an Eastern non-Catholic in the Eastern non-Catholic church, permission to be excused from the observance of the canonical form is required for liceity only. For validity, the marriage must take place before the Eastern non-Catholic priest, because the blessing of the priest is required for the validity of the marriage in the Eastern churches.

It is forbidden, either before or after the celebration of the marriage in the Eastern non-Catholic church, to have another religious celebration of the same marriage to give or renew marital consent. It is likewise forbidden to have any religious celebration in which a Catholic assistant and non-Catholic minister together, following their own rite, ask for the consent of the parties. (See can. 1127, §3.) Not forbidden by this law is a second ceremony, following the Catholic form, in which the Eastern non-Catholic priest imparts a marriage blessing without a renewal of consent. (SCDF, reply, June 16, 1966, CLD 6:22–23)

B. Dispensation from Form in Mixed Marriages

If serious difficulties prevent the observance of the canonical form, the local Ordinary of the Catholic party has the right to dispense from it in individual cases, after consulting the Ordinary of the place where the marriage is celebrated. For validity, there must be some public form of celebrating the marriage. The episcopal conference may enact norms by which the above stated dispensation can be granted uniformly. (Can. 1127, §2)

In any mixed marriage other than one with an Eastern non-Catholic, the canonical form is required for validity. Therefore a dispensation is necessary for the validity of such a marriage if the canonical form is not going to be observed.

A requirement for the dispensation is the presence of serious difficulties. Any dispensation requires a just and reasonable cause (can. 90), so the serious difficulties mentioned here must be something more than that. According to the statement on mixed marriages of the NCCB, the following are types of reasons which qualify for granting the dispensation: to achieve family harmony or to avoid family alienation, to obtain parental agreement to the marriage, to recognize the significant claims of relationship or special friendship with a non-Catholic minister, to permit the marriage in a church that has particular importance to the non-Catholic. (NCCB, Nov. 16, 1970, CLD 7:737)

For validity, there must be some *public form* of a marriage celebrated with a dispensation from form. This can be in the non-Catholic church, before a justice of the peace, in the reception hall, etc., so long as it is a public celebration with witnesses present. Although a common law marriage is valid in some civil jurisdictions, it would not be valid in canon law in this case because it lacks a public form of celebration. (On the other hand, if two non-Catholics contract a common law marriage, it is recognized as valid by canon law provided the civil law recognizes its validity.)

A dispensation from form for marriages involving two Catholics can be given only by the Holy See.

C. Supplied Faculty

In common error, whether of fact or of law, and also in positive and probable doubt, whether of law or fact, the Church supplies executive power of governance both for the external and internal forum. This also applies to the faculty for marriage. (See can. 144.)

The use of canon 144 to supply the faculty for assisting at marriage in the case of common error can be done only in very limited circumstances. It is not sufficient for the community mistakenly to believe the minister has the faculty when in fact he does not. Rather, the circumstances must be such that the community errs concerning the *status* of the priest or deacon, e.g., believing the priest to be the pastor, or the parochial vicar with general delegation, or the deacon as being assigned to the parish with general delegation for marriages. This can happen, for example, when a priest is merely in residence in the rectory, and is not assigned as parochial vicar, such that the community would think he has a general delegation for marriages when in fact he does not; or when a priest is involved on a regular basis with the pastoral care of a parish, even if not in residence. Thus, there must be some public fact as the basis for the error. The Church supplies the faculty here for the *common good*, because the community errs in thinking that this priest can be approached for any weddings in that parish. On the other hand, a visiting priest or deacon, who lacks special delegation for one or a few marriages, is not supplied with the faculty in virtue of canon 144. The reason is that the Church supplies the faculty for cases that affect the common good, and in the case of a lack of special delegation, the good of the community is not at stake because it is only one or several determinate marriages in question.

A 1972 decision of the Rota summarizes well the question of supplied jurisdiction for marriage in the case of common error:

"a) In the practical order, *common error* exists whenever there is publicly placed a fact from which, if it were known by the community in question (e.g., a parish), all or nearly all would prudently think that power to assist at marriage belongs to a specified priest or deacon who as a matter of fact lacks it.

"b) The sole and adequate reason for which the Church supplies a lack of power is the necessity *of promoting the common good* or *of avoiding a common evil*. But not for a merely private good. . . .

"Consequently, it is not probable that the Church supplies power in cases where, even though common error exists, no danger of public harm is had, because . . . there is no probable danger that many other members of the community would, as a matter of fact, approach the priest and celebrate invalid marriages. Therefore, there would be question of a purely speculative, not a really practical common error. In such a situation the Church would not supply jurisdiction . . . because it is not to be believed that the supreme authority wishes to repair violation of a law . . . for the sake of a purely private good which can be met by the convalidation of the marriage, even by granting a radical sanation for it.

"From what has been said, it is clear that power is supplied when common error is verified relative to a priest to whom the parishioners can freely have recourse to celebrate marriages. . . . It is not applied, however, when the common error concerns a priest who is thought to have been delegated to assist at a specified marriage." (SRR, sentence, Dec. 11, 1972, CLD 8:172–73; see also SRR, sentence, June 25, 1977, CLD 9:660–76.)

The above interpretation of supplied jurisdiction, as it applies to marriage, has not been changed with the revised Code. (See B. Primetshofer, "Die Eheschliessung," in *Handbuch*, pp. 785–86; SRR, sentence, Apr. 29, 1983, *Monitor Ecclesiasticus* 109 (1984) 308–26.)

D. Lay Officiant

Where priests and deacons are lacking, the diocesan bishop, with the previous favorable vote of the episcopal conference and permission obtained from the Holy See, can delegate lay persons to assist at marriages. A worthy lay person is to be chosen who is capable of giving instructions to the couples to be married and who can properly perform the marriage rite. (Can. 1112)

E. The Extraordinary Form

If a person who is competent to assist at marriages in accord with the law cannot be present or cannot be approached without grave inconvenience, a couple who intends to enter a true marriage can validly and licitly contract before witnesses alone: (a) in danger of death; (b) outside the danger of death, provided it is prudently foreseen that this state of affairs will last for one month. In both cases, if another priest or deacon is available and can be present, he must be called upon for the celebration of the marriage together with the witnesses, without prejudice to the validity of the marriage before witnesses alone. (Can. 1116)

1. *In danger of death.*

To contract marriage before witnesses only, it must be a case of *true danger of death*, either from an intrinsic cause (sickness) or an extrinsic cause (war, flood, etc.). The *articulum mortis* is not required, i.e., death need not be imminent.

It is also necessary that it be either *absolutely* or *morally impossible* for an authorized witness to be present or approached. It is absolutely impossible when there is no time to approach the official witness or to obtain from him delegation to assist at the marriage. It is morally impossible when this cannot be done without grave inconvenience, e.g., a dangerous journey during time of war, persecution, floods, etc.

It is also morally impossible for the official witness to be present or approached when he, although materially present in the place, is unable by reason of grave inconvenience to assist at the marriage asking and receiving the consent of the contracting parties. (CodCom, reply, July 25, 1931) E.g., if the pastor is forbidden by civil law to assist at the marriage of certain parties under penalties to be inflicted either on the pastor or on the parties, the pastor can be considered absent and unavailable in the sense of canon 1116. (SCSacr, private response, Apr. 24, 1935) Note that the grave inconvenience mentioned in the canon is not only one which threatens the official witness, but also one which threatens both parties or either party to the marriage. (CodCom, reply, May 3, 1945)

226

2. *Outside the danger of death.*

To contract marriage before witnesses only, it is required that it be either absolutely or morally impossible for an authorized witness to be present or approached. It is also necessary that it be prudently foreseen that this situation is to last for a month.

The *impossibility* of an authorized witness being present or approached has been explained above. This is the case especially in mission countries and remote areas, and also in other places during time of war and persecution.

It must be foreseen that *this situation will last for a month*. Hence a past month's absence does not suffice, but it is required that one prudently judge that the situation will last for a month yet. For the valid and licit use of canon 1116 the mere fact of the official witness' absence does not suffice, but it is required that there exist moral certainty, based either on common knowledge or on inquiry, that for one month the pastor, delegated priest or deacon (or lay officiant where applicable) will be neither available nor accessible without grave inconvenience. (CodCom, reply, Nov. 10, 1925) The marriage would not, however, be invalid if the assistance of a competent minister became possible before the month elapsed, provided that at the time of the marriage there was little hope of this. (Sipos, §134)

3. *The priest or deacon of canon 1116, §2.*

If there is another priest or deacon at hand, he is to be called to the wedding to assist together with the witnesses. The priest or deacon of canon 1116, §2 is one who has no delegation or authorization to assist at marriages as the official witness. However, he is given ample faculties to dispense from matrimonial impediments and from the form of marriage according to the norms of canons 1079–1081. (See above, pp. 176-179.)

This priest or deacon is to be called both in danger of death and also outside the danger of death for marriages legally celebrated before two witnesses alone.

Canon 1116 speaks of a priest or deacon who is

available; hence, if there is none available, one need not be sought out. (V.C., II, n. 406) Even if he is available, the marriage is celebrated validly without him, provided two witnesses are used. (Mathis/Bonner, 267–68) Another opinion holds that in extreme circumstances a marriage would be valid before one witness or even no witnesses. (See Doyle, 797.)

CHAPTER VI
The Celebration of Marriage

I. The Marriage Liturgy

A. General Principles

1. Except for a case of necessity, the rites contained in the liturgical books approved by the Church, or those received by legitimate customs, are to be observed in the celebration of marriage. (Can. 1119)

> The *Rite of Marriage* (RM) is found in the *Roman Ritual*. It must be followed except in a case of necessity, such as danger of death, when the exchange of consent suffices. There are three different rites of marriage in the Ritual as follows below.

2. When a marriage is celebrated during Advent or Lent or other days of penance, the parish priest should advise the couple to take into consideration the special nature of these liturgical seasons. (RM, 11)

B. Rite of Marriage During Mass

1. *Catholic marriages.* The *Rite for Celebrating Marriage During Mass* should normally be used for the marriages of two Catholics. (See RM, 6 and RM, Chapter II, note 13.)

2. *Mixed marriages.* This rite may also be used in mixed marriages involving a Catholic and a baptized non-Catholic if the situation warrants it and the local Ordinary gives permission, except that communion is not given to the non-Catholic, since the general law does not allow it. (See RM, 8)

In most places where mixed marriages are commonplace, the local Ordinary's permission for a marriage celebration during Mass can often be presumed. The non-Catholic must be validly baptized.

To the extent that Eucharistic sharing is not permitted by the general discipline of the Church, this is to be considered when plans are being made to have the mixed marriage at Mass or not. (NCCB statement on mixed marriages, n. 17, Nov. 16, 1970, CLD 7:739)

It is forbidden, either before or after the celebration of a mixed marriage according to the canonical form, to have another religious celebration of the same marriage to give or renew marital consent. It is likewise forbidden to have any religious celebration in which a Catholic assistant and non-Catholic minister together, following their own rite, ask for the consent of the parties. (See can. 1127, §3.) Not forbidden by this law is a second ceremony, after the Catholic form, in which the non-Catholic minister imparts a blessing or has a ceremony without the exchange or renewal of consent.

With the permission of the local Ordinary and the consent of the appropriate authority of the other church or community, a non-Catholic minister may be invited to participate in the Catholic marriage service by giving additional prayers, blessings, or words of greeting or exhortation. (NCCB statement, n. 15, CLD 7:738)

3. *Exceptions to use of nuptial Mass texts*
a) If the marriage is celebrated on a Sunday or solemnity, the Mass of the day is used with the nuptial blessing and the special final blessing according to the circumstances.
b) On the Sundays of the Christmas season and in Ordinary Time, the entire wedding Mass may be used in Masses that are not parish Masses. (See RM, 11.)

C. Rite of Marriage Outside Mass

1. *Choice of texts.* The liturgy of the word as adapted to the marriage celebration is a highly effective means for the catechesis on the sacrament of marriage and its duties. Therefore when the wedding Mass may not be held, one of the readings from the texts provided for the marriage celebration (nn. 67–105 of the rite) may be chosen,

except from Holy Thursday to Easter, on the solemnities of Epiphany, Ascension, Pentecost, or Corpus Christi, or on holydays of obligation. (See RM, 11.)

2. *Catholic marriages.* If good reasons are present, the *Rite for Celebrating Marriage Outside Mass* may be used for Catholic marriages also. (See RM, Chapter II, note 13.)

> It is desirable that the wedding of two Catholics take place during the celebration of the Eucharist. Some good reasons for having it outside the Eucharist include the observance of canon 905 which permits the local Ordinary to grant permission only for binations on weekdays (including Saturdays) and trinations on Sundays and holy days; lack of time due to other pressing pastoral needs; when a deacon (or, in countries where applicable, a lay minister) assists at the marriage.

3. *Mixed marriages.* In a marriage between a Catholic and a baptized person who is not a Catholic, the rite of marriage outside Mass shall be used. (RM, 8)

> The *Rite for Celebrating Marriage During Mass* may also be used for mixed marriages as above.

> The minister of the non-Catholic party, with permission of the local Ordinary and the consent of the appropriate authority of the other church or ecclesial community, may be invited to read a lesson and/or preach at a wedding outside of Mass. (NCCB statement, CLD 7:738)

> Holy communion should not be given at a mixed marriage outside of Mass, not only because the law (can. 918) prefers that communion be given during Mass, but also because it is more ecumenically sensitive not to give communion when only the Catholic party is permitted by law to receive.

D. Rite of Marriage of a Catholic and Unbaptized

In a marriage between a Catholic and one who is not baptized, the *Rite for Celebrating Marriage Between a Catholic and an Unbaptized Person* is to be used. (See RM, 8.)

> There may be no Mass or Communion with this rite of marriage.

II. Place of Celebration

A. Sacramental Marriages

1. A marriage between two Catholics or between a Catholic party and a baptized non-Catholic is to be celebrated in the parish church; with the permission of the local Ordinary or the pastor, it may be celebrated in some other church or oratory.

> The parish church of the Catholic party, whether of the bride or the groom, is the typical place for the marriage celebration. The pastor of the bride or the groom could give permission for it to be celebrated in another *Catholic* church or oratory only; the local Ordinary's permission would be needed for some non-Catholic place. Also necessary is the permission of the rector or competent superior of the church or oratory where the wedding is to be held.

> An oratory is a place for divine worship for the benefit of some community or assembly of the faithful to which other members of the faithful may go with permission of the competent superior. (See can. 1223.) Oratories would include the places of worship in a religious house, seminary, Catholic school, etc. A church is a place of worship to which the faithful have a *right* to go, such as a parish church or cathedral. (See can. 1214.)

2. *Outside a sacred place.* The local Ordinary may permit marriages to be celebrated in some suitable place besides a church or oratory. (See can. 1118, §2.)

> This permission is needed only for sacramental marriages. For non-sacramental marriages, see below.

> A suitable place would include a non-denominational chapel, or a place of worship of another Christian church or ecclesial community when there is good reason for having it there, such as a mixed marriage. The local Ordinary is free to determine what constitutes a suitable place, and thus he may exclude certain kinds of places, such as garden weddings, reception hall weddings, etc. since the ecclesial signifi-

cance of a sacramental marriage is not well signified in such places.

N.B. This permission does not constitute a dispensation from form; it presumes the Catholic minister will assist at the wedding. On the other hand, when a dispensation from form is obtained, this permission is unnecessary.

B. Non-sacramental Marriages

A marriage between a Catholic party and a non-baptized party can be celebrated in a church or in some other suitable place.

Permission of the local Ordinary is not necessary to have a non-sacramental marriage outside a church or other sacred place. However, it would be within the diocesan bishop's authority to establish guidelines for what constitutes "suitable" places even for non-sacramental marriages.

III. The Secret Celebration of Marriage

A. When Permitted

The local Ordinary can permit a marriage to be celebrated in secret for a serious and urgent reason. (Can. 1130)

Some examples of a serious and urgent reason for a secret marriage are: marriages contrary to civil law if the prohibition is contrary to natural or ecclesiatical law, such as interracial marriages; marriages in countries where the church is persecuted and religious marriages are forbidden; marriages of those living in concubinage when they are believed by the community to be married. (See Doyle, 807.)

B. Obligation of Secrecy

The permission to celebrate a marriage in secret also requires: (a) that the investigations which must precede marriage be conducted in secret; and (b) that secrecy concerning the marriage be observed by the local Ordinary, the one who assists at the marriage, the witnesses, and the spouses. (Can. 1131)

> The obligation to observe the secret on the part of the local Ordinary ceases if there arises from the observance of the secret either serious scandal or serious harm to the sanctity of marriage. This fact is to be made known to the parties before the marriage celebration. (Can. 1132)

> For the law on the recording of a secret marriage, see below.

IV. Recording of Marriages

A. Duties of Pastor of Place of Marriage

1. After a marriage has been celebrated the pastor of the place of celebration, or the one who takes his place, even if neither has assisted at the marriage, should record in the marriage register as soon as possible the names of the spouses, the minister who assisted, and the witnesses, and the place and date of celebration, in accord with the manner prescribed by the episcopal conference or by the diocesan bishop. (Can. 1121, §1)

2. Marriages are also to be recorded in the baptismal register of the place in which the baptism of the spouses has been recorded. If a spouse has contracted marriage in a place other than the parish of baptism, the pastor of the place of celebration should send as soon as possible notification of the marriage to the pastor of the place where baptism was conferred. (Can. 1122)

> Convalidations, annulments, and dissolutions of marriage should also be recorded by the pastor in both the marriage and baptismal registers. (See can. 1123.)

B. Other Cases

> 1. *Marriages with a dispensation from form.* The local Ordinary who granted the dispensation is responsible for recording the dispensation and the celebration of the marriage in accord with canon 1121, §3.

> 2. *The extraordinary form.* When a marriage is cele-

brated according to canon 1116 without a competent minister assisting either in danger of death or a month's absence of the minister, the priest or deacon, if present at the celebration, is obliged to inform the pastor or local Ordinary; if there was no priest or deacon present, the witnesses have this obligation. (See can. 1121, §2.)

3. *A marriage celebrated in secret* is recorded only in the special register kept in the secret archives of the curia. (Can. 1133)

4. *Convalidations, annulments, dissolutions.* Whenever a marriage is convalidated in the external forum, or is declared null, or is legitimately dissolved except for death, the pastor of the place of the celebration of marriage must be notified so that a notation may be duly made in the marriage and baptismal registers. (Can. 1123)

V. Common Law Marriage

1. Common law marriage, i.e., one in which a man and a woman contract marriage by the expression of true matrimonial consent but without any ceremony, i.e., without the intervention of a civil or religious official or of witnesses, is considered valid in some states of the union. In most states it is required by law that marriage be celebrated before a qualified civil or religious official, and common law marriages are considered invalid.

Since the laws of the states change in this matter, no attempt is made to enumerate the states in which common law marriages are considered valid. In marriage cases involving common law marriages, the following information must be ascertained: the date of the marriage, the domicile of the parties, the place of the marriage, and the law of the states involved as the law existed at the time the marriage was celebrated. Investigations may also be necessary to ascertain the competence of the civil or religious official who assisted at a marriage in states which do not recognize common law marriages. As is evident, a civil lawyer should be consulted in these matters.

2. Common law marriage between two non-Catholics is valid only

in the manner recognized by the civil law to which the parties are bound. If the civil law recognizes the validity of such a marriage, the marriage is valid; if the civil law does not recognize the validity of common law marriage, such a union is invalid, even though the parties give a consent that by the law of nature would suffice.

3. *1917 Code.* For marriages contracted before November 27, 1983, the following rule applies: Common law marriage between two *baptized* non-Catholics or between a baptized non-Catholic and an unbaptized person was valid, even in states which did not recognize common law marriage, provided there was no impediment or defective consent. The reason for this is that marriages involving the baptized were not subject to the civil authority under the former law. (See Mathis/Bonner, 274–75.)

CHAPTER VII
Convalidation of Marriage

Convalidation is a legal remedy by which a couple's original marriage consent, which was invalid, is subsequently made valid. (Doyle, 822) The consent may have been invalid for reasons of a diriment impediment, defective consent, or a defect of form. While the consent was invalid, the marital relationship still exists. The marriage is generally recognized as valid in the civil law, and the couple consider themselves to be married. Thus, convalidation is a means for granting Church recognition to a marriage that had been considered invalid according to canon law. Convalidations can only be given when there is an appearance of marriage; concubinage cannot be convalidated. (*Handbuch*, 809)

There are two categories of convalidation: simple convalidation which takes place by a private renewal of consent or according to the canonical form; and radical sanation (*sanatio in radice*) which involves no action on the part of the couple themselves but is a "healing to the roots" of the marriage by the intervention of competent ecclesiastical authority.

Pastoral ministers should not agree to a convalidation if they have serious doubts concerning the stability of the marriage, as, e.g., an immature couple, a hastily arranged civil marriage with a pregnancy involved, etc. It is better to wait for a suitable period, several years if necessary, to determine the stability of the marriage. If such a couple or the parents insist on a convalidation, the case should be referred to the local Ordinary. Such cases should be handled with extreme sensitivity so that the couple are not lost to the faith.

I. Simple Convalidation

A. Convalidation of Marriage Invalid Because of an Impediment

1. To convalidate a marriage that is invalid because of a diriment impediment, it is required that the impediment cease or it be dispensed, and that at least the party who knows of the impediment renew consent. This renewal of consent is required by ecclesiastical law for the validity of the convalidation, even if both parties gave consent in the beginning and have not since revoked it. (Can. 1156)

> *The impediment* may cease in three ways: (a) automatically (e.g., prior bond, by the death of the former spouse; disparity of cult, by the conversion of the unbaptized; age, by mere lapse of time); (b) by dispensation; or (c) by a change in law (e.g., the former impediments of spiritual relationship and adultery with a promise to marry or with an attempted marriage). In danger of death or in the *omnia parata* case when everything is prepared for the wedding, canons 1079–1081 may be used to dispense.

> *The renewal of consent* is required by ecclesiastical law only. It is not required by the natural law, for after the removal of the impediment, the consent given in the beginning and not since revoked would now take effect and effect the validation of the marriage. Hence an invalid marriage of two non-Catholics would be validated upon the cessation of the impediment by mere continuation of conjugal life. This rule is generally recognized also in civil law, especially when the impediment was nonage or defective consent; however, in some states limitations are placed, so that marriages invalid because of certain types of impediments are not convalidated by mere marital cohabitation upon the cessation of the impediment. Hence marriages involving non-Catholics only call for special investigation in individual cases. (Mathis/Bonner, 298)

> In the former law, all the baptized, including non-Catholics, were bound to renew consent.

> If a confessor discovers an impediment and the marriage cannot be convalidated, he should ordinarily

leave the parties in good faith if they are inculpably ignorant of the invalidity of their marriage, especially if
he foresees that they cannot be induced to separate, or
that grave harm would come to them on their children
by a separation. (See Sipos, §142; Genicot, II, nn. 703,
706.)

2.   The renewal of consent must be a new act of the will directed to
a marriage which the renewing party knows or thinks was invalid
from the beginning. (Can. 1157)

Knowledge or belief of the invalidity of the marriage must be had before the renewal of consent will effect the convalidation of the marriage. This is also a
requirement of ecclesiastical law (Sipos, §142), and
hence if only the non-Catholic party is aware of the
impediment, a renewal of consent is not necessary. If
the non-Catholic party, however, accepts the force of
canon law and believes the original consent to have
been invalid, then he or she also must renew consent
by a new act of the will in accord with canon 1158.
(Doyle, 824)

3.   *If the impediment is public*, consent must be renewed by both
parties by the canonical form, without prejudice to canon 1127, §2.

The impediment is public when it can be proved in
the external forum (e.g., consanguinity, age, prior
bond); otherwise it is *occult*. (See can. 1074.) Note,
however, that the possibility of proof must be practical,
i.e., one can find witnesses who are able and willing to
testify, documents are available to prove the existence
of the impediment, etc. Theoretical possibility of proof,
e.g., the impediment is of its nature public and therefore should be able to be proved, does not suffice.
(V.C., II, n. 297) Hence if the parties are related, e.g.,
but the fact cannot be proved, the impediment is occult.

The form required by law is the presence of the
local Ordinary or pastor (or delegated priest or deacon)
and two witnesses. However, if the impediment is by
law public but in fact occult, the form can be observed
quietly and secretly; if the impediment is also factually
public, the form is to be observed publicly and openly.

(Sipos, §142) Under the former law, baptized non-Catholics, when marrying other non-Catholics, were not bound to the form, but they were bound to the law to renew consent in a convalidation by means of some *external act*, provided they were conscious of the invalidity of the marriage. (Mathis/Bonner, 299)

The consent must be renewed by both parties. If the impediment is public by law but nevertheless unknown to one of the parties, he or she should be told and the marriage consent renewed with the observance of the canonical form; and if this cannot be done, a *sanatio in radice* should be requested. (Genicot, II, n. 707)

Since a non-Catholic marrying a Catholic is bound to observe the canonical form for the validity of the marriage, in the case of public impediments, the renewal of consent by the non-Catholic according to the canonical form is also necessary for the validity of the convalidation. However, the canonical form may be dispensed from in mixed marriages in accord with canon 1127, §2 when there are serious difficulties that prevent the observance of the form. For example, the non-Catholic might refuse to renew consent before a priest or deacon, because he or she believes that the marriage was valid from the beginning. In such a case, a dispensation from the canonical form for the convalidation of a mixed marriage could be given, provided the non-Catholic gives assurances that the original consent still exists. A dispensation from canonical form requires some public form of celebration for validity, and therefore a convalidation with a dispensation from form would require some public renewal of consent at least before witnesses, with the Catholic party renewing consent and the non-Catholic at least affirming that his or her original consent still exists. (See Doyle, 824.) A better pastoral solution in such a case would be to request a *sanatio in radice*.

Whenever the case is public, the convalidation should be recorded in the marriage register. No record is made of a convalidation when the impediment cannot be proved.

4. If the impediment cannot be proved to exist, it suffices that consent be renewed privately and in secret, either by the party aware of the impediment, provided that the other's consent perseveres, or by both parties if the impediment is known to both of them. (Can. 1158, §2)

> In occult cases the canonical form need not be observed and the consent is renewed without the intervention of the minister and witnesses. If, however, the marriage is also invalid because the canonical form was not observed in the first place, it is now necessary to renew consent in the presence of the minister and two witnesses. If only one party knows of the impediment, it suffices that consent be renewed internally. If both know of the impediment, they should renew consent by some appropriate words or signs, such as sexual intercourse with affection as a sign of giving oneself in marriage. (See Gasparri, II, n. 1200.)

> If both parties are Catholic, and both know of the occult impediment, both must renew consent. If one party is Catholic and the other non-Catholic, only the Catholic party must renew the consent, and the non-Catholic *may* do so. However, the non-Catholic party must affirm that the original consent still exists. If the non-Catholic party accepts the force of canon law and holds the original consent to be invalid, then he or she must renew consent. (Doyle, 824) If only the non-Catholic party knows of the impediment, no renewal of consent is necessary unless the non-Catholic accepts the force of canon law and believes the marriage to be invalid.

B. Convalidation of Marriage Invalid Because of Defective Consent

1. A marriage that is invalid because of defective consent is convalidated if the party who did not consent, now consents, provided that the consent given by the other party perseveres. (Can. 1159, §1)

> For the convalidation of a marriage where the original consent was defective for some reason or other (see canons 1095–1105), it is necessary that a new and

valid consent be given. According to the norm of canon 1157, this renewal of consent must be a new act of the will directed to a marriage which is known or thought to be invalid from the beginning. Hence, if the party was unaware of the invalidity of the marriage, subsequent consent or the granting of marital rights would not convalidate the marriage. (SRR, case, July, 29, 1926, CLD 1:523.)

Since true consent is necessary for the validity of any marriage, the necessity of a renewal of consent where it is defective is necessary for the validity of the convalidation of the marriages of Catholics and non-Catholics alike.

2.   If the defect of consent cannot be proved, it is sufficient that the party who had not consented gives consent privately and in secret. If the defect of consent can be proved, it is necessary that the consent be given according to the canonical form. (Can. 1159, §§2–3)

The defect cannot be proved in the external forum if, e.g., witnesses refuse to testify, there are no witnesses, the witnesses can prove nothing (as is often the case with intentions contrary to the substance of marriage). In such cases, the party or parties who are aware of the defect need only consent internally.

If the defect can be proved in the external forum, the canonical form is required for the convalidation. A dispensation from the form in mixed marriages can be given as explained above under canon 1158.

Non-Catholics can convalidate a marriage that was invalid due to a defect of consent only if they are aware that the marriage was invalid from the beginning, and then through a new act of the will consent to the marriage.

C.   Convalidation of Marriage Invalid for Want of Form

In order that a marriage which is invalid because of a defect of form be made valid, it must be contracted anew according to the canonical form, without prejudice to canon 1127, §2.

There are two kinds of defect of form: total lack of form when there was no appearance of a marriage according to the form, as when a couple marries outside the Catholic Church without a dispensation; and lack of substantial form when there was an appearance of the form but the form was invalid due to an absence of an essential element, namely, lack of the faculty to assist on the part of the minister, lack of witnesses or only one witness, omission of the exchange of consent, or omission of the asking for and receiving the consent by the minister who assists. (Doyle, 826)

If the nullity is occult, the marriage may be contracted secretly before the minister and two witnesses. If the nullity is publicly known, the form should be observed publicly.

If the non-Catholic party in a mixed marriage refuses to renew consent before a priest or deacon, or does not acknowledge the invalidity of the original consent, a dispensation from canonical form can be obtained as explained above under canon 1158, or a *sanatio in radice* can be requested.

II. Radical Sanation

A. Nature and Effects of Radical Sanation

1. The radical sanation (*sanatio in radice*) of an invalid marriage is its convalidation, without renewal of consent, granted by competent authority, that includes a dispensation from an impediment, if there is one, and from the canonical form, if had not been observed, as well as the retroactivity to the past of the effects of the marriage. The convalidation occurs from the moment the favor is granted; however, it is understood as being retroactive to the moment of the celebration of the marriage, unless something else is expressly stated. A radical sanation should not be granted unless it is probable that the parties wish to persevere in their conjugal life. (Can. 1161)

The principal feature of a radical sanation, as opposed to a simple convalidation, is that no renewal of consent is necessary for the convalidation of the marriage. Once the impediment or lack of form has been dispensed by the sanation, the consent previously given, which was naturally valid but juridically invalid,

243

becomes efficacious and produces its effect, namely, a valid marriage. Therefore, a radical sanation is not to be given unless it is likely that the original consent still exists.

2. A sanation can be granted validly even if one party or both parties do not know about it, but this cannot be done without a serious reason. (**Can.** 1164)

Sanations made without the knowledge of either of the parties are sometimes such as are granted *in globo*, e.g., sanations of marriages invalidly contracted due to lack of authorization of the minister officiating. (See sanations granted in this way by the SCSacr, July, 21, 1919, CLD 3:451.) They are also given in cases where the invalidity of the marriage is the fault of an ecclesiastical personage; thus the Holy Office sanated a marriage contracted by an erroneous application of the Pauline privilege. (SCOf, June 19, 1947, CLD 3:482)

Before granting a radical sanation without the knowledge of both parties, there should be discreet inquiries into the stability of the marriage in question. If there are any somewhat serious problems in the marriage, a sanation should not be granted.

It can also happen, especially in a mixed marriage, that one party desires the sanation and the other is opposed, believing the marriage to have been valid from the beginning. In such a case a sanation can be granted even with the other party not knowing of it provided there is no reason to think that his or her consent no longer exists.

B. Conditions for Radical Sanation

1. If the consent is wanting in both parties or in one party, the marriage cannot be radically sanated, whether the consent was lacking from the beginning or was originally given but later revoked. But if consent was lacking in the beginning but is later given, the sanation can be granted from the moment when the consent was given. (Can. 1162)

Since consent makes the marriage, a sanation given where consent is lacking would be invalid.

2. A marriage that is invalid due to an impediment or a defect of legitimate form can be sanated provided the consent of both parties perseveres. (Can. 1163, §1)

> The consent must be naturally valid, i.e., not defective by reason of intentions contrary to the essential elements or properties of marriage, nor by error or fraud, or lack of due competence or lack of due discretion, etc. Note, however, that the knowledge or belief that a marriage is null does not necessarily exclude a valid matrimonial consent, for, together with the knowledge or the opinion of nullity there can exist a will to enter marriage insofar as one can. True matrimonial consent can certainly exist even though the marriage itself is known to be invalid by reason of some diriment impediment. (See can. 1100.)

> Even though a marriage has been contracted invalidly because of an impediment or lack of form, *the consent which has been given is presumed to persevere* until its revocation has been proven. (Can. 1107) In a sanation, the consent must exist at the time the marriage is convalidated; however, if the consent was once given, it is presumed that it still exists unless one can prove that it was revoked.

> Marriages sanated for reason of an impediment or lack of form include a dispensation from observing the canonical form. (See can. 1161, §1.)

3. A marriage which is invalid on account of an impediment of the natural law or the divine positive law can be sanated only after the impediment has ceased. (Can. 1163, §2)

> Impotence is an impediment of the natural law which is by definition perpetual and therefore does not cease to exist. Even if impotence had ceased by some extraordinary means such as a miracle, doubtfully successful or illicit means, or surgery involving probable danger to one's life or serious harm to one's health, a sanation would not be necessary due to the presumption of canon 1060.

> Likewise the impediments of consanguinity in the direct line and in the second degree collateral cannot cease. Even if they are to be considered impediments

of ecclesiastical law, they cannot be sanated since they are never dispensed. (See can. 1078, §3.)

A marriage which is invalid due to the divine positive law impediment of prior bond can be sanated by the Apostolic See after the death of the first spouse.

C. Competent Authorities

1. *The Apostolic See* can grant radical sanations for any possible case. Only the Apostolic See can grant sanations of marriages invalid by reason of the impediments of holy orders, a public perpetual vow of chastity in a religious institute of pontifical right, crime, or the impediments of the natural law and divine positive law which have ceased to exist. (See can. 1165.)

2. *The diocesan bishop*, in individual cases, even if there are several grounds for nullity in the same marriage, can grant a radical sanation for all cases other than those which can be given only by the Apostolic See; in the sanation of a mixed marriage the conditions of canon 1125 are to be fulfilled. (See can. 1165, §2.)

The diocesan bishop can grant radical sanations only in individual cases, i.e., not to whole groups of people.

The diocesan bishop can grant a sanation in a mixed marriage only if the conditions of canon 1125 have been fulfilled. The Catholic party must declare that he or she is prepared to remove dangers of falling away from the faith and make a since promise to do all in his or her power to have all the children baptized and raised in the Catholic Church; the non-Catholic is to be informed of this declaration and promise; and both parties must be instructed on the essential ends and properties of marriage. It suffices that these conditions were fulfilled when the marriage was originally attempted invalidly. If they were not fulfilled then and cannot now be fulfilled, the case should be referred to the Apostolic See.

CHAPTER VIII
The Dissolution of the Bond

I. General Principles

A. The Bond of Marriage

From a valid marriage there arises between the spouses a bond which by nature is perpetual and exclusive. In Christian marriage, additionally, the spouses are strengthened and, as it were, consecrated by a special sacrament for the duties and dignity of their state. (Can. 1134)

> The bond of marriage arises from a valid marriage when true consent is given. This bond is exclusive and perpetual. Even when the two parties divorce, the bond persists and remarriage is considered invalid and adulterous. Hence, it is necessary for prior marriages to be annulled or dissolved before a subsequent marriage is permitted in the Catholic Church.

B. Ratified-Consummated Marriage

A ratified and consummated marriage cannot be dissolved by any human power or by any other cause except death. (Can. 1141)

> A ratified marriage (*matrimonium ratum*) is a valid marriage between baptized persons; ratified and consummated (*matrimonium ratum et consummatum*) is a valid marriage between baptized persons after there occurs the conjugal act in a human manner which is per se apt for the generation of children to which marriage is ordained by its very nature and by which the spouses become one flesh. (See can. 1061.) For consummation

to occur, therefore, it must be the act of sexual intercourse *after* the marriage is validly contracted, and it must be done in a "human manner," i.e., not with force, fear, or induced by drugs or other means against one's will. Rape, for example, is not consummation.

Once the spouses have lived together after the celebration of marriage, consummation is presumed until the contrary is proved. (Can. 1061, §2)

The principle enunciated in canon 1141 obtains for the marriage of *all* the baptized, even of non-Catholics provided both parties are validly baptized. No authority, civil or ecclesiastical, can dissolve such marriages after they have been consummated. The civil authority has no power to dissolve any kind of valid marriage, even the marriage of the unbaptized.

II. Non-Consummated Marriages

A non-consummated marriage between baptized persons or between a baptized party and a non-baptized party can be dissolved by the Roman Pontiff for a just cause, either by both parties requesting it, or by one of them, even if the other party is opposed. (Can. 1142)

The procedure to be followed in non-consummation cases is found in Book VII of the Code, canons 1697–1706. The dissolution is granted only by the pope, but the petition for the dissolution is handled by the diocese of the petitioner and then forwarded to the Apostolic See for adjudication. There must be proof of the fact of non-consummation, or that it did not take place in a human manner, as, e.g., in the case of forced sexual intercourse. There must also be proof of the existence of a just cause for granting the dispensation. (See cans. 1698–1699.)

Just causes for granting the dispensation include: subsequent impotence; possible existence of antecedent impotence; irreconcilable discord; contagious disease contracted or discovered after the marriage; desertion; partial proof that the marriage was invalid for want of consent. Often in impotence cases the impediment cannot be proved with certainty, but it can be proved that the marriage was not consummated and hence a dis-

248

pensation from a non-consummated marriage is sought. (Mathis/Bonner, 282)

The papal power spoken of in canon 1142 extends to the following marriages: (1) ratified non-consummated marriage (between two baptized persons); (2) non-consummated marriage between a baptized and non-baptized person; (3) a legitimate consummated marriage which becomes a ratified non-consummated marriage, i.e., the marriage is contracted between two unbaptized persons and consummated by them, then both are baptized but the marriage is not consummated again after the baptism; (4) the same as in n. 3 if only one party receives baptism and the marriage is not again consummated after baptism. (Gasparri, II, n. 1131) Non-consummated marriages between two unbaptized persons are not dissolved in virtue of canon 1142.

Non-consummated marriages can no longer be dissolved by solemn religious profession as was possible under the 1917 Code.

III. The Privilege of the Faith: Introduction

1. The *privilege of the faith* may be defined as the right to act in a way that is favorable to the acquiring or preserving of the faith. In reference to marriage the term is used to designate the Pauline privilege, the Petrine privilege, and the special cases provided for in canons 1148 and 1149.

a) *The Pauline privilege* is based on I Cor 7:12–15. It applies to the marriage of two unbaptized persons, even if consummated, when one of the spouses later is baptized.

b) *The Petrine privilege* is the dissolution of a legitimate marriage of a baptized party with an unbaptized person granted by the pope in favor of the faith.

c) *Canons 1148 and 1149* are based on missionary faculties granted by Paul III (Constitution, *Altitudo*, June 1, 1537), Pius V (Constitution, *Romani Pontificis*, Aug. 2, 1571), and Gregory XIII (Constitution, *Populis*, Jan. 25, 1585). They deal with cases of converts who had been in polygamous marriages and converts separated from their first spouse by reason of captivity or persecution.

2. *Presumption in favor of faith.* In a doubtful matter the privilege of the faith enjoys the favor of the law. (Can. 1150)

> According to this principle, doubtful matters in privilege of the faith cases are resolved in favor of the convert or baptized party to marry again. A matter is doubtful when every effort has been made to ascertain the truth but the doubt remains insoluble, i.e., certitude cannot be obtained either by evidence or by presumptions. The doubt may concern the validity of the former marriage, the identity of the first spouse, the sincerity of the answers of the party requesting the privilege, the baptism of one party, etc. N.B. If the doubt concerns the baptism of *both* parties the privilege of the faith is not given because it may be a *ratum et consummatum* marriage from which the pope does not dispense. (SCOf, response, June 10, 1937, CLD 2:343)

IV. The Pauline Privilege

A. The Privilege

A marriage of two unbaptized persons can be dissolved by the Pauline privilege in favor of the faith of the party who received baptism by the very fact that a new marriage is contracted by that party, provided the unbaptized party departs. The unbaptized party is considered to have departed if he or she does not wish to cohabit with the baptized party or to cohabit peacefully without contumely toward the Creator, unless the baptized party after baptism has given just cause for the unbaptized party's departing. (Can. 1143)

> The privilege can be used in the following cases: (a) a Catholic who wishes to marry a convert to Catholicism, who was previously non-baptized and married to another non-baptized; (b) a Catholic who wishes to marry a validly baptized non-Catholic, who was previously non-baptized and married to another non-baptized; (c) a convert to Catholicism who was formerly non-baptized and married to a non-baptized

person who now wishes to marry a baptized or non-baptized person. (Doyle, 814) In short, the Pauline privilege only applies to marriages where both parties were unbaptized, and then one of them receives baptism. If both of them receive baptism, the marriage could be handled as a non-consummation case provided there was no sexual intercourse in a human manner after the baptism of both, since that would make the marriage *ratum et consummatum*.

Two further conditions are necessary for the privilege: (a) that one of the parties is baptized before the second marriage; and (b) that the non-baptized departs. The departure of the non-baptized party is usually indicated by the civil divorce of the parties who were married as unbaptized persons. If the parties are not separated at the time of the baptism of one of them, the Pauline privilege can be used only in two circumstances: (a) if the non-baptized is the cause of the later separation; or (b) if the non-baptized, though not separating or divorcing, will not live in peace with the baptized party without contumely toward the Creator. The phrase, "without contumely toward the Creator" refers to the case of a non-baptized spouse who does not depart but makes it difficult for the baptized party to fulfill the obligations of the Christian life or to live peacefully. (Doyle, 814–15)

The privilege may not be used if the fault for the departure of the unbaptized spouse was that of the baptized spouse, *after* the latter had received baptism. *A just cause for the departure of the non-baptized* would be adultery or some other offense, provided it is not condoned by the unbaptized spouse. Adultery on the part of the convert would not be the cause of the departure if the unbaptized had also been guilty of adultery, or had condoned it, or was unaware of it so that it had no influence on the breakdown of the marriage. If there is a doubt about the cause of departure, the judgment is to be given in favor of the faith according to the presumption of canon 1150. (See SCOf, decr, Aug. 5, 1759; SCProp, instr, Jan. 16, 1797; SCOf, reply, Apr. 19, 1899.) If the party who causes the unbaptized party's departure is baptized only *after* this departure occurred, the privilege may still be used.

The dissolution of the marriage of the parties who had married as unbaptized occurs at the moment when the party now baptized marries again. Such a new marriage can be permitted only after the interpellation has been conducted by the local Ordinary according to canons 1144–1146.

B. The Interpellation

1. In order for the baptized party validly to contract a new marriage, the non-baptized party must be asked whether: (a) he or she also wishes to receive baptism; (b) he or she at least is willing to cohabit peacefully with the baptized party without contumely toward the Creator. (Can. 1144, §1)

Asking the unbaptized party these two questions is called the interpellation or interrogation. Both questions must be asked of the non-baptized party for the *validity* of the new marriage, unless the interpellation is dispensed.

The interpellation is ordinarily conducted under the authority of the local Ordinary of the converted party. The local Ordinary must grant the unbaptized party, if he or she requests it, a period of grace before responding, warning the said party, however, that if this period of grace elapses without reply, the person's silence will be considered a negative response. (Can. 1145, §1) The reason for this rule is to give the unbaptized person sufficient time to consider his or her reply without creating undue delays, whether deliberate or unintentional.

An interpellation made privately by the converted party is also valid and, if the form prescribed above cannot be observed, it is also licit. (Can. 1145, §2) It is *licit* for the party to make the interpellation on his or her own authority only when it cannot be made on the authority of the local Ordinary. In this case the party should see to it that several witnesses can testify to the answers given by the non-baptized party, or to the fact that letters have been sent to that party and a negative answer or no answer has been received. In the absence of witnesses, a letter signed by the unbaptized party or the sworn testimony of a knowledgeable witness would be sufficient proof. (See V.C., II, n. 432.)

In either case, the fact of the interpellation and its outcome must be legitimately established in the external forum. (Can. 1145, §3) Hence, there must be some external forum proof that the interpellation took place and the responses to the two questions must be stated.

2. *Dispensation from the interpellation.* The interpellation must be done after the baptism; but the local Ordinary, for a serious reason, can permit the interpellation to be conducted before the baptism; or he can even dispense from the interpellation, whether before or after baptism, provided it is established by means of at least a summary and extra-judicial process that the interpellation could not be done or would be useless. (Can. 1144, §2)

A decree of the civil divorce of the marriage originally contracted between the unbaptized parties is sufficient reason for dispensing from the interpellation, unless there is contrary evidence that the non-baptized party still desires to be married to the baptized party and would answer affirmatively to either of the questions asked in the interpellation. Other reasons for a dispensation should be established by some process, either judicial or extra-judicial, depending on the nature of the evidence.

C. The New Marriage

1. The baptized party has the right to contract a new marriage with a Catholic party: (a) if the other party has responded negatively to the questions, or if the interpellation has been legitimately omitted; (b) if the unbaptized party, whether already interpellated or not, first persevered in peaceful cohabitation without contumely toward the Creator, but afterward departed without a just cause, with due regard for canons 1144 and 1145. (Can. 1146)

Even though the baptized party may have continued the marriage after baptism, he or she does not lose the right to contract a new marriage with a Catholic party, and therefore can use this right if the unbaptized party later has a change of mind and departs without just cause or ceases to cohabit peacefully without contumely toward the Creator. Hence, the right to use the Pauline privilege lasts as long as the other party remains unbaptized.

A *negative response* would also include long delays on the part of the unbaptized party; or obstinate silence; or subterfuges to impede the serving of the interpellation, etc., if from these acts moral certitude is had that he or she does not wish to convert or at least to cohabit peacefully without contumely toward the Creator.

2. The local Ordinary, for a serious reason, can permit the baptized party using the Pauline privilege to contract a marriage with a non-Catholic or another unbaptized party, observing the canons on mixed marriages. (Can. 1147)

A serious reason for permitting the Catholic convert to remarry a non-Catholic would be evidence that this would strengthen the baptized party's faith rather than endanger it. In case of doubt, the local Ordinary may grant permission for a marriage with a baptized non-Catholic, or a dispensation from disparity of cult for a marriage with another non-baptized.

V. The Petrine Privilege

A. Dissolution of Marriage of Baptized and Unbaptized

For a just cause, the pope can dissolve any marriage that is not both ratified and consummated, provided at least one of the parties is baptized at the time the dissolution is given. Whereas the Pauline privilege is used in cases where two unbaptized persons marry and one converts, the Petrine privilege may be used in a non-sacramental marriage contracted by one baptized and one unbaptized, even if consummated.

B. Conditions for the Dissolution

1. In order that a dissolution may be validly granted, *three* conditions are *absolutely (sine quibus non)* required:
a) lack of baptism of one of the two spouses during the whole time of their married life;
b) nonuse of the marriage [no consummation] after the baptism

perchance received by the party who was not baptized;

c) that the person who is not baptized or baptized outside the Catholic Church yields freedom and ability to the Catholic party to profess his or her own religion and baptize and educate the children as Catholics: this condition must be safeguarded in the form of a promise *(cautio)*. (SCDF, instr, Dec. 6, 1973, CLD 8:1177) The person in question who is unbaptized or baptized outside the Catholic Church is the party who wishes to marry the Catholic after the dissolution of the first marriage. Such a person must promise that the Catholic will be able to practice the Catholic faith and raise the children in the faith. This promise is required to ensure that the privilege will truly be granted "in favor of the faith" of the Catholic party.

2. It is further required:

a) that there is no possibility of restoring married life because of persistent radical and irremediable discord;

b) that from the grant of the favor no danger of public scandal or serious wonderment be had;

c) that the petitioner is not the culpable cause of the breakdown of the valid, non-sacramental marriage and the Catholic party with whom the new marriage is to be contracted or convalidated did not provoke separation of the spouses by reason of fault on his or her part;

d) that the other party of the previous marriage be interpellated if possible, and does not offer reasonable opposition;

e) that the party seeking the dissolution take care that children who may have been born of the previous marriage be brought up in a religious manner;

f) that equitable provisions be made according to the laws of justice for the abandoned spouse and for the children who may have been born;

g) that the Catholic party with whom a new marriage is to be entered live in accord with his or her baptismal promises and take care of the new family;

h) that when there is question of a catechumen with whom marriage is to be contracted, moral certitude be had regarding the baptism to be received shortly, if the baptism itself cannot be waited for (which is to be encouraged). (Ibid., 1178)

These conditions are all for liceity.

3. Dissolution is more readily granted if on some other ground there is serious doubt about the validity of the marriage itself.

4. A marriage between a Catholic party and a party not baptized entered into with a dispensation from disparity of cult can also be dissolved provided that the conditions set down in nn. 2 and 3 are verified and provided it is established that the Catholic party, because of the particular circumstances of the region, especially because of the very small number of Catholics in the region, could not have avoided marriage and lead a life consonant with the Catholic religion in that marriage. Moreover, the Congregation for the Doctrine of the Faith must be instructed about the publicity of the marriage celebrated.

5. Dissolution of a valid, non-sacramental marriage entered into with a dispensation from the impediment of disparity of cult is not granted to a Catholic party who petitions to enter a new marriage with a non-baptized person who is not a convert.

6. Dissolution of a valid, non-sacramental marriage is not granted if it was contracted or convalidated after a dissolution had been obtained from a previous valid non-sacramental marriage. (Ibid., 1178–79)

Petrine privilege cases are prepared under the jurisdiction of the local Ordinary who is competent to handle marriage annulment cases. (See below, Chapter IX; see also CLD 8:1179, art. 1.)

VI. Special Cases

A. Polygamous Converts

A non-baptized man who simultaneously has several unbaptized wives, after he receives baptism in the Catholic Church, can keep one of them and dismiss the others if it is hard on him to remain with the first wife. The same is applicable to a non-baptized woman who simultaneously has several unbaptized husbands. (Can. 1148, §1)

> In these cases the marriage, after the reception of baptism, must be contracted in the legitimate form, also observing, if necessary, the norms on mixed marriage and any other requirements of the law. (Ibid., §2)

> The local Ordinary, bearing in mind the moral, social, and economic condition of the area and the persons, should see to it that adequate provision is made for the needs of the first wife and the other wives dismissed in accord with the norms of justice, Christian charity, and natural equity. (Ibid., §3)

B. Separation Due to Captivity or Persecution

A non-baptized person who, after receiving baptism in the Catholic Church, is unable to restore cohabitation by reason of captivity or persecution, may contract another marriage even if the other party has meanwhile received baptism, with due regard for canon 1141.

> Canon 1141 states that a ratified and consummated marriage cannot be dissolved by any human power or for any reason except death. Therefore, this privilege can be used only in cases where there has been no consummation of a marriage after both parties were baptized.

CHAPTER IX
Annulments and Internal Forum Solution

I. Annulments

An annulment is a declaration by a competent tribunal of the Church that what had the appearance of marriage was in fact invalid according to canon law. Annulments are granted as a result of some impediment or on various grounds related to defective consent or lack of form. The most frequent grounds for marriage nullity is defective consent, especially lack of due discretion and lack of due competence (can. 1095, 2°, 3°).

A. Who May Petition for an Annulment

Anyone, whether baptized or not, who was a party to a marriage involving at least one baptized person, whether Catholic or not, may petition a competent tribunal for an annulment. (See can. 1671.) The Church has no jurisdiction over the marriage of two unbaptized persons, although the Pauline privilege may be possible if one spouse was baptized anytime after the marriage was celebrated. The party who petitions the tribunal for an annulment is called the petitioner. The party who is asked to respond to the petition for a declaration of nullity is called the respondent or defendant. Annulment cases are handled as contentious processes, even if both parties wish to obtain the annulment.

B. The Competent Tribunal

In matrimonial cases which are not reserved to the Apostolic See, the following are competent:
1. the tribunal of the place where the marriage was celebrated;

2. the tribunal of the place where the respondent has a domicile or quasi-domicile;

3. the tribunal of the place where the petitioner has a domicile, provided that both parties live in the territory of the same episcopal conference and that the judicial vicar of the respondent's domicile, having heard the respondent, gives his consent;

4. the tribunal of the place where de facto most of the proofs are to be collected, provided the judicial vicar of the respondent's domicile gives consent and, before doing so, asks the respondent whether he or she has any objection. (Can. 1673)

> The following cases are reserved to the Apostolic See: heads of state, including governors (can. 1405, §1, 1°); non-consummation cases (can. 1698); and Petrine privileges.

> Useful resources for preparing a marriage nullity case are Lawrence G. Wrenn's volumes, *Annulments* (4th ed. rev., 1983) and *Decisions* (2nd ed. rev., 1983), both published by the Canon Law Society of America, Washington, D.C. On a popular level, see Terence E. Tierney, *Annulment: Do You Have a Case?* (N.Y.: Alba House, 1978) and Joseph P. Zwack, *Annulment: Your Chance to Remarry Within the Catholic Church* (Cambridge: Harper & Row, 1983).

II. The Internal Forum Solution

1. With regard to admission to the sacraments [of those in invalid marriages], the local Ordinaries are asked on the one hand to stress observance of current discipline and, on the other hand, to take care that pastoral ministers exercise special care to seek out those who are living in an irregular union by applying to the solution of such cases, in addition to other right means, the Church's approved practice in the internal forum. (SCDF, letter, Apr. 11, 1973; CLD 8:632)

2. The "approved practice of the Church in the internal forum" means: These couples may be allowed to receive the sacraments on two conditions, that they try to live according to the demands of Christian moral principles, and that they receive the sacraments in churches in which they are not known so that they will not create any scandal. (SCDF, letter, Mar. 21, 1975, CLD 9:504–5)

It is preferable that marriage cases be handled in the external forum by means of a process of annulment or dissolution. Under certain conditions, however, canonists and moral theologians have taught that couples living in an irregular second union can approach the sacraments by means of the internal forum solution. Since this is a very involved subject and not strictly a canonical matter, the reader is referred to several articles where a more adequate treatment is developed. See James H. Provost, "Intolerable Marriage Situations Revisited," *The Jurist* 40 (1980) 141–96; James J. Young, *Ministering to the Divorced Catholic* (N.Y.: Paulist, 1979), especially the articles by Richard A. McCormick, Karl Lehmann, and Thomas J. Green; "Report of the Canon Law Society of America's Committee on Alternatives to Tribunal Procedures," in James J. Young, ed., *Divorce Ministry and the Marriage Tribunal* (N.Y.: Paulist, 1982) 117–39; and John Huels, "The Eucharist and the Divorced and Remarried," *Emmanuel* 91 (1985) 268–75.

Blessings

Note: At the time of this writing, an American rite of blessings has not been published. The norms which follow are from the Latin typical edition of the *Roman Ritual, De benedictionibus* (1984), and from the *Code of Canon Law*.

I. Offices and Ministries

A. The Community

For blessings of greater significance, which pertain to the local church, it is fitting for the diocesan or parochial community to assemble under the presidency of the bishop or pastor. But it is efficacious for the faithful to take part also in other blessings because what is done for one group redounds in a certain way to the whole community. (See *Rite of Blessings* (RB), 16.)

B. Presbyters

Any presbyter can give blessings except for those which are reserved to the Roman Pontiff or to bishops. (Can. 1169, §2) Presbyters may preside at blessings, especially those for the community to whose service they are assigned, and therefore they may celebrate all the blessings in the *Ritual*, unless there is present a bishop, who should then preside over them. (See RB, 18, b.)

C. Deacons

A deacon can give only those blessings which are expressly permitted him by law. (Can. 1169, §3) A deacon is competent to preside at some blessings as indicated in the *Ritual*. But whenever a priest is present, the function of presiding is more fittingly relegated to him, while the deacon is to assist him by performing his proper functions in the liturgical action. (See RB, 18, c.)

A deacon can give blessings which are part of the liturgical celebration at which he presides, including marriage, baptism, Holy

Communion and Viaticum outside Mass, Morning and Evening Prayer, and non-sacramental penance services. In addition, a deacon can give the following blessings:

1. The blessing with the Holy Eucharist at benediction (can. 943);
2. The blessing of a family (RB, 42–61);
3. The annual blessing of families in their homes (RB, 68–89);
4. The blessing of spouses (RB 115–134);
5. The blessing of children (RB, 135–194);
6. The blessing of engaged couples (RB, 195–214);
7. The blessing of a woman before or after giving birth (RB, 215–257);
8. The blessing of an old person who is housebound (RB, 258–276; 283–289);
9. The blessing of sick persons (RB, 290–320);
10. The blessing of those deputed for catechesis (RB 361–372);
11. The blessing of a group gathered for catechesis or prayer (RB, 378–387);
12. The blessing of an association which provides help for public needs (RB, 388–403)
13. The blessing of pilgrims (RB, 404–430);
14. The blessing of those going on a trip (RB, 431–452);
15. The blessing of the site for a new building (RB, 456–473);
16. The blessing of a new home (RB, 474–491);
17. The blessing of a new religious house when the deacon is the superior of the house and the Ordinary cannot be there (RB, 515–537);
18. The blessing of other buildings as given in RB, 538–650;
19. The blessing of things, places, animals, harvests, and the blessing before and after meals as given in RB, 651–827;
20. The blessing of holy water outside Mass (RB, 1085–1096);
21. The blessing of objects of devotion, including rosaries, medals, and crosses as given in RB, 1137–1207;
22. The blessing of thanksgiving for favors received and the blessing for various circumstances (RB, 1225–1271).

D. Laypersons

The minister of sacramentals is a cleric who has the necessary power. Certain sacramentals, in accord with the liturgical books and in the judgment of the local Ordinary, can also be administered by laypersons who have the appropriate qualities. (Can. 1168)

In the judgment of the local Ordinary, *acolytes and lectors* can be given the faculty to give those blessings which the law allows laypersons to give. Also *other laypersons*, both men and women, whether by virtue of their proper roles (as parents for their children), or exercising an extraordinary ministry, or performing other special tasks in the Church (as do religious and catechists in some regions), can celebrate certain blessings in accord with the *Rite of Blessings*. However, when a priest or deacon is present, the task of presiding should be relinquished to him. (See RB, 18, d.)

The *Rite of Blessings* allows laypersons, in accord with the law above, to give the following blessings:

1. The blessing of a family (RB, 42–61);
2. The blessing of spouses (RB 115–134);
3. The blessing of children (RB, 135–194);
4. The blessing by one of the parents of an engaged couple (RB, 195–214);
5. The blessing of a woman before or after giving birth (RB, 215–257);
6. The blessing of an old person who is housebound (RB, 258–276; 283–289);
7. The blessing of sick persons (RB, 290–320);
8. The blessing of a group gathered for catechesis or prayer (RB, 378–387);
9. The blessing of those going on a trip (RB, 431–452);
10. The blessing of a new home (RB, 474–491);
11. The blessing of a new religious house by the superior of the house when the Ordinary cannot be there (RB, 515–537);
12. The blessing of things, places, animals, harvests, and the blessing before and after meals as given in RB, 651–827);
13. The blessing of thanksgiving for favors received and the blessing for various circumstances (RB, 1225–1271).

II. The Celebration of Blessings

A. The Principal Parts and Signs

1. The typical celebration of blessings consists of two principal parts: the first is the proclamation of God's word, and the second is

the praise of God's goodness and intercession for heavenly aid. (See RB, 20.)

2. The principal signs used in blessings are these: extending, elevating, or folding of the hands, the imposition of hands, the sign of the cross, sprinkling with blessed water, and incensation. (See RB, 26.)

> When the minister of the blessing is a priest or deacon, he extends his hands to give the blessing; when lay ministers give a blessing they fold their hands.

B.   Persons Who May Be Blessed

Blessings are to be given in the first place to Catholics and they can also be given to catechumens and, unless there is a Church prohibition, even to non-Catholics. (Can. 1170)

C.   Vestments

The presbyter and deacon, when they preside over blessings in a communitarian form, especially in the church or with some external solemnity, should wear an alb with a stole. A surplice may replace the alb when a cassock is worn. In more solemn celebrations a cope may be used. The color of the stole or cope should be white or the color of the liturgical season or feast. (See RB, 36–37.)

Properly instituted ministers, when they preside at celebrations of the community, should wear the vestments which are prescribed for liturgical celebrations by the episcopal conference or by the local Ordinary. (RB, 38)

The Liturgy of the Hours

Part IX

I. The Celebration of the Liturgy of the Hours

A. Ecclesial Nature of the Celebration

1. The Church, fulfilling Christ's priestly function, celebrates the liturgy of the hours in which, hearing God speaking to his people and remembering the mystery of salvation, it praises God without interruption in song and prayer and intercedes for the salvation of the whole world. (Can. 1173)

2. Whenever it is possible to have a celebration in common, with the people present and actively taking part, this kind of celebration is to be preferred to one that is individual and, as it were, private. It is also advantageous to sing the office in choir and in community as opportunity offers, in accordance with the nature and function of the individual parts. (See *General Instruction of the Liturgy of the Hours* (GILH), 33.)

B. Time of Celebration

1. In celebrating the liturgy of the hours, the true time of each hour is to be observed as much as possible. (Can. 1175)

> The purpose of the liturgy of the hours is to sanctify the day and the whole range of human activity. Therefore its structure has been revised in such a way as to make each hour once more correspond as nearly as possible to natural time and to take account of the circumstances of life today. (GILH, 11)

2. *The Office of Readings* may be recited at any hour of the day, even during the night hours of the previous day, after evening prayer has been said. (See GILH, 59.)

> Some religious are obliged by their proper law and others may commendably wish to retain the character of this office as a night office of praise (either by saying

it at night or very early in the morning and before
Morning Prayer). (See GILH, 58.)

3. *Night Prayer* is the last prayer of the day, said before retiring,
even if that is after midnight. (GILH, 84)

II. Those Who Celebrate the Liturgy of the Hours

A. The Laity

1. Inasmuch as it is an action of the Church, lay members of the
faithful should earnestly be invited to participate in the liturgy of the
hours in accord with the circumstances. (See can. 1174, §2.)

2. Wherever possible, groups of the faithful should celebrate the
liturgy of the hours communally in church. This especially applies to
parishes—the cells of the diocese, established under their pastors,
taking the place of the bishop. (See GILH, 21.)

3. Those in holy orders or with a special canonical mission have
the responsibility of initiating and directing the prayer of the community. . . . They must therefore see to it that the people are invited, and prepared by suitable instruction, to celebrate the principal
hours in common, especially on Sundays and holydays. (See GILH,
23.)

4. Lay groups gathering for prayer, apostolic work, or any other
reason are encouraged to fulfill the Church's duty by celebrating part
of the liturgy of the hours. . . . Finally, it is of great advantage for
the family, the domestic sanctuary of the Church, not only to pray
together to God but also to celebrate some parts of the liturgy of the
hours as occasion offers, in order to enter more deeply into the life
of the Church. (See GILH, 27.)

5. Morning Prayer and Evening Prayer are to be accorded the
highest importance as the prayer of the Christian community. Their
public or communal celebration should be encouraged, especially in
the case of those who live in community. Indeed, the recitation of
these hours should be recommended also to individual members of

the faithful unable to take part in a celebration in common. (GILH, 40)

B. Priests and Deacons

1. *Priests and deacons aspiring to the presbyterate* are bound to fulfill daily the liturgy of the hours according to the proper and approved liturgical books; *permanent deacons*, however, should fulfill the same regarding the parts specified for them by the episcopal conference. (Can. 276, §2, 3°)

2. Sacred ministers have the liturgy of the hours entrusted to them in such a particular way that even when the faithful are not present they are to pray it themselves with the adaptations necessary under these circumstances. The Church commissions them to celebrate the liturgy of the hours so as to ensure at least in their persons the regular carrying out of the duty of the whole community and the unceasing continuance of Christ's prayer in the Church. (GILH, 28, §1)

3. Even when having no obligation to communal celebration, all sacred ministers and all clerics living in a community or meeting together should arrange to say at least some part of the liturgy of the hours in common, particularly Morning Prayer and Evening Prayer. (GILH, 25)

4. Hence, bishops, priests, and deacons aspiring to the priesthood who have received from the Church the mandate to celebrate the liturgy of the hours are bound by the obligation of reciting the full sequence of hours each day.
a. They should, first and foremost, attach due importance to those hours that are, so to speak, the two hinges of the liturgy of hours, that is, *Morning Prayer and Evening Prayer*, which should not be omitted except for a serious reason.
b. They should faithfully pray the Office of Readings, which is above all a liturgical celebration of the word of God. In this way they fulfill daily a duty that is peculiarly their own, that is, of receiving the word of God into their lives, so that they may become more perfect as disciples of the Lord and experience more deeply the unfathomable riches of Christ.
c. In order to sanctify the whole day more completely, they will

273

also treasure the recitation of Daytime and Night Prayer, to round off the whole *Opus Dei* and to commend themselves to God before retiring. (GILH, 29)

d.   Outside choir, without prejudice to particular law, it is permitted to choose from the three hours the one most appropriate to the time of day, so that the tradition of prayer in the course of the day's work may be maintained. (GILH, 77) Vatican Council II decreed that these lesser hours are to be retained in choir. The liturgical practice of saying these three hours is . . . recommended also for all, especially those who take part in retreats or pastoral meetings. (GILH, 78)

> The law obliges priests and deacons to celebrate the entire liturgy of the hours every day. This is the ideal, but the law itself admits of exceptions.

> There is a serious obligation to celebrate Morning Prayer and Evening Prayer, preferably in common, but also individually when there is no communal celebration. This is a serious obligation and can be omitted only for serious reasons, e.g. illness.

> There is also an obligation to celebrate the Office of Readings. Since this does not have to be done at any particular time during the day, it should not be difficult ordinarily to fulfill this obligation. However, it can be omitted in a particular case for a reason less serious than the omission of Morning Prayer and Evening Prayer.

> The canonical obligation requires the priest or temporary deacon to recite only one of the three midday hours, depending on the time of day. It seems that these lesser hours, as well as Night Prayer, can be omitted for a reason even less serious than omitting the Office of Readings, and even on a regular basis when the reasons apply, e.g., due to the demands of the apostolate, travel, fatigue, etc.

C. Religious

1.   In accord with the prescriptions of their proper law, religious and members of societies of apostolic life should worthily celebrate the liturgy of the hours. (See cans. 663, §3; 1174, §1.)

2. Men and women religious not bound to a common celebration, as well as members of any institute of perfection, are strongly urged to gather together, by themselves or with the people, to celebrate the liturgy of the hours or part of it.

An institute of perfection was a former term for an institute of consecrated life, i.e., a religious institute or a secular institute.

3. Religious communities bound to the recitation of the liturgy of the hours and their individual members should celebrate the hours in keeping with their own particular law. Communities bound to choir should celebrate the whole sequence of the hours daily in choir; when absent from choir their members should recite the hours in keeping with their own particular law. The prescriptions in no. 29 are always to be respected. (See GILH, 31, b.)

> No. 29 is the obligation of priests and temporary deacons to celebrate the liturgy of the hours daily. Hence, a priest or temporary deacon who is a member of a religious community is bound to recite the liturgy of the hours as above even when the community does not celebrate a particular hour in common.

> The liturgical practice of saying the three daytime hours is to be retained, without prejudice to particular law, by those who live the contemplative life. (See GILH, 76.)

4. Other religious communities and their individual members are advised to celebrate some parts of the liturgy of the hours, in accordance with their own situation, for it is the prayer of the Church and makes the whole Church, scattered throughout the world, one in heart and mind. (GILH, 32)

Funeral Rites

Part X

I. Celebration of Funeral Rites

A. Prohibited Days for Funeral Mass

The funeral Mass has first place among the Masses for the dead and may be celebrated on any day except solemnities that are days of obligation, Holy Thursday, the Easter triduum, and the Sundays of Advent, Lent, and the Easter season. (GIRM, 336)

> If funeral rites take place on these excluded days, it is fitting that there be a liturgy of the word with a rite of commendation and farewell as provided in the Funeral Ritual (n. 6). Readings should be selected according to their appropriateness to the liturgical season. Whereas singing is permitted during the celebration, the distribution of Communion is not. (*Notitiae* 11 (1975) 288; trans. in *BCL Newsletter* 12 (1976) 8)

> A memorial Mass for the deceased may then be celebrated later at the convenience of the family and the rector of the church.

B. Place of Celebration

1. *The church.* Generally the funeral rites of any deceased member of the faithful must be celebrated in one's own parish church. However, each of the faithful is allowed to choose another church for the funeral with the consent of the rector of that church. One's pastor should be notified of this arrangement. One may personally choose the other church, or it may be done by the person who is in charge of the funeral arrangements. If death occurs outside one's parish and the body was not returned to it, and another church was not legitimately chosen for the funeral, the funeral rites should be celebrated in the parish church within whose boundaries the death occurred, unless particular law has specified another church. (Can. 1177)

> Ordinarily funeral rites are celebrated in one's

parish church. However, the faithful have a right to choose some other church with the consent of its rector, notifying the proper pastor. Since the canon speaks only of some other *church*, it seems that the possibility of choosing an oratory or other sacred place is not included. A dispensation from the diocesan bishop would be necessary to hold funeral rites in, e.g., the oratory of a religious house, unless legitimate custom, acquired rights, or a privilege is in force.

Ordinarily the funeral rites of religious or members of a society of apostolic life are celebrated in their own church or oratory by the superior, if the institute or society is clerical, or by the chaplain if not. (Can. 1179)

2. *The cemetery.*

a. If the parish has its own cemetery, the faithful departed are to be buried in it unless another cemetery was legitimately chosen by the deceased or by those who have charge of the burial. However, all may choose their own cemetery, unless they are prohibited by law. (Can. 1180)

Parishes and religious institutes may have their own cemetery. Also, other juridic persons or families may have a special cemetery or burial place to be blessed according to the judgment of the local Ordinary. (Can. 1241) Corpses are not to be buried in churches, unless it is a question of the Roman Pontiff or cardinals or diocesan bishops, even retired, being buried in their own church. (Can. 1242)

b. The Church is to have its own cemeteries, where possible, or at least space in the secular cemeteries destined for the faithful departed. If this cannot be done, individual graves are to be properly blessed as often as necessary. (Can. 1240)

In those situations in which a Catholic is to be interred in a non-Catholic cemetery, the priest [or deacon] after the liturgy in church, may conduct the committal service at the graveside. He should bless the individual grave and then follow the usual ritual for the burial of a Catholic. On those occasions when a non-Catholic is to be buried in a Catholic cemetery, the ordained minister of the church in which he shared belief or communion may conduct the committal service. (NCCC Guidelines, The Burial Rite, A, B, CLD 9:687.)

C. Cremation

1. The Church earnestly recommends that the pious custom of burying the bodies of the dead be observed. However, cremation is not prohibited unless it is chosen for reasons contrary to Christian doctrine. (Can. 1176, §3)

> An example of a reason for choosing cremation contrary to Christian doctrine would be the denial of the resurrection of the body.

2. The funeral is to be celebrated according to the model in use in the region. It should be carried out in a way, however, that clearly expresses the Church's preference for the custom of burying the dead, after the example of Christ's own will to be buried, and that forestalls any danger of scandalizing or shocking the faithful. The rites usually held in the cemetery chapel or at the grave may in this case take place within the confines of the crematorium and, for want of any other suitable place, even in the crematorium room. Every precaution is to be taken against the danger of scandal or religious indifferentism. (RF, 15)

> When cremation has been chosen, the various elements of the funeral rite will be conducted in the usual way, and normally, with body present, if practical. The remains of the deceased after cremation must always be treated with respect and placed in consecrated ground. (NCCC Guidelines, C, F, CLD 9:698)

> Although the rite of final commendation at the catafalque or pall is excluded, it is permitted to celebrate the funeral service, including the commendation, in those cases where it is physically or morally impossible for the body of the deceased person to be present. (*BCL Newsletter* 7 (1971) 274)

D. Offices and Ministries

1. *The faithful and priests.* In the celebration of a funeral all the members of the people of God must remember that to each one a

role and an office is entrusted: to relatives and friends, funeral directors, the Christian community as such, finally, the priest, who as the teacher of faith and the minister of comfort presides at the liturgical rites and celebrates the Eucharist. (RF, 16)

2. *Deacons and lay ministers.* Except for the Mass, a deacon may conduct all the funeral rites. As pastoral needs require, the conference of bishops, with the Apostolic See's permission, may even depute a lay person for this. (RF, 19)

> The funeral rites consist of three principal parts, called stations. These are: (a) the service in the home of the deceased person, the funeral parlor, a chapel or other place where the body of the deceased has been placed during the period before the funeral rite; (b) the Eucharistic celebration in the church; (c) the rite of burial.
>
> In the United States, in the absence of a priest or deacon, it is desirable that a lay person should lead the first and third stations. In addition, the local Ordinary may depute a lay person, in the absence of a priest or deacon, to lead the station in the church i.e., the liturgy of the word and the commendation. (*BCL Newsletter* 7 (1971) 274)

E. Adaptations in the United States

(See *BCL Newsletter* 7 (1971) 274.)

1. *Adaptations by the minister.* If an individual prayer or other text is clearly inappropriate to the circumstances of the deceased person, it is the responsibility of the priest to make the necessary adaptation.

2. *Holy water and incense.* The use of holy water may not ordinarily be omitted, but it should be explained with reference to Christian baptism. The use of incense may be omitted. Neither holy water nor incense should ordinarily be used more than once during the station in the church.

3. *Vestments.* White, violet, or black vestments may be worn at funeral services and at other offices and Masses for the Dead.

II. Those Granted and Denied Church Funerals

A. Non-Catholics who are Granted Funeral Rites

1. *Catechumens* are equated with the faithful in matters pertaining to funeral rites.

2. The local Ordinary can permit ecclesiastical funeral rites for *children who died before baptism* if their parents had intended to have them baptized.

> Unless the local Ordinary has given general permission, this permission from the local Ordinary is required for each individual case.

> The Roman Missal contains a funeral Mass for a child who died before baptism.

3. In the prudent judgment of the local Ordinary, ecclesiastical funeral rites can be granted to *baptized persons belonging to some non-Catholic church or ecclesial community*, provided they are unable to have their own minister. This cannot be done if it is against their wishes. (Can. 1183)

> The judgment of the local Ordinary must be made on a case by case basis. However, he could give general delegation to pastors to make this judgment.

> The inability to have the proper non-Catholic minister may result from moral as well as physical unavailability. Physical unavailability would be, e.g., when there is no minister of the non-Catholic deceased in the area. Moral unavailability would be, e.g., when there is a minister of the non-Catholic deceased in the area, but the non-Catholic has not practiced his or her faith, and the practicing Catholic spouse or other next of kin would like to have the funeral in the Catholic Church.

> If a non-Catholic had been practicing his or her religion during life, it should be presumed that that individual would have wanted to have the funeral in his or her own church, and therefore it would be contrary to the wishes of the departed to have it in the Catholic church. To presume otherwise would be ecumenically insensitive.

N.B. This permission cannot be granted to those who were unbaptized or baptized invalidly.

B. Catholics who are Denied Funeral Rites

1. Unless before death there was some indication of repentance, ecclesiastical funeral rites are denied to:

a) Notorious apostates, heretics, and schismatics.

This restriction applies only to those who had been baptized Catholic or had been received into full communion with the Catholic Church.

Heresy is the obstinate post-baptismal denial of some truth which must be believed by divine and Catholic faith, or the obstinate doubt about the same; apostasy is the total repudiation of the Christian faith; schism is the refusal of subjection to the Supreme Pontiff or of communion with the members of the Church subject to him. (Can. 751)

Unlike the former Code (can. 2197), the revised Code makes no distinction between a crime that is notorious in law or notorious in fact. Hence, notoriety should be understood in the normal sense of the word, namely, anything that is "publicly known."

One who commits the crimes of apostasy, heresy, or schism automatically incurs the penalty of excommunication. To deny funeral rites, it is not necessary that such persons be *declared* excommunicate, but only that their crime be notorious, i.e., publicly known. (For a different opinion of what constitutes notoriety, see R. Thomas, CLSA Comm., 839.)

Since it is often difficult in practice to determine who is a notorious apostate, heretic, or schismatic, some doubt will usually arise. Thus it is prudent in all such cases to consult the local Ordinary.

b) Those who have chosen cremation of their bodies for reasons contrary to the Christian faith.

The faithful who choose cremation are presumed to have the proper motives and good intentions, unless

284

the contrary is clear. When a doubt persists as to the proper motivations of the person who has chosen cremation, the matter should be referred to the local Ordinary. (Cf. NCCC Guidelines, Cremation, G–J, CLD 9:698.)

c) Other manifest sinners for whom ecclesiastical funeral rites cannot be conducted without public scandal to the faithful. (Can. 1184, §1)

A manifest sin is one for which there are eyewitnesses who can give testimony about it. (R. Thomas, CLSA Comm., 840) Excluded from funeral rites are only those who are both manifest sinners and whose funeral will cause public scandal, such as gangsters who have given no signs of repentance. A sign of repentance would include summoning a priest at the time of death, entering a confessional shortly before death, making an act of perfect contrition, or making some other evident attempt to be reconciled with God and the Church.

Also included as public sinners are those under an imposed or declared penalty of excommunication or interdict, but even such manifest sinners are not to be deprived of funeral rites unless there is public scandal to the faithful.

Ordinarily, those who are divorced and remarried may have a church funeral. (See SCDF, letter, May 29, 1973, CLD 8:962–63.) Indeed, in many localities it would be a greater scandal to the faithful if a deceased divorced and remarried person were to be denied ecclesiastical funeral rites.

Persons committing suicide should not as a rule be deprived of full burial rites in the Church. (NCCC Guidelines, CLD 9:694)

The continued neglect of Mass and sacraments, even though the neglect of the delinquent Catholic is generally known, is not sufficient cause for the denial of funeral rites. (Ibid., B)

2. If any doubt occurs in this matter, one should consult the local Ordinary whose decision is to be followed. (Can. 1184, §2)

Because Christian burial is not to lead the faithful away from the Church, but to draw them closer to God, the priest confronted with a case of denial of Church burial should lean to leniency and mercy. (NCCC Guidelines, CLD 9:694)

3. Any funeral Mass whatsoever is also to be denied to someone who is excluded from ecclesiastical funeral rites. (Can. 1185)

Not excluded is a priest offering Mass for the intention of such a person, provided the Mass is not a funeral Mass, even a funeral Mass without the body present. (See can. 901.)

III. Special Questions

(The following norms are from the NCCC Guidelines, CLD 9:700–702.)

A. Burial of Stillborns and Fetuses

The Church urges that stillborns and fetuses of Catholic parents be interred in a Catholic cemetery, or another cemetery of the parents' choosing. [See cans. 1180 and 1183, §2.] The decision and procedure for the internment will be left to the parents and their pastor.

B. Disposal of Amputated Limbs

It is recommended that amputated limbs be buried in a blessed place. However, hospital personnel may dispose of portions of bodies in a manner they deem most suitable and hygienic. Cremation is not excluded but the preference of the person and his family are not to be disregarded.

C. Organ Transplants and Donations of Bodies for Medical Science

Because of the achievements of science and medicine, particularly in the matter of organ transplants, occasionally requests are made to donate organs or to donate one's body to science. Such requests are legitimate and not contrary to Christian principles. However, in keeping with Christian respect for the body, when it is possible and practicable, there should be reasonable assurance that the remains be disposed of in a proper, reverent, and dignified manner upon completion of the scientific research. In these donations, when the body is not embalmed, a wake or a Funeral Mass is usually impossible. The family should be urged to schedule the celebration of a Memorial Mass as soon after death as is practical. The Mass texts would be those of the Funeral Mass.

D. Removal of a Body

While internment is *per se* permanent, removal of a body from its place of burial may at times become necessary or appropriate. Other than legal necessities such as the exercise of eminent domain, examples would be where scattered family members may wish to be joined together in a common lot, where preferred burial facilities not previously available become available (including the establishment of a Catholic cemetery where none existed), and where relocation of a family may suggest the possibility of removal. For whatever reason, in addition to obtaining the required permission of the civil authorities, the permission of the Chancery Office or Cemetery Office must be obtained to disinter a body from a Catholic cemetery.

If the funeral rites at the gravesight were observed in the first burial, none are prescribed in the second. However, they may be held, especially if the body is being returned to the deceased's domicile as, e.g., in the case of someone killed in the military and buried in a foreign country. (See SCConc, Jan. 12, 1924.)

Sacred Times

Part XI

I. Feast Days

A. Sundays and Holy Days

Feast days are all Sundays and holy days of obligation. In the United States, besides Sundays, also the following feasts are celebrated as days of obligation: Christmas (Dec. 25), Ascension (Thursday of the sixth week of Easter), Mary Mother of God (Jan. 1), the Immaculate Conception (Dec. 8), the Assumption (Aug. 15), All Saints (Nov. 1). (See *BCL Newsletter* 20 (1984) 9.)

B. Feast Day Obligations

On Sundays and holy days of obligation the faithful are bound to participate in the Mass. (See can. 1247.)

1. The precept of participating in the Mass is satisfied by one who assists at Mass wherever it is celebrated in a Catholic rite either on the feast day itself or on the evening of the preceding day. (Can. 1248, §1)

> Participating at Mass minimally means one's physical presence at Mass. In the United States, custom dictates that anticipated evening Masses not begin before 4:00 p.m. on the day preceding the obligation. It is unlikely that the precept is fulfilled at a Mass earlier than this time, as the law clearly states that it be an evening Mass.

2. If an ordained minister is lacking or for some other serious reason it is impossible to participate in the Eucharistic celebration, it is highly recommended that the faithful take part in a liturgy of the Word, if it is celebrated in a parish church or some other sacred place in accord with the norms of the diocesan bishop, or by praying for a suitable time either personally, as a family or, as the occasion may offer, in groups of families. (Can. 1248, §2)

3. On Sundays and holy days the faithful also should abstain from those works and business concerns which impede the worship to be rendered to God, the joy proper to the Lord's day, or the fitting relaxation of mind and body. (See can. 1247.)

According to moral theologian Bernard Haring, the aspect of disturbance of divine worship and conflict with it is particularly significant and decisive. Work which interferes with the performance of one's religious duties would more easily fall under the ban than work which can be performed without making any inroad on time to be spent worshiping God. Thus, some lighter manual work may at times be permitted; e.g., a laborer who has worked elsewhere all week may cultivate his little garden on Sunday. In any case, the customs of one's region must be taken into consideration, and scandal must be avoided. The Church approves of local custom and the informed conscience of its members as an acceptable form of interpretation of the law, which is itself only a means to guard and guide Catholics in their essential relation to divine worship. Therefore, the explanation and interpretation of the law prohibiting work which impedes divine worship must be free from every species of rigorism. There can be no comprehensive solution for all cases that will be valid everywhere under every condition; an equitable, common-sense approach is necessary to avoid anxiety of conscience and confusion concerning the very meaning of the law itself. (See Haring, II, pp. 335–36; Matthis/Bonner, p. 338.)

II. Days of Penance

A. Fast and Abstinence

1. *Fast.* The law of fast prescribes that only one full meal a day be taken; but it does not forbid taking some nourishment in the morning and evening, observing, however, as to the quantity and quality, the approved customs of the place. (Paul VI, apconst, *Paenitemini*, Feb. 17, 1966, n. III, CLD 6:676–78)

Although the law does not expressly contain any reference to the eating of one's full meal in the evening, it seems that the time of the full meal and the evening collation may be interchanged without any special reason. An interchange between the evening collation and the breakfast snack, or between the breakfast snack and the main meal, may be permitted for a reasonable cause, since the essence of the fast consists in this—that only one full meal be taken in a day. The time of that full meal is not of the essence of the law.

On days of fast and abstinence, eggs and milk products may everywhere be eaten, both in the morning and in the evening, i.e., both at breakfast and at the collation. (SCConc, Jan. 28, 1949) In the United States, local usage indicates that the two smaller meals should be sufficient to maintain strength according to each one's needs, but together they should not equal another full meal. Eating between meals is not permitted, but liquids, including milk and fruit juices, are allowed. Only ordinary or homogenized milk should be taken between meals. Such combinations as malted milks, milk shakes and the like are not included in the term "milk." On the other hand, combinations based on skim milk and a coloring or special flavoring, such as "chocolate milk," are considered a drink rather than a food and are allowed. (See Report of Episcopal Committee, Nov. 14, 1951; Mathis/Bonner, 340–341.)

2. *Abstinence.* The law of abstinence forbids the eating of meat, but not eggs, milk products, nor condiments of any kind, even though made from animal fat. (*Paenitemini*, III, §1)

Forbidden are the flesh meat of warm-blooded animals and all parts of such animals, e.g., marrow, bones, brains, sweet-breads, liver, kidneys, etc. This does not include meat juices and liquid foods made from meat.

Permitted, therefore, are such foods as chicken and beef broth, consomme, or, in general, any kind of soup cooked or flavored with meat, meat gravies and sauces. Moreover, seasonings or condiments derived from the fat of warm-blooded animals are allowable; thus it is allowed on a day of abstinence to make use of oleomargarine, lard, and like substances. Even bacon fryings which contain little bits of meat can be poured over lettuce as a seasoning. Also allowed are fish and all cold-blooded animals, e.g., frogs and all shell-fish such as clams, turtles, oysters, crabs, lobsters, etc. Permitted also are eggs, milk and milk products such as butter and various kinds of cheese. Nor is there any prohibition attached to the eating of foods which have some nutritive value derived from meat, but which have lost the flavor of meat, e.g., cream of mushroom soup which contains beef extract, and gelatin desserts like "Jello" which are made from meat. No one considers these things as meat; indeed they have long been permitted by established custom. In doubt whether a given food is to be considered meat, one need only look to the *common estimation* of persons in the locality. (Mathis/Bonner, 340)

B. Days of Fast and Abstinence

1. *Prescribed days.* In the United States, Catholics who are obliged to *abstain* from eating meat must do so on Ash Wednesday and on all Fridays during the season of Lent. Those obliged to *fast* must do so on Ash Wednesday and Good Friday. (NCCB, pastoral statement, Nov. 18, 1966, CLD 6:679–84) The *substantial* observance of the laws of fast and abstinence is a serious obligation. (*Paenitemini*, II, §1)

> The substantial observance of the laws of fast and abstinence does not pertain to individual days, but to the whole complexus of penitential days, i.e., one only sins gravely who, without an excusing cause, omits a notable part, quantitative or qualitative, of the penitential observance which is prescribed as a whole. (See SCConc, reply, Feb. 24, 1967, CLD 6:684–85.)

> Therefore, the individual violations of the laws of fast and abstinence are not to be regarded as seriously sinful. Rather, it is the *substantial* disregard of them that constitutes grave matter, i.e., the repeated and habitual violation of the obligation of penance enjoined by these norms. In general, the more sincerely and seriously one tries to practice penance on the days and in the manner determined by the Church, the less reason is there to conclude that any departure from

these norms is seriously sinful. Where a proportionately serious reason exists, there is surely no sin in departing from them. Thus, one may very well be excused by sickness or any infirmity which requires that one eat meat even on Friday during Lent, by the need to take one's meals in common, by travel when it is not possible to obtain readily permissible foods, by great poverty, etc. (See G. Bertrams, "Il valore spirituale della penitenza christiana nella Costituzione Apostolica 'Paenitemini,' " *L'Osservatore Romano*, Feb. 20. 1966, p. 1; Mathis/Bonner, 342.)

2. *Recommended days.*

a. Self-imposed observance of fasting on all weekdays of Lent is strongly recommended.
b. Abstinence from flesh meat on all Fridays of the year is especially recommended to individuals and to the Catholic community as a whole. (NCCB pastoral statement, Nov. 18, 1966) Also recommended is prayer, penance (especially by eating less food), and almsgiving on all Fridays of the year for the sake of world peace. (NCCB, *The Challenge of Peace: God's Promise and Our Response*, May 3, 1983, n. 298)

> "Prayer by itself is incomplete without penance. Penance directs us toward our goal of putting on the attitudes of Jesus himself. Because we are all capable of violence, we are never totally conformed to Christ and are always in need of conversion. The twentieth century alone provides adequate evidence of our violence as individuals and as a nation. Thus, there is continual need for acts of penance and conversion. The worship of the Church, particularly through the sacrament of reconciliation and communal penance services, offers us multiple ways to make reparation for the violence in our own lives and in our world." (Ibid., n. 297)

> The bishops are also concerned to maintain the salutary penitential character of the Lenten season. Besides the recommended fasting, they also strongly urge the traditional Lenten devotions, the practice adopted by many of going to daily Mass during Lent, the sharing of resources, time, and energy to relieve the needs of the poor, the sick, the underprivileged.

Concerning the recommendation to preserve the custom of abstaining on Friday, besides the reason of world peace, there is also the reason of self-denial in remembrance of the passion of the Lord as well as a sense of solidarity with our forebears in the faith: "we shall thus freely and out of love for Christ crucified show our solidarity with the generations of believers to whom this practice frequently became, especially in times of persecution and of great poverty, no mean evidence of fidelity to Christ and His Church." It is also a continuous reminder of our need of repentance and conversion: "we shall thus also remind ourselves that as Christians, although immersed in the world and sharing its life we must preserve a saving and necessary difference from the spirit of the world. Our deliberate abstinence from meat, more especially because no longer required by law, will be an outward sign of the spiritual values that we cherish." (NCCB Pastoral Statement, CLD 6:682–84)

C. Those Bound to Fast and Abstain

1. All those who have completed their fourteenth year are bound to the law of abstinence.

2. All those from eighteen years of age to the beginning of their sixtieth year are bound by the law of fast. (See can. 1252.)

Persons are not bound on their fourteenth or eighteenth birthday respectively, but begin to abstain or fast on the next day. Persons are still bound to fast on their fifty-ninth birthday; the obligation ceases at midnight between their birthday and the next day.

3. Pastoral ministers and parents are to see to it that even those who by reason of minor age are not bound to the law of fast and abstinence nevertheless develop a genuine sense of penance. (See can. 1252.)

III. Dispensations and Commutations

A. Pastors

The pastor, for a just cause and in accord with the norms of the diocesan bishop, in individual cases can grant a dispensation from the obligation of observing a feast day or a day of penance, or he can commute them to other pious works. (See can. 1245.)

The pastor cannot grant a general dispensation for the whole parish. He may, however, by one and the same act, dispense several individuals or several families to whom the same reason for dispensation is applicable, e.g., a number of families taking part in a wedding celebration, as well as the various individuals invited to the celebration. He may dispense his own parishioners anywhere as well as others in his territory.

Since this faculty of the pastor is ordinary power, it may be delegated to others, even habitually. Parochial vicars, deacons, and confessors have no power to dispense from the observance of feast days and days of penance unless it is delegated to them by others. The diocesan *pagella* may grant such a faculty.

Latin rite pastors and Ordinaries may grant dispensations to individuals and families subject to them from Oriental rite regulations concerning feasts and fasts.

B. Superiors

The superior of a religious institute or a society of apostolic life, if they are clerical institutes or societies and of pontifical right, for a just cause and in accord with the norms of the diocesan bishop, in individual cases, and on behalf of his own subjects and others staying day and night in the house, can grant a dispensation from the observance of a feast day or day of penance or he can commute them to other pious works. (See can. 1245.)

Superiors can grant a dispensation or commutation of the obligation of feast days and days of penance to individual members or groups of those subject to them. Since this faculty of superiors is placed on a par with that of pastors, it seems that the local superior, *per se*, cannot use it to dispense his entire community as such, nor a provincial superior his entire province. However, by one and the same act, a local superior may dispense several individual members to whom the same reason for the dispensation applies, e.g., celebration of a community feast day, even though in fact the dispensation is granted to every single member of the community. The same applies to a provincial superior who, for a reason applicable to each of them, dispenses every individual community in the entire province. The dispensing power of superiors is ordinary power of governance, and can be delegated to others, even habitually.

It seems that lay brothers who are superiors in clerical institutes of pontifical right also have this faculty. (See can. 129, §2.)

Besides members, those who stay day and night in the house include servants, pupils, guests or patients who stay overnight.

Ecumenism and the Liturgy

Part XII

I. Baptism and Confirmation

A. Doubts Regarding Validity

1. *Eastern non-Catholics.* There can be no doubt cast upon the validity of baptism as conferred among separated Eastern Christians. It suffices, therefore, to establish the fact that baptism was administered. Since in the Eastern churches the sacrament of confirmation is always lawfully administered by the priest at the same time as baptism, it often happens that no mention is made of the confirmation in the canonical testimony of baptism. This does not give grounds for doubting that the sacrament was conferred. (*Ecumenical Directory*, Part I, (ED), 12)

2. *Other Christians.*

a. If there is a doubt whether someone was baptized, or whether the baptism was conferred validly, and this doubt remains after a serious investigation, then baptism should be administered conditionally.

b. Those baptized in a non-Catholic ecclesial community are not to be baptized conditionally unless there is a serious reason for doubting the validity of the baptism after examining the matter and the form of the words used in the baptism as well as the intention of the adult being baptized and of the baptizing minister. (Can. 869, §§1–2)

c. *Concerning matter and form.* Baptism by immersion, pouring, or sprinkling, together with the Trinitarian formula, is of itself valid, though consideration should be given to the danger of invalidity when the sacrament is administered by sprinkling, especially of several people at once. Hence, if rituals, liturgical books, or customs of a church or community prescribe one of these ways of baptizing, doubt can arise only if it happens that the minister does not observe the regulations of his own church or community. What is necessary and sufficient, therefore, is evidence that the minister of baptism was faithful to these norms. For this purpose, one should generally

301

obtain a written baptismal certificate with the name of the minister. In many cases, the other community may be asked to cooperate in establishing whether or not, in general or in a particular case, a minister is to be considered as having baptized according to the approved ritual. (ED, 13, a)

d. *Concerning faith and intention.* Insufficient faith on the part of the minister never, of itself, makes baptism invalid. Sufficient intention in the baptizing minister is to be presumed, unless there is serious ground for doubting that he intends to do what Christians do. (ED, 13, b)

e. *Concerning the application of the matter.* When doubt arises in this area, both reverence for the sacrament and respect for the ecclesial nature of other communities demand that a serious investigation of the practice of the separated community and the circumstances of a particular baptism be made before any judgment is passed on the validity of a baptism by reason of its manner of administration. (ED, 13, c)

f. Indiscriminate conditional baptism of all who desire full communion with the Catholic Church cannot be approved. Conditional rebaptism is not allowed unless there is prudent doubt of the fact or invalidity of a baptism already administered. (ED, 14)

> Since baptism cannot be repeated, conditional baptism or rebaptism should be done only after a thorough investigation has taken place, the results of which demonstrate that the baptism did not take place or was not conferred validly. If water and the Trinitarian formula was used, one can presume that the intention of the minister was to do what the Church does when it baptizes, unless there are contrary indications. A baptismal certificate is sufficient proof of baptism in ordinary circumstances.

> The following are some non-Catholic churches which have valid baptism: all Eastern non-Catholics (Orthodox), Adventists, African Methodist Episcopal, Amish, Anglican, Assembly of God, Baptists, Evangelical United Brethren, Church of the Brethren, Church of God, Congregational Church, Disciples of Christ, Episcopalians, Evangelical Churches, Lutherans, Methodists, Liberal Catholic Church, Old Catholics, Old Roman Catholics, Church of the Nazzerine, Polish

National Church, Presbyterian Church, Reformed Churches, United Church of Christ, Church of the Latter Day Saints (Mormons).

Some churches without valid baptism are: Apostolic Church, Bohemian Free Thinkers, Christian and Missionary Alliance, Christian Scientists, Church of Divine Science, Masons (no baptism at all), Peoples Church of Chicago, Quakers, Salvation Army, Pentecostal Churches, Christadelphians, Jehovah's Witnesses, and Unitarians.

In the absence of a baptismal certificate, proof of baptism can be had as described above, p. 53.

g. In cases 1 and 2 above, if doubt remains whether the baptism was conferred or whether it was valid, baptism should not be administered until after the one being baptized, if he or she is an adult, has received instruction on the doctrine of the sacrament of baptism. Also the reasons for doubting the validity of the previous baptism should be explained to the person or, in the case of infant baptism, to the parents. (Can. 869, §3)

h. The local Ordinary shall determine, in individual cases, what rites are to be included or excluded in conditional baptism. (RCIA, appendix, n. 7. See also can. 845, §2.) The formula for conditional baptism is: If you are not baptized, I baptize you in the name of the Father, and of the Son, and of the Holy Spirit.

i. *Confirmation.* Those baptized in ecclesial communities which do not have valid orders and apostolic succession should be confirmed when they are being received into full communion with the Catholic Church. (See can. 883, 2° and RCIA, appendix, *Rite of Receiving Baptized Christians into the Full Communion of the Catholic Church*, n. 8.)

Note: The reception of a baptized Christian into full communion is treated in Part III above on confirmation, chapter IV.

B. Godparents and Witnesses

1. *Eastern non-Catholics.* Because of the close communion between the Catholic Church and the separated Eastern churches, it is permissible for a just cause that a member of a separated Eastern church act as godparent together with a Catholic godparent, at the

baptism of a Catholic infant or adult, so long as there is provision for the Catholic education of the person being baptized, and it is clear that the godparent is a suitable one. A Catholic is not forbidden to stand as godparent in a separated Eastern church if he or she is invited. In this case the duty of providing for the Christian education of the baptized person binds in the first place the godparent who belongs to the church in which the child is baptized. (ED, 48)

2. *Other Christians.* A baptized person who belongs to a non-Catholic ecclesial community may be admitted only as a witness to baptism together with a Catholic godparent. (Can. 874, §2) It is not permissible for a member of a separated community to act as godparent in the liturgical and canonical sense at baptism or confirmation. Nor may a Catholic be permitted to fulfill this function for a member of a separated community. However, because of ties of blood or friendship, a Christian of another communion, since he or she has faith in Christ, can be admitted with a Catholic godparent as a Christian witness of the baptism. In comparable circumstances, a Catholic can do the same for a member of a separated community.

> The reason for these rules is that the godparents are not merely assuming responsibility for the Christian education of the person receiving baptism or confirmation; they are also representatives of the community of faith, standing as sponsor for the faith of the candidate. When a person is admitted as Christian witness of baptism in another communion, the responsibility for the Christian education of the candidate belongs to the godparent who is a member of the church in which the candidate is baptized. Pastors should carefully explain to the faithful the evangelical and ecumenical reasons for this regulation, so that all misunderstanding of it may be prevented. (See ED, 57.)

II. Eucharist, Penance, Anointing of the Sick

A. Reception from non-Catholic Ministers

1. As often as need requires it or true spiritual advantage recommends it, and provided that the danger of error or indifferentism is avoided, the faithful for whom it is physically or morally impossible

to go to a Catholic minister may receive the sacraments of penance, Eucharist, and anointing of the sick from non-Catholic ministers in those churches in which these sacraments are valid. (Can. 844, §2)

The general rule is that the Catholic faithful receive the sacraments from Catholic ministers. (See can. 844, §1.) The above law is an exception to the rule by which Catholics may receive the three sacraments mentioned under certain conditions.

The principal condition is that these sacraments can be received only from ministers in whose churches these sacraments are valid. These are the "churches which have preserved the substance of the Eucharistic teaching, the sacrament of orders, and apostolic succession." (See SPCU, communication, Oct. 17, 1973, CLD 8:471, n. 9.) This would include all Orthodox churches, the Polish National Church, Old Catholics, Old Roman Catholics.

A second condition is physical or moral impossibility of approaching a Catholic minister. Cases of physical impossibility would include any situations in which a person is unable to approach a Catholic minister, as, e.g., when one is attending services at an Orthodox church. Moral impossibility means that a person is physically able to approach a Catholic minister, but cannot do so for some reason, e.g., in a country where the Catholic Church is persecuted or held in disfavor; a divorced and remarried person using the internal forum solution who wishes to avoid scandal in the Catholic community when there is only one Catholic church in the area; one who has a psychological aversion of some kind to the Catholic minister or church; etc.

Another requirement is that of need or spiritual advantage. This can be interpreted broadly in keeping with the canonical axiom, "favors are to be multiplied, burdens are to be restricted."

Finally, it is required that error and indifferentism be avoided. This refers to the erroneous and indifferent attitude that holds that there is no real difference between the churches and it does not matter to which church one belongs.

2. It is particularly opportune that Catholic authorities not extend permission to share in the sacraments of separated Eastern Christians until satisfactory consultations with the Eastern authorities have been completed, at least on the local level. Serious attention should be given to reciprocity in this matter. Moreover, since practice differs between Catholics and separated Eastern Christians in the matter of frequency of Communion and the Eucharistic fast, care must be taken to avoid wonderment and suspicion among the separated brethren caused by Catholics not following the Eastern usage. A Catholic who legitimately receives Communion with separated Eastern Christians should observe their discipline insofar as possible. (ED, 42–43, 45)

> Although a Catholic may have met all the requirements of canon law to receive the Eucharist, penance, or anointing from an Eastern non-Catholic minister (or his equivalent), the non-Catholic church may not admit of such reception. In the absence of local guidelines, permission from the non-Catholic minister should be obtained as an ecumenical courtesy before approaching the sacrament.

B. Reception by Non-Catholics

1. *Eastern non-Catholic and equivalent churches.* Catholic ministers may licitly administer the sacraments of penance, Eucharist, and anointing of the sick to members of the Eastern churches which do not have full communion with the Catholic Church, if these persons spontaneously ask for the sacrament and are properly disposed. This also applies to members of other churches which, in the judgment of the Apostolic See, are in a condition equal to the Eastern churches in reference to the sacraments. (Can. 844, §3)

> This norm refers to a Catholic minister giving any of the three specified sacraments to a member of an Eastern non-Catholic church or some other equivalent church as exemplified in the commentary under A, 1 above. Although the *Decree on Ecumenism* from Vatican II singled out the Anglican communion as having "a special place among those communions in which Catholic traditions and institutions in part continue to exist," there has not yet been a formal judgment published by the Apostolic See concerning the Anglican

communion or other communions as a church or churches "in a condition equal to the Eastern churches." (See UR, 13; McManus, 610.) However, if the church in question has preserved the substance of Eucharistic teaching, the sacrament of orders, and apostolic succession, it would be comparable to the Eastern churches and therefore its members would be eligible to receive the three specified sacraments in accord with the requirements of this law.

The requirement that the non-Catholic person in question "spontaneously ask" for the sacrament means that the person requests it on his or her own initiative and not at the instigation of the minister. The minister ordinarily can presume the person has the proper disposition unless there is reason to doubt it as, e.g., when the person wishes to receive Communion and does not practice his or her own faith.

2. *Other non-Catholic churches.* If there is danger of death or, in the judgment of the diocesan bishop or the episcopal conference, there is some other serious need, Catholic ministers also licitly administer these same sacraments to other Christians who are not in full communion with the Catholic Church. This may be done when they are unable to go to a minister of their own community and they spontaneously ask for the sacrament, and provided they manifest Catholic faith concerning these sacraments and are properly disposed. (Can. 844, §4)

This law provides for Christians other than the Eastern non-Catholics and those who are in a condition equal to them. They must always be validly baptized Christians, because no one who is unbaptized can validly receive any other sacraments.

For a person belonging to such an ecclesial communion to receive any of the three specified sacraments from a Catholic minister, there must be a danger of death or other serious need. The *Ecumenical Directory*, n. 55, gives two examples of serious need—during persecution and in prisons. A June 1, 1972 instruction of the Secretariate for Promoting Christian Unity mentioned another case of serious need, that of non-Catholic Christians who live in an area where they are unable to have access to their own ecclesial community. (See CLD 7:590, n. 6.) In other cases the judgment concerning what constitutes serious need is made by the episcopal conference or the diocesan bishop.

Most of the other requirements of this law have been discussed above with the exception of the requirement that the non-Catholic person in question manifest Catholic faith concerning these sacraments. It is not necessary that the person have a detailed knowledge of the sacramental theology of the sacrament in question. For example, in reference to the reception of the Eucharist, it would suffice that the person believes the consecrated bread and wine is spiritual food, the body and blood of the Lord. (See cans. 899, §1 and 913, §2.) For the anointing of the sick, it would be sufficient that he or she believe that the sacrament is a spiritual means of promoting healing and comfort and, if necessary, the forgiveness of sins. (See RA, 6, 7, and 12.) For penance it would be sufficient that the person believes that the priest is able to absolve from sins and this brings reconciliation with God and the Church. (See can. 959.)

A note of caution should be added about an October 17, 1973 communication of the SPCU regarding the Eucharist: "In order that other Christians may be admitted to the Eucharist in the Catholic Church, . . . they must manifest a faith in conformity with that of the Catholic Church concerning this sacrament. This faith is not limited only to an affirmation of the "real presence" in the Eucharist but virtually includes the doctrine of the Eucharist as taught by the Catholic Church." (See n. 7, CLD 8:471.) This should not be interpreted to mean that the non-Catholic persons in question need precise "knowledge" of Catholic doctrine. It suffices for them to answer in the affirmative to the question, "Do you believe that what the Catholic Church teaches about the Eucharist is true?" The issue is not how much knowledge the persons have, but whether their *faith* is in conformity to that of the Catholic Church's.

C. Prohibition Against Interdenominational Concelebration

Catholic priests are prohibited from concelebrating the Eucharist together with priests or ministers of churches or ecclesial communities that do not have full communion with the Catholic Church. (Can. 908)

D. Celebrating the Eucharist in a Non-Catholic Church

For a just cause, with the express permission of the local Ordinary, and with scandal avoided, a priest may celebrate the Eucharist in the place of worship of another Church or ecclesial community that does not have full communion with the Catholic Church. (Can. 933)

> Examples of a just cause include pastoral advantage and ecumenical good will.

> Since the canon requires permission of the local Ordinary to celebrate the Eucharist in non-Catholic *Christian* churches only, no permission is needed to celebrate in an interdenominational chapel or a non-Christian church if there is a particular case of need. (See can. 923, §1.)

E. Participation in Eucharistic Liturgies

1. *Participation in Eastern Non-Catholic Liturgy.*

a. A Catholic who, for lawful reasons, attends the Holy Liturgy (Mass) on a day of obligation in a separated Eastern church is not then bound by the precept to assist at Mass in a Catholic church. It is likewise a good thing for Catholics who, on such days, for just reasons cannot attend the Holy Liturgy in their own church, to attend the Liturgy of their separated Eastern brothers and sisters. (ED, 47)

b. Catholics may attend liturgical services of separated Easterners if there is a just reason, e.g., a reason arising out of public office or function, blood relationship, friendship, desire to be better informed, etc. In such cases, they may take part in the common responses, hymns, and actions of the church whose guests they are. Reception of Holy Communion is governed by what is said above under A. Local Ordinaries can give permission for Catholics to read lessons at a liturgical service if they are invited to do so. These same principles govern the manner in which a separated Eastern Christian may assist at services in Catholic churches. (See ED, 50.)

2. *Other Christians.*

a. Catholics may be allowed to attend occasionally the liturgical services of separated Christians if they have reasonable grounds for so doing, e.g., for reasons of public office or function, blood relationship or friendship, desire to be better informed, an ecumenical gathering, etc. In these cases Catholics may take part in the common responses, hymns, and actions of the community of which they are guests, so long as they are not at variance with Catholic faith. The same principles govern the manner in which separated Christians may assist at services in Catholic churches. This participation, from which reception of the Eucharist is always excluded [except as provided for above by canon 844, §2], should lead the participants to esteem the spiritual riches we have in common, and at the same time make them more aware of the gravity of our separations. (See ED, 59.)

b. A separated brother is not to act as a Scripture reader or to preach during the Eucharistic celebration in a Catholic church. The same holds for a Catholic at the celebration of the Lord's Supper in a Protestant church, or at the principal liturgical service of the Word held by separated Christians.

> This restriction does not apply to other services of
> the Word and other liturgical celebrations.

III. Marriage

For the treatment on mixed marriages, the reader should consult the appropriate sections of Part VII above, especially in Chapter II, on the preparation for marriage; Chapter III, under the impediment of disparity of cult; Chapter V, under dispensations from the form in mixed marriages; Chapter VI, under the sections on the rite of marriage outside Mass, the rite of marriage of a Catholic and an unbaptized, and the place of marriage; and Chapter VIII on the dissolution of the bond.

IV. Other Acts of Divine Worship

A. Blessings

Blessings can be given to Catholics in the first place and also to catechumens, and even to non-Catholics unless a prohibition of the Church prevents this. (Can. 1170; see also RB, 31.)

B. Funeral Rites

1. *Non-Catholics who are Granted Funeral Rites*

a. *Catechumens* are equated with the faithful in matters pertaining to funeral rites.

b. The local Ordinary can permit ecclesiastical funeral rites for *children who died before baptism* if their parents had intended to have them baptized.

> Unless the local Ordinary has given general permission, this permission from the local Ordinary is required for each individual case.

> The *Roman Missal* contains a funeral Mass for a child who dies before baptism.

c. In the prudent judgment of the local Ordinary, ecclesiastical funeral rites can be granted to *baptized persons to some non-Catholic church or ecclesial community*, provided they are unable to have their own minister. This cannot be done if it is against their wishes. (Can. 1183)

> The judgment of the local Ordinary must be made on a case by case basis. However, he could give general delegation to pastors to make this judgment.

> The inability to have the proper non-Catholic minister may result from moral as well as physical unavailability. Physical unavailability would be, e.g., when there is no minister of the non-Catholic deceased in the area. Moral unavailability would be, e.g., when there is a minister of the non-Catholic deceased in the area but the non-Catholic has not practiced his or her faith, and the practicing Catholic spouse or other next of kin would like to have the funeral in the Catholic Church. However, if there is evidence that the deceased had altogether abandoned the Christian faith, there can be no Church funeral rites. (See can. 1184, §1, 1°.)

> If a non-Catholic had been practicing his or her religion during life, it should be presumed that that indi-

vidual would have wanted to have the funeral in his or her own church, and therefore it would be contrary to the wishes of the departed to have it in the Catholic church. To presume otherwise would be ecumenically insensitive.

N.B. This permission cannot be granted to those who were unbaptized or baptized invalidly.

2. *Burial in Non-Catholic Cemetery*

In those situations in which a Catholic is to be interred in a non-Catholic cemetery, the priest [or deacon] after the liturgy in church, may conduct the committal service at the graveside. He should bless the individual grave and then follow the usual ritual for the burial of a Catholic. On those occasions when a non-Catholic is to be buried in a Catholic cemetery, the ordained minister of the church in which he shared belief or communion may conduct the committal service. (NCCC Guidelines, The Burial Rite, A, B, CLD 9:687)

Parish
Administration

Part XIII

CHAPTER I
Pastors

I. Installation, Term and Cessation of Office

A. Installation

The one who is promoted to carry out the pastoral care of a parish obtains that care and is bound to exercise it from the moment of taking possession of the parish. The local Ordinary or the priest delegated by him places the pastor in possession of the parish, observing the manner accepted by particular law or legitimate custom. However, for a just reason the same Ordinary can dispense from this procedure, in which case notification of the dispensation to the parish replaces the act of taking possession. (Can. 527, §§1–2) At the beginning of his term of office, the pastor is obliged to make a profession of faith personally, in accord with a formula approved by the Apostolic See, before the local Ordinary or his delegate. (See can. 833, 6°.)

The profession of faith begins:

"I, N., with firm faith, believe and profess all and everything that is contained in the Symbol of Faith, that is:

[Recitation of the Nicene Creed followed by]:

"I firmly embrace and accept all and everything which has been either defined by the Church's solemn deliberations or affirmed and declared by its ordinary magisterium concerning the doctrine of faith and morals, according as they are proposed by it, especially those things dealing with the mystery of the Holy Church of Christ, its sacraments and the sacrifice of the Mass, and the primacy of the Roman Pontiff.'' (See CLSA Comm, 1093.)

B. Term of Office

The pastor must have stability in office and therefore is to be appointed for an indefinite time. He can be appointed for a definite term by the diocesan bishop only if this has been allowed by a decree of the episcopal conference. (Can. 522) In the United States, the N.C.C.B. has decided that diocesan bishops may appoint pastors for a six-year term which can be renewed. (Janicki, 422)

> It is up to the bishop of each diocese to determine whether there is a term of office, whether it can be renewed, and how many times it can be renewed.

C. Cessation of Office

1. *Retirement.* When he completes his 75th year, the pastor is asked to submit to the diocesan bishop his resignation from office. The bishop should decide whether to accept or defer the resignation after considering all the circumstances of the person and the place. (See can. 538, §3.)

> The letter of resignation should be submitted on or before the day after the pastor's 75th birthday.

> The requirement also applies to a pastor who belongs to a religious institute or clerical society. If the superior wishes the pastor to remain in office after completing his 75th year, the superior should petition the bishop accordingly.

2. *Completion of term.* The office of pastor is lost by the completion of his term in accord with the prescriptions of particular law. (See can. 538, §1.)

> At the end of the term, the bishop may reappoint the pastor to a new term or assign him elsewhere.

3. *Transfer and removal.* A diocesan pastor ceases from office by removal or transfer by the diocesan bishop done in accord with the norm of law. A pastor who is a member of a religious institute or a society of apostolic life is removed either by the diocesan bishop,

316

having notified the superior, or by the superior, having notified the bishop; neither requires the consent of the other. (See cans. 538, §§1–2 and 682, §2.)

The procedures for the removal of diocesan pastors are found in canons 1740–1747, and for their transfer in canons 1748–1752.

4. *Resignation.* A pastor may resign for a just cause; the resignation, for validity, must be accepted by the diocesan bishop. (See can. 538, §1.)

Just causes for resignation would be poor health, inadequacy, retirement, etc. The pastor is not free to vacate the office unless the resignation is accepted by the bishop.

A pastor who is a member of a religious institute or clerical society, and who wishes to resign, should first submit his resignation to his competent superior.

II. Some Rights and Duties of Pastors

A. Functions Especially Committed to Pastors

The following functions are especially committed to the pastor:

1. The administration of baptism.

If baptism was administered neither by the pastor nor in his presence, the minister of baptism, whoever the person is, must give notification of the conferral of baptism to the pastor of the parish in which the baptism was administered so that he may record the baptism in keeping with canon 877, §1. (Can. 878)

Except in a case of necessity, no one, without permission, may confer baptism in the territory of another, not even on his own subjects. (Can. 862)

2. The administration of the sacrament of confirmation to those who are in danger of death in accord with canon 883, n. 3.

Canon 833, 3° permits not only the pastor but indeed any presbyter to confirm in danger of death.

3.   The administration of Viaticum and the anointing of the sick, with due regard for canon 1003, §§ 2 and 3, and the imparting of the apostolic blessing.

> All priests who have been entrusted with the office of pastoral care have the duty and right to administer the anointing of the sick on behalf of the faithful committed to their pastoral office. For a reasonable cause, any other priest can administer this sacrament with at least the presumed consent of the priest entrusted with the pastoral office. (See can. 1003, §2.)

> Every priest may carry blessed oil so that, in a case of necessity, he may administer the sacrament of the anointing of the sick. (Can. 1003, §3)

4.   Assistance at marriages and the nuptial blessing.

> Pastors have the faculty to assist at marriages in their parish in virtue of their office. (See cans. 1108, §1 and 1109.)

> If one other than the pastor is to assist at the marriage conducts the pre-marital investigations, that person should inform the pastor of the results as soon as possible by means of an authentic document. (See can. 1070.)

5.   The celebration of funerals.

6.   The blessing of the baptismal font in the Easter season, the leading of processions outside the church, and solemn blessings outside the church.

> The *Rite of Blessings* from the *Roman Ritual* specifies that the bishop should bless a new baptistery or baptismal font that is built in his diocese, or he may entrust this to another presbyter. (See RB, 839.) Thus, when the bishop does not bless a baptismal font *that is built*, the pastor would need his permission to do so; but the pastor does not need permission to bless a portable baptismal font. The blessing of baptismal fonts should take place on Sundays, especially in the Easter season, or on the feast of the Baptism of the Lord. (See RB, 840.)

> To have an outdoor procession for the veneration

of the Eucharist, the permission of the diocesan bishop is required. (See can. 944.)

The solemn blessings outside church would mainly be those found in Part II of the *Rite of Blessings*.

7. The more solemn celebration of the Eucharist on Sundays and holy days of obligation.

Canon 530 "especially commits" the functions listed above to the pastor. This does not mean that these functions are reserved exclusively to the pastor, but that he is entrusted with them in a special way. Some of the functions, since they are honorific, should more frequently be performed by the pastor, e.g., the blessing of the baptismal font, the leading of processions outside church, and the imparting of solemn blessings outside church. The other functions, insofar as they are regular pastoral responsibilities, can be performed by other priests or appropriate ministers at the pastor's discretion in accord with the law.

B. Residence, Vacations and Absences

1. The pastor must reside in the parish house near the church. Nevertheless, in particular cases, if there is a just reason, the local Ordinary can permit him to live elsewhere, especially in a house common to several presbyters, as long as there is proper and due provision for the performance of parochial functions.

2. Unless a serious reason prevents it, the pastor is allowed to be away from the parish on vacation each year for at most one continuous or intermittent month. Not counted in the vacation time are the days in which the pastor makes a retreat once a year. Moreover, the pastor, when he is to be absent from the parish for more than a week, is bound to notify the local Ordinary of this. (Can. 533, §§1–2)

C. Missa pro populo

After taking possession of the parish, the pastor is obliged to apply a Mass for the people entrusted to him on every Sunday and holy day of obligation observed in the diocese. If he is legitimately impeded from this celebration, he should apply a Mass on these same days through another priest or he himself should do it on other days. A pastor who has the care of several parishes need apply only one Mass on Sundays and holy days for all the people entrusted to him. A pastor who has not satisfied these obligations shall as soon as possible apply as many Masses for the people as he has omitted. (See can. 534.)

> A parochial vicar who acts as a substitute for the pastor is not bound to this obligation; a parochial administrator is bound. (See cans. 549 and 540, §1.)

D. Keeping Parish Registers, the Seal, Archives

1. In every parish there are to be parish registers for baptisms, marriages, deaths, and other registers in accord with the prescriptions of the episcopal conference and the diocesan bishop. The pastor should ensure that these books are accurately inscribed and diligently preserved. In the baptismal register there also should be recorded confirmations as well as those things which pertain to the canonical status of the faithful by reason of marriage, without prejudice to canon 1133, by reason of adoption, and likewise by reason of the reception of holy orders, perpetual profession in a religious institute, and a change of rite. These notations should always be mentioned on a baptismal certificate. (Can. 535, §§1–2)

> Canon 1133 refers to the celebration of a marriage in secret which is recorded only in a special register kept in the secret archive of the diocesan curia.

2. Every parish should have its own seal. Testimonies which are given concerning the canonical status of the faithful, as well as all acts which can have juridical import, should be signed by the pastor himself or his delegate and sealed with the parish seal. (Can. 535, §3)

3. In every parish there should be a register or archive in which the parish books are kept together with letters of the bishops and other documents which must be preserved due to need or utility. At visitation or at another opportune time all these things are to be inspected by the diocesan bishop or his delegate. The pastor should take care lest these materials fall into the hands of outsiders. The older parish books should also be carefully kept in accord with the prescriptions of particular law. (Can. 535, §§4–5)

III. Co-Pastors

1. Where circumstances require it, the pastoral care of a parish or of several parishes together can be entrusted to several priests jointly (*in solidum*). Nevertheless, one of them is to be appointed moderator for the exercise of pastoral care, namely, he should oversee the joint activity and is answerable for it before the bishop. (Can. 517, §1)

2. The priests who serve as co-pastors obtain the pastoral care only from the moment of taking possession of the parish. The moderator is placed in possession in the same way as the pastor in accord with can. 527, §2. For the other priests a profession of faith legitimately made replaces the taking of possession. (See can. 542, 3°.)

3. If the pastoral care of some parish or several parishes together has been committed to priests jointly, each of them, in accord with an arrangement determined by themselves, are bound to fulfill the duties and functions of the pastor given in canons 528, 529, and 530. They all have the faculty to assist at marriages as well as all powers of dispensation granted by law to the pastor which, nevertheless, must be exercised under the direction of the moderator. (Can. 543, §1)

4. All the priests who belong to the group are bound to the obligation of residence. Through common agreement they should establish a rule whereby one of them celebrates the *Missa pro populo* in accord with canon 534. Only the moderator represents in juridic affairs the parish or parishes entrusted to the group. (Can. 543, §2)

5. When one of the priests from the group, or the moderator, ceases from office, or when one of them becomes incapable of exercising his pastoral duties, the parish or parishes, whose care is entrusted to the group, do not become vacant. However, the diocesan bishop is to appoint another moderator. Before another moderator is appointed by the bishop, the senior priest of the group by reason of appointment should fulfill this role. (Can. 544)

CHAPTER II
Other Parish Ministries

I. Parochial Vicars and Administrators

1. Unless something else is expressly stated in the letter of the diocesan bishop, the parochial vicar is bound by reason of his office to assist in the entire parochial ministry, except for the application of the *Missa pro populo*, and likewise, if the case calls for it, to take the place of the pastor in accord with the norm of law. (Can. 548, §1)

> The parochial vicar is the canonical term for the office more commonly known as assistant pastor, associate pastor, or curate. Only a priest may be appointed parochial vicar. (See can. 546.)

2. The parochial vicar should report regularly to the pastor concerning prospective and initiated pastoral undertakings. In this way the pastor and the vicar or vicars, through their joint efforts, can provide for the pastoral care of the parish for which they are together responsible. (Can. 548, §3)

3. The parochial vicar is bound to reside in the parish or, if he was appointed for several parishes together, he is bound to reside in one of them. Nevertheless, the local Ordinary, for a just reason, can permit him to live elsewhere, especially in a house common to several presbyters, provided no harm is done thereby to the performance of his pastoral duties. (Can. 550, §1)

4. The parochial vicar enjoys the same right as the pastor for a vacation. (Can. 550, §3)

Thus the parochial vicar may have an annual vacation of one month, whether continuous or interrupted, not counting the time spent away for his annual retreat. (See can. 533, §2.)

5. Concerning offerings given to the vicar by some member of the faithful on the occasion of his performing a pastoral ministry, the prescriptions of canon 531 are to be observed. (Can. 551)

Canon 531 is presented below in Chapter III on financial administration of parishes, pp. 330-331.

6. When the pastor is absent the parochial vicar is bound to all the obligations of the pastor except for the obligation of applying the *Missa pro populo*. (See can. 549.)

7. When the parish is vacant and likewise when the pastor is impeded from exercising his pastoral duty, the parochial vicar assumes the governance of the parish in the interim before a parochial administrator is appointed. If there are several parochial vicars, this is done by the one who is senior by appointment, or if there are no vicars, the pastor specified in particular law. The one who has assumed the governance of the parish should immediately notify the local Ordinary of the vacancy of the parish. (Can. 541)

A *parish is vacant* when the pastor dies or when his office ceases due to the expiration of his term, resignation, transfer, or removal. The pastor is impeded when he is unable to function for a significant period of time for any reason. This is to be distinguished from a pastor who is merely absent temporarily for reason of vacation, retreat, etc. in which case no administrator will be appointed and the parochial vicar assumes the pastor's obligations as under n. 6 above (can. 549).

The parochial vicar who is senior by appointment is the one who was first assigned to the parish in question.

II. Deacons, Lay Ministers, Parish Councils

A. Deacons and Lay Ministers

If by reason of a scarcity of priests the diocesan bishop decides that a share in the exercise of the pastoral care of a parish is to be entrusted to a deacon, or some other person who is not a priest, or to a community of persons, he should appoint some priest who, endowed with the powers and faculties of a pastor, shall moderate the pastoral care. (Can. 517, §2)

This law allows deacons and lay ministers, including a community of laypersons such as lay religious, to be appointed parish administrators in areas where there are not enough priests. This should not be confused with the canonical term "administrator" which is used of the priest who assumes the pastor's function when the parish is vacant or the pastor is impeded. The priest who is appointed moderator of the pastoral care of a parish with a deacon or lay administrator need not reside in the parish.

The section on parishes in the Code says very little about the role of deacons and lay persons in parish ministry. The reader should consult other parts of this handbook, especially the parts on baptism, Eucharist, marriage, funeral rites, blessings, and the Liturgy of the Hours.

B. Parish Council

If it is opportune in the judgment of the diocesan bishop after consulting the presbyteral council, a pastoral council is to be established in each parish. The pastor presides over the council in which the faithful, together with those who in virtue of office participate in the pastoral care of the parish, offer their assistance in fostering pastoral action. The parish council enjoys a consultative vote only and is governed by norms enacted by the diocesan bishop. (Can. 536)

Although the Code does not require a parish council, it does permit the diocesan bishop to require it if he wishes. In the absence of a determination by the bishop, the pastor may decide whether to establish a parish council.

CHAPTER III
Financial Administration of Parishes

I. Financial Administrators

A. The Pastor

1. In accord with the law, the pastor represents the parish in all juridical affairs. He should see to it that the goods of the parish are administered in accord with canons 1281–1288. (Can. 532)

2. The administration of ecclesiastical goods is the responsibility of the one who immediately governs the [juridic] person to which the same goods belong, unless something else is provided by particular law, statutes, or legitimate custom, and without prejudice to the right of the Ordinary to intervene in case of negligence by the administrator. (Can. 1279, §1)

B. The Finance Council

In each parish there is to be a council for financial affairs which, in addition to universal law, is regulated by norms established by the diocesan bishop. The faithful, selected for this council in accord with these same regulations, assist the pastor in the administration of the parish goods, with due regard for canon 532. (Can. 537)

> A finance council is mandatory for each parish. Since it is constitutive law, the diocesan bishop may not dispense from it. (See can. 86.) This requirement is a specification of the general law that states: Every juridic person should have its own council for financial affairs, or at least two advisers, who in accord with the norm of the statutes assist the administrator in fulfilling his or her duties. (Can. 1280)

The finance council is distinct from the parish council, although there is nothing to prevent certain members of the parish council from acting as a finance council provided this is not prohibited by diocesan statutes. On the other hand, if the diocesan statutes give the right to the pastor to choose the members of the finance council, he is not obliged to choose any members of the parish council.

II. Duties of Financial Administrators

A. General Duties

1. All persons, whether cleric or lay, who by legitimate title take part in the administration of ecclesiastical goods, are bound to fulfill their duties in the name of the Church in accord with the norm of law. (Can. 1282)

2. Before administrators begin their duties they must take an oath before the Ordinary or his delegate that they will be good and faithful administrators. (Can. 1283, 1°)

> The pastor fulfills this law by his installation. Since the members of the finance council have a part in the financial administration of the parish, they too should take an oath in accord with this law.

3. All administrators are bound to fulfill their duties with the diligence of a good *paterfamilias*. Thus, they must:

a. Be vigilant that the property entrusted to their care is not lost or damaged in any way; to this end, inasmuch as may be necessary, they are to take out insurance policies;

b. See to it that the ownership of ecclesiastical goods is safeguarded in civilly valid ways;

c. Observe the regulations of canon and civil law, as well as regulations imposed by a founder or donor or by legitimate authority, and beware lest the non-observance of the civil law result in harm to the Church;

d. Collect income and profits promptly and in full, keep them safe, and use them in accord with the intention of the founder or legitimate norms;

e. Pay the interest on a loan or mortgage at the time it is due and see to it that the capital debt itself is paid in due time;

f.   Keep well-ordered accounts of receipts and expenditures;

g.   Prepare a report of their administration at the end of every year;

h.   Keep in good order in the archives all documents and legal papers upon which depend the rights of the Church or the institution to its goods, and deposit authentic copies of all such papers in the archives of the curia when this can conveniently be done. (Can. 1284, §§1–2)

4.   Even though they may not be bound to administration by title of an ecclesiastical office, administrators may not arbitrarily relinquish the duties they have undertaken; if from their arbitrary neglect of duty any harm comes to the Church, they are bound to make restitution. (Can. 1289)

> Pastors are administrators by title of office. The members of the finance council participate in this administration even though they do not have the principal responsibility for finances; thus they are subject to this canon. Likewise bound to this canon are any employees or even volunteers in the parish who have any kind of financial responsibility. (See Myers, 878.)

B. Budget and Reports

1.   It is highly recommended that administrators each year prepare budgets of income and expenses; however, it is left to particular law to require them and to determine more precisely the manner in which they are to be presented. (Can. 1284, §3)

2.   Administrators, whether cleric or lay, of any ecclesiastical goods whatsoever, which have not been legitimately exempted from the power of governance of the diocesan bishop, are obliged by their office to give a report every year to the local Ordinary, who shall present it to the [diocesan] finance council for examination. Any custom to the contrary is reprobated. (Can. 1287, §1)

> This law also applies to the property and funds of parishes administered by religious and members of societies of apostolic life, but not the property, including the church, which is owned by the religious institute or clerical society.

3.   Administrators should give an account to the faithful, according to the norms established in particular law, of the goods which are donated to the Church by the faithful. (Can. 1287, §2)

The canon only requires the particular law to establish regulations to account to the faithful for the donations made by the faithful, although particular law may require a more complete financial report to parishioners.

C. Duties Regarding Employees

In the employment of workers, administrators of goods must faithfully observe also the civil laws which pertain to work and social life, in accord with the principles handed down by the Church. They are to pay those who work for them under contract a just and honest wage so that they can appropriately provide for themselves and their dependents. (Can. 1286)

D. Inventory of Parish Goods

Before administrators begin their duties, they are to prepare an accurate and precise inventory, signed by themselves, of immovable goods, movable goods that are precious or of significant cultural value, and other goods, with a description and appraisal of them; after this is prepared, it should be reviewed. One copy of this inventory should be kept in the administration's archives, another in the archives of the curia. Any change that the patrimony may undergo should be recorded on both copies. (Can. 1283, 2° and 3°)

III. Offerings and Stole Fees

1. Although another person may have performed a certain parochial function, the offerings received on this occasion from the faithful are to be turned over to the parish fund, unless it is evident that it would be contrary to the will of the donor as far as voluntary donations are concerned. The diocesan bishop, having heard the presbyteral council, is competent to enact norms which provide for the allocation of these offerings as well as for the remuneration of the clerics who fulfill the same parochial function. (Can. 531)

2. Unless the law provides otherwise, the meeting of bishops of a province is competent to establish the amount of the offerings given on the occasion of the administration of sacraments and sacramentals. (See can. 1264, 2°.) In the absence of such a determination, diocesan law or custom is to be followed.

According to these laws, all stole fees and other

voluntary offerings given to pastors, other priests, deacons, and lay ministers who perform parochial functions are to be turned over to a parish fund to be used for the purpose specified by the bishop. Thus, the established amount of an offering for any service is to go entirely to this fund, unless part of it is set aside for the payment for a particular service, e.g., organist, cantor, janitor, etc., as is sometimes the case with weddings and funerals and the like. Any voluntary offering given over and above the established amount can be kept by the minister only if it is clear that this was the donor's intention. In doubt about the donor's intention, the offering goes entirely to the parish fund.

N.B.: This provision *does not apply to Mass offerings (stipends)*. Each priest has a right to keep Mass offerings in accord with the provisions of canons 945–958. In those places where the practice of the diocese is for priests to hand over all Mass offerings to the parish in exchange for a uniform salary, this diocesan practice would not apply to visiting priests who would be entitled by law to the Mass offerings for Sunday Masses, weddings, etc. in addition to any payment for their services to which they may be entitled. On the other hand, visiting priests are subject to the same rule governing stole fees and voluntary offerings as stated above, that is, they must turn them in to the parish fund unless a voluntary donation above the established amount was given to them personally.

3. Unless the contrary is established, offerings given to the superiors or administrators of any ecclesiastical juridic person, even a private one, are presumed to have been given to the juridic person itself. (Can. 1267, §1)

In the absence of any determination by the diocesan bishop concerning the allocation of the special fund for stole fees and offerings, the money should go into the general parish account in virtue of the law requiring offerings to go to the juridic person.

IV. Ordinary and Extraordinary Administration

Ordinary administration includes the ordinary upkeep of church property, paying bills, making necessary repairs, buying supplies, opening regular checking accounts, accepting ordinary donations, and the collection of debts, rents, interest, or dividends. *Extraordinary administration* covers acts which do not occur periodically or which are by their nature of greater importance, e.g., making long-term investments, changing investments, acts of alienation, the acceptance or refusal of major bequests, land purchases, construction of new buildings or extensive repairs on old buildings, leasing or renting property for an extended period, the opening of a cemetery, the establishment of a school, taking up special collections. (See Myers, 874.) Special permission is needed for acts of extraordinary administration, as seen below under section B.

A. Donations from the Parish

Within the limits of ordinary administration only, administrators are at liberty to make donations for purposes of piety or Christian charity from movable goods which do not belong to the stable patrimony. (Can. 1285)

> Hence, pastors may make donations from parish funds but not from any investments, property, etc. which belong to the stable patrimony. Such donations may not exceed the limits of ordinary administration. This means that such donations should be budgeted, or at least not exceed the amount established by the diocesan bishop for extraordinary expenses.

> Movable goods include investments, money, furnishings, art objects, etc.; immovable goods are land and buildings. Immovable goods belong to the stable patrimony. Movable goods which have great historical or artistic value, or which have been invested for a specific purpose, also belong to the stable patrimony, e.g., a fund for a new church.

B. Acts of Extraordinary Administration

Unless they have obtained the prior written permission from the Ordinary, administrators invalidly place acts which exceed the limits and manner of ordinary administration, with due regard for the norms of the statutes. (Can. 1281, §1)

> After he has consulted his finance council, the

diocesan bishop is competent to determine the limits and procedures for acts of extraordinary administration by parish administrators (pastors, co-pastors, administrators in priestless parishes, etc.). (See can. 1281, §2.) Thus, any act of extraordinary administration by a pastor or other parish administrator requires permission of the diocesan bishop who must consult his financial council.

If a pastor or other person charged with the financial administration of a parish exceeds the limits or does not follow procedures affecting validity, he or she acts invalidly. The parish, as juridic person, is not held to answer for invalid acts of its administrators except and insofar as the invalid acts benefit the parish. The parish is responsible for acts which are illicit but valid, but it has the right to sue or to have recourse against administrators who have caused financial damage to the parish when they have acted illicitly. (See can. 1281, §3.) Note: Even though a financial act is canonically invalid or illicit, this is not usually recognized by the civil law.

V. Contracts and Alienation

A. Contracts

Whatever the civil law establishes in the territory concerning contracts, both in general and in particular, and concerning their dissolution, is to be observed regarding matters subject to the Church's power of governance with the same effects, unless it is contrary to the divine law or canon law specifies something else, with due regard for canon 1547.

This means that canon law defers to the civil law on all matters governing legal contracts, except when the civil law is contrary to divine law or when canon law makes other provision, as it does in canon 1547. Canon 1547 says that witnesses are a means of judicial proof. Hence, witnesses to a contract could establish proof of a contract in the absence of a written document, even if the civil law would not admit such evidence as conclusive.

B. Alienation

1. In the strict sense, "alienation" (also called "conveyance") is "any act by which the right to ownership of ecclesiastical property is transferred to another." In the broad sense, alienation is "any act by which the use of the right, or the right itself, of ownership is or could be diminished, restricted, or endangered." (F. Morrisey, "The Conveyance of Ecclesiastical Goods," PCLSA 38 (1976) 126–127) The laws of alienation in canons 1291–1298 of the Code apply to acts of alienation both in the strict and broad sense. Transactions involving the payment of money from *free capital* are not subject to the laws of alienation, but they are subject to the laws governing acts of extraordinary administration. Subject to the laws of alienation are transactions involving sale, mortgage, lien, easement, option, compromise, settlement, renting, and leasing of property, as well as expenditure of funds that are part of the parish's patrimony, i.e., its *stable capital* such as funds invested for a specific purpose. (See Myers, 879–80.)

The laws on alienation of goods in canons 1291–1294 apply also to any transaction through which the patrimonial condition of a juridic person can be worsened. (See can. 1295.)

2. The permission of the authority competent by law is required for the valid alienation of goods which by legitimate designation constitute the stable patrimony of a public juridic person and whose value exceeds the amount defined by law. (Can. 1291)

> To alienate validly the goods of the parish whose value exceeds the minimum amount established by the episcopal conference, the administrator is required to obtain permission of the diocesan bishop who must have the consent of his finance council and the college of consultors. In the absence of the determination of a minimum amount, diocesan statutes prevail. (See can. 1292, §1.)

> The permission of the Holy See is necessary to alienate goods whose value exceeds the amount that the bishop can authorize, which is presently $1,000,000 in the United States. Permission is also necessary to alienate goods donated to the Church through a vow or goods which are especially valuable due to their artistic or historical value. (See can. 1292, §2.)

> Those who must take part in alienations through

their counsel or consent are not to give counsel or consent unless they have first been precisely informed both of the economic status of the juridic person which is proposing to alienate goods as well as of alienations already made. (Can. 1292, §4)

Whenever ecclesiastical goods have been alienated without observing the canonical formalities, yet the alienation is civilly valid, it is up to the competent authority to decide, after mature consideration of all circumstances, whether and what kind of action, either personal or real, by whom and against whom, is to be taken to vindicate the rights of the Church. (Can. 1296)

3. If the thing to be alienated is divisible, one must mention all parts already alienated in the petition for permission for further alienation; otherwise the permission is invalid. (Can. 1292, §3)

4. To alienate goods whose value exceeds the minimum amount specified [by the episcopal conference], it is moreover required:
a. that there be a just cause, such as urgent necessity, evident usefulness, piety, charity, or another serious pastoral reason;
b. a written estimate by experts of the value of the thing to be alienated. (Can. 1293, §1)

Also other precautions prescribed by legitimate authority are to be observed to prevent harm to the Church. (Can. 1293, §2)

5. An object ordinarily must not be alienated for a lower amount than that indicated by the estimate. The money gained from an alienation either should be carefully invested for the benefit of the Church or prudently spent in accord with the purposes of the alienation. (Can. 1294)

6. Unless an object is of small value, ecclesiastical goods must not be sold or leased to their administrators or to the administrators' relatives up to the fourth degree of consanguinity or affinity without special written permission from the competent authority. (Can. 1298)

The competent authority in the case of parish administrators is the diocesan bishop.

VI. Law Suits

Administrators are neither to begin a law suit in the name of a public juridic person nor act as a defendant against one in civil court unless they have obtained the written permission of their Ordinary. (Can. 1288)

Thus, parish administrators must have the written permission of the diocesan bishop before initiating a law suit in the name of the parish or even contesting a suit against the parish. If the parish is owned (as opposed to merely administered) by a religious institute or society of apostolic life of pontifical right, the major superior is the competent Ordinary to give this permission.

ABBREVIATIONS
Series I

AAS   *Acta Apostolicae Sedis*, Rome 1909–

apconst   apostolic constitution

BCL   Bishops' Committee on the Liturgy

can.   canon

CIC   1917 Code of Canon Law (*Codex Iuris Canonici*)

CLD   *Canon Law Digest*. Edited by T. Bouscaren and J. O'Connor. Vols. 1–6, Milwaukee-New York: The Bruce Publishing Co., 1934–1969. Vols. 7–9 and supplements, Chicago: Canon Law Digest, 1975–

CLSA   Canon Law Society of America

CodCom   Pontifical Commission for the Authentic Interpretation of the Canons of the Code of Canon Law

decl   declaration

decr   decree

DMC   Congregation for Divine Worship, *Directory for Masses with Children*, Nov. 1, 1973, AAS 66 (1974) 30–46; DOL, n. 276, CLD 8:497

DOL   *Documents on the Liturgy 1963–1979, Conciliar, Papal and Curial Texts*, Collegeville, Minn.: Liturgical Press, 1982

ED   Secretariat for Promoting Christian Unity, *Ecumenical Directory*, part I, May 14, 1967, AAS 59 (1967), 564–92; CLD 6:716–34

ency   encyclical

GILH   *General Instruction of the Liturgy of the Hours*

GIRM   *General Instruction of the Roman Missal*

HCW   *Roman Ritual, Rite of Holy Communion and Worship of the Eucharistic Mystery Outside Mass*

ICEL   International Committee on English in the Liturgy

IGIC   *Roman Ritual, Introduction to the Rite of Christian Initiation.*

instr	instruction
LFM	*Lectionary for Mass*
Mp	The *motu proprio, Crebrae allatae.* Codification of the marriage legislation for the Eastern Catholic Churches
NCCB	National Conference of Catholic Bishops
NCCO-Guidelines	National Catholic Cemetery Conference, *Christian Burial Guidelines*, Jan. 28, 1975, CLD 9:688–702
OE	Vatican II, decree *Orientalium Ecclesiarum*, AAS 57 (1965), 76–89
PCLSA	*Proceedings of the Canon Law Society of America*
PCS	*Pastoral Care of the Sick: Rites of Anointing and Viaticum*, approved for use in the dioceses of the U.S.A. by the NCCB
RA	*Roman Ritual, Rite of Anointing*
RB	*Roman Ritual, Rite of Blessings*
RBaptC	*Roman Ritual, Rite of Baptism of Children*
RCIA	*Roman Ritual, Rite of Christian Initiation of Adults*
RConf	*Roman Pontifical, Rite of Confirmation*
RF	*Roman Ritual, Rite of Funerals*
RM	*Roman Ritual, Rite of Marriage*
SCB	Congregation for Bishops
SCC	Congregation for the Clergy
SCCE	Congregation for Catholic Education
SCConc	Sacred Congregation of the Council
SCDF	Congregation for the Doctrine of the Faith
SCDW	Congregation for Divine Worship
SCOf	Sacred Congregation for the Holy Office (former title of the SCDF)
SCProp	Congregation for the Evangelization of Nations/ Congregation for the Propagation of the Faith
SCRIS	Congregation for Religious and Secular Institutes

SCRit	Sacred Congregation of Rites
SCSacr	Congregation for the Discipline of the Sacraments
SPCU	Secretariate for Promoting Christian Unity
SRR	Roman Rota
UR	Vatican II, decree *Unitatis Redintegratio*, AAS 57 (1965), 90–107
VatCom	Pontifical Commission for the Interpretation of the Decrees of the Second Vatican Council

Series II

ABBO-HANNAN—Abbo, J. and Hannan J. *The Sacred Canons*. 2 vols. St. Louis: B. Herder, 1st ed., 1952; 2nd ed., 1960.

ALFORD—Alford, C. *Jus Matrimoniale Comparatum*. Rome: Anonima Libraria Cattolica Italiana, 1938.

BOUSCAREN-ELLIS—Bouscaren, T. and Ellis, A. *Canon Law, a Text and Commentary*. 3rd ed. Milwaukee: Bruce, 1957.

CAPPELLO—Cappello, F. *Tractatus Canonico-Moralis de Sacramentis*. 5 vols. Roma: Marietti, 1949–1958. Vol 1, 6th ed., 1953; Vol. 2, 6th ed., 1953; Vol. 3, 3rd ed., 1949; 4th ed., 1958; Vol. 4, 3rd ed., 1951; Vol. 5, 6th ed., 1950.

CLSA COMM.—*The Code of Canon Law: A Text and Commentary Commissioned by the Canon Law Society of America*. Edited by J. Coriden, T. Green, and D. Heintschel. New York: Paulist, 1985

CORIDEN—Coriden, J. "The Teaching Office of the Church." CLSA Comm., pp. 543–589.

CORONATA—Conte a Coronata, M. *Institutiones Iuris Canonici ad Usum Utriusque Cleri et Scholarum*. 2nd ed. 5 vols. Rome: Marietti, 1939–1947.

DOYLE—Doyle, T. "Marriage." CLSA COMM., pp. 737–833.

GASPARRI—Gasparri, P. *Tractatus Canonicus de Matrimonio*. Ed. post Codicem. 2 vols. Rome: Vatican Press, 1932.

GENICOT—Genicot, E., Salsmans, J., and Gortebecke, A. *Institutiones Theologiae Moralis*. 17th ed. 2 vols. Brussels: 1951.

GREEN—Green, T. "Sanctions in the Church". CLSA COMM., pp. 891–941.

HANDBUCH—*Handbuch des katholischen Kirchenrechts*. Edited by J. Listl, H. Müller, and H. Schmitz. Regensburg: Friedrich Pustet, 1983.

HARING—Häring, B. *The Law of Christ*. 2 vols. Westminster, MD: Newman, 1963.

JANICKI—Janicki, J. CLSA COMM., pp. 414–449.

McMANUS—McManus, F. CLSA COMM.: "Baptism," pp. 605–630; "Confirmation," pp. 631–642; "Penance," pp. 673–701; "Anointing of the Sick," pp. 702–712.

MATHIS/BONNER—Mathis M. and Bonner, D. *The Pastoral Companion: A Handbook of Canon Law*. 14th ed. Chicago: Franciscan Herald, 1976.

MYERS—Myers, J. "The Temporal Goods of the Church." CLSA COMM., pp. 857–890.

NOLDIN—Noldin, H., Schmitt, A., and Heinzel, G. *Summa Theologiae Moralis*, 3 vols. Oeniponte: Typis et Sumptibus Feliciani Rauch, 1953–1954. Vol. 2, 30th ed., 1954; Vol. 3, 30th ed., 1954; Vol. 1, 31st ed., 1953.

POSPISHIL/FARIS—Pospishil, V. and Faris, J. *The New Latin Code of Canon Law and Esatern Catholics*. Brooklyn: Diocese of Saint Maron, 1984.

SIPOS—Sipos, S. and Galos, L. *Enchiridion Iuris Canonici*. 6th ed. Rome: Herder, 1954.

V.C.—Vermeersch, A. and Creusen, J. *Epitome Iuris Canonici*. 3 vols. Mechlinia and Rome: H. Dessain. Vol. 1, 7th ed., 1949; Vol. 2, 7th ed., 1954; Vol. 3, 6th ed., 1946; 7th ed., 1956.

VLAMING—Vlaming, T. and Bender, L. *Praelectiones Iuris Matrimonii*. 4th ed. Bussum: Paul Brand, 1950.

WOYWOD—Woywod, S. and Smith, C. *A Practical Commentary on the Code of Canon Law*. New York: Joseph Wagner. 1 vol. ed., 1952; revised and enlarged ed., 1962.

WRENN, ANNULMENTS—Wrenn L. *Annulments*. 4th ed. rev. Washington, D.C.: CLSA, 1983.

WRENN, DECISIONS—Wrenn L. *Decisions*. 2nd ed. rev. Washington, D.C.: CLSA, 1983.

GENERAL INDEX

Abandoned infants, 41
Abduction, 190
Aborted fetuses, 41, 286
Abortion, 135, 142–44, 210
Abstinence, 293, 294, 296–98
Acolyte, 87
Administrator, 324
Adoption, 54, 195, 320
Adult, 19
Adultery, 191
Affinity, 26, 193–95
Age
    for confirmation, 59
    for marriage, 166, 180–81
    of discretion, 59
Alcoholic intoxication, 200
Alcoholic priests, 94
Alcoholism, 202–3, 205
Alienation, 334
Altar, 101
Altar server, 87
Annulment, 235, 259–60
Anointing of the sick,
    before surgery, 152
    by pastor, 318
    by several priests, 149
    communal, 149–50
    doubt about eligibility for, 153–54
    during Mass, 150
    ecumenical law on, 304–08
    eligibility to receive, 151
    form of, 147
    in necessity, 149
    matter of, 147–48
    minister of, 151
    place of, 150
    prohibition of, 153
    repetition of, 154
    rite of, 147
    role of family and friends at, 151
    time for, 152
    with additional anointings, 149
    with an instrument, 149
Apostate, 284
Apostolic blessing, 318
Ash Wednesday, 294
Assistance at marriage, 217, 221, 318
Assistant pastor. *See Parochial vicar.*

Banns, 163
Baptism,
    adult, 37–38
    by bishop, 38
    by pastor, 317
    capability for, 35
    churches with invalid, 51
    churches with valid, 50
    conditional, 49–51, 302–3
    consequences of for marriage, 185
    day of, 44
    doubt regarding, 49, 187, 301–3
    emergency, 46–48
    extraordinary minister of, 42
    form of, 34, 49, 301
    in danger of death, 47
    in necessity, 46–47
    infant, 39–41
    juridical effects of, 33
    matter of, 34, 49, 301–2
    membership in Church by, 33, 185
    necessity of, 33
    non-repeatability of, 35
    of abandoned infants, 41
    of aborted fetuses, 41
    of adopted children, 54
    of illegitimate children, 54
    offices and ministries of, 42–44
    place of, 46
    postponement of, 40–41
    proof of, 53
    recording of, 53–54
    relation to full initiation, 33
    rite established by, 27–28
    rites of, 37, 39, 47, 48
    time of, 44–45
    validity of non-Catholic, 50–51
Baptismal certificate, 53, 302, 303
Baptismal font, 318
Benediction, 107
Bination, 98–100
Blessing,
    by deacons, 265–66
    by laypersons, 266–67
    by pastor, 318
    by presbyters, 265
    celebration of, 267–68
    of baptismal font, 318

343

Name, baptismal, 41
Night Prayer, 272, 274
Nonage, 180
Non-consummation, 248
Nuptial blessing, 318

Occult, 172, 239, 241
Offerings, 330–31
Office of Readings, 271, 273
Oil,
    blessing of, 148
    of catechumens, 34
    of the sick, 148, 318
    retention of, 318
    use of, 149
Omnia parata, 191, 177–79
Oratory, 232
Ordinary administration, 331–32
Ordinary power, 2, 6
Organ transplants, 286
Oriental Churches. *See Eastern rite Catholics.*
Orthodox. *See Eastern non-Catholics.*

Paschal precept, 84
Parents,
    duties of regarding baptism, 39–40, 44
    non-practicing, 40
    role of at confirmation, 60
    role of for First Communion, 81
    preparation of for infant baptism, 39
Parish
    administrator, 324
    archives, 320
    budget, 329
    council, 325, 328
    employees, 330
    finance council, 327
    financial administration, 327–36
    financial report, 329
    goods, 330
    registers, 320
    seal, 320
    vacancy, 324
Parochial vicar, 323–24
Partial simulation, 209
Particular law, 20–22
Past condition, 212
Pastor,
    absence of, 319
    as financial administrator, 327, 329
    by domicile, 23–24
    dispensation by, 296–97
    faculty of for marriage, 219

functions especially committed to, 317–19
    installation of, 315
    record-keeping by, 53–54, 67, 234, 320
    removal of, 316
    residence of, 319
    resignation of, 317
    retirement of, 316
    term of, 316
    transfer of, 316
    vacation of, 319
Patrimony, 330, 334
Pauline privilege, 250–53
Penalties,
    automatic, 136, 139, 140, 141
    exemptions from, 138–39
    general principles of, 137
    remission of, 141
    reserved, 141
Penance, days of, 292–95
Penance for sin, 132
Penance, sacrament of. *See also Confessors.*
    before marriage, 162
    before reception into full communion, 133
    disposition for, 131
    ecumenical law on, 304–8
    faculty for, 121–27
    in danger of death, 116, 128, 129
    individual, 115
    minister of, 121
    obligation of, 131
    place of, 120
    seal of, 128
    short rite of, 116
    time of, 119
    with general absolution, 116
Perpetual vow, 189
Perpetuity, intention against, 210
Personal laws, 21
Petrine privilege, 254–56
Physical impossibility, 14
Polygamy, 206, 256
Pouring, 301
Preaching, 77–78
Pregnancy, 173, 201
Pre-marital investigation, 162, 163, 318
Presbyters, 265
Present condition, 212
Presumption, 158, 250
Prior bond, 184, 246
Privilege of faith,
    explanation of, 249–50

349

INDEX OF CANONS OF 1983 CODE

351

Index of Canons

Index of Canons